Focus on
GRAMMAR 5B

FOURTH EDITION

Focus on GRAMMAR 5B

FOURTH EDITION

Jay Maurer

ALWAYS LEARNING

PEARSON

Focus on Grammar 5B: An Integrated Skills Approach, Fourth Edition

Pearson Education, 10 Bank Street, White Plains, NY 10606

Staff credits: The people who made up the *Focus on Grammar 5B, Fourth Edition*
team, representing editorial, production, design, and manufacturing, are John Barnes, Andrea
Bryant, Elizabeth Carlson, Tracey Cataldo, Aerin Csigay, Dave Dickey, Christine Edmonds,
Nancy Flaggman, Ann France, Shelley Gazes, Lise Minovitz, Barbara Perez, Robert Ruvo, and
Debbie Sistino.

Cover image: Shutterstock.com
Text composition: ElectraGraphics, Inc.
Text font: New Aster

PEARSON LONGMAN ON THE **WEB**

Pearsonlongman.com offers online
resources for teachers and students. Access
our Companion Websites, our online catalog,
and our local offices around the world.

Visit us at **pearsonlongman.com**.

Printed in the United States of America

ISBN 10: 0-13-216983-5
ISBN 13: 978-0-13-216983-7

1 2 3 4 5 6 7 8 9 10—V082—16 15 14 13 12 11

ISBN 10: 0-13-216984-3 (with MyLab)
ISBN 13: 978-0-13-216984-4 (with MyLab)

1 2 3 4 5 6 7 8 9 10—V082—16 15 14 13 12 11

CONTENTS

WELCOME TO *FOCUS ON GRAMMAR*

Now in a new edition, the popular five-level ***Focus on Grammar*** course continues to provide an integrated-skills approach to help students understand and practice English grammar. Centered on thematic instruction, ***Focus on Grammar*** combines controlled and communicative practice with critical thinking skills and ongoing assessment. Students gain the confidence they need to speak and write English accurately and fluently.

NEW for the FOURTH EDITION

VOCABULARY

Key vocabulary is highlighted, practiced, and recycled throughout the unit.

PRONUNCIATION

Now, in every unit, pronunciation points and activities help students improve spoken accuracy and fluency.

LISTENING

Expanded listening tasks allow students to develop a range of listening skills.

UPDATED CHARTS and NOTES

Target structures are presented in a clear, easy-to-read format.

NEW READINGS

High-interest readings, updated or completely new, in a variety of genres integrate grammar and vocabulary in natural contexts.

NEW UNIT REVIEWS

Students can check their understanding and monitor their progress after completing each unit.

MyFocusOnGrammarLab

An easy-to-use online learning and assessment program offers online homework and individualized instruction anywhere, anytime.

Teacher's Resource Pack   One compact resource includes:

THE TEACHER'S MANUAL: General Teaching Notes, Unit Teaching Notes, the Student Book Audioscript, and the Student Book Answer Key.

TEACHER'S RESOURCE DISC: Bound into the Resource Pack, this CD-ROM contains reproducible Placement, Part, and Unit Tests, as well as customizable Test-Generating Software. It also includes reproducible Internet Activities and PowerPoint® Grammar Presentations.

THE *FOCUS ON GRAMMAR* APPROACH

The new edition follows the same successful four-step approach of previous editions. The books provide an abundance of both controlled and communicative exercises so that students can bridge the gap between identifying grammatical structures and using them. The many communicative activities in each Student Book provide opportunities for critical thinking while enabling students to personalize what they have learned.

- **STEP 1: GRAMMAR IN CONTEXT** highlights the target structures in realistic contexts, such as conversations, magazine articles, and blog posts.
- **STEP 2: GRAMMAR PRESENTATION** presents the structures in clear and accessible grammar charts and notes with multiple examples of form and usage.
- **STEP 3: FOCUSED PRACTICE** provides numerous and varied controlled exercises for both the form and meaning of the new structures.
- **STEP 4: COMMUNICATION PRACTICE** includes listening and pronunciation and allows students to use the new structures freely and creatively in motivating, open-ended speaking and writing activities.

Recycling

Underpinning the scope and sequence of the *Focus on Grammar* series is the belief that students need to use target structures and vocabulary many times, in different contexts. New grammar and vocabulary are recycled throughout the book. Students have maximum exposure and become confident using the language in speech and in writing.

Assessment

Extensive testing informs instruction and allows teachers and students to measure progress.

- **Unit Reviews** at the end of every Student Book unit assess students' understanding of the grammar and allow students to monitor their own progress.
- Easy to administer and score, **Part and Unit Tests** provide teachers with a valid and reliable means to determine how well students know the material they are about to study and to assess students' mastery after they complete the material. These tests can be found on MyFocusOnGrammarLab, where they include immediate feedback and remediation, and as reproducible tests on the Teacher's Resource Disc.
- **Test-Generating Software** on the Teacher's Resource Disc includes a bank of *additional* test items teachers can use to create customized tests.
- A reproducible **Placement Test** on the Teacher's Resource Disc is designed to help teachers place students into one of the five levels of the *Focus on Grammar* course.

COMPONENTS

In addition to the Student Books, Teacher's Resource Packs, and MyLabs, the complete *Focus on Grammar* course includes:

Workbooks Contain additional contextualized exercises appropriate for self-study.

Audio Program Includes all of the listening and pronunciation exercises and opening passages from the Student Book. Some Student Books are packaged with the complete audio program (mp3 files). Alternatively, the audio program is available on a classroom set of CDs and on the MyLab.

THE *FOCUS ON GRAMMAR* UNIT

Focus on Grammar introduces grammar structures in the context of unified themes. All units follow a **four-step approach**, taking learners from grammar in context to communicative practice.

STEP 1 GRAMMAR IN CONTEXT

This section presents the target structure(s) in a natural context. As students read the **high-interest texts**, they encounter the form, meaning, and use of the grammar. **Before You Read** activities create interest and elicit students' knowledge about the topic. **After You Read** activities build students' reading vocabulary and comprehension.

Vocabulary exercises improve students' command of English. Vocabulary is **recycled** throughout the unit.

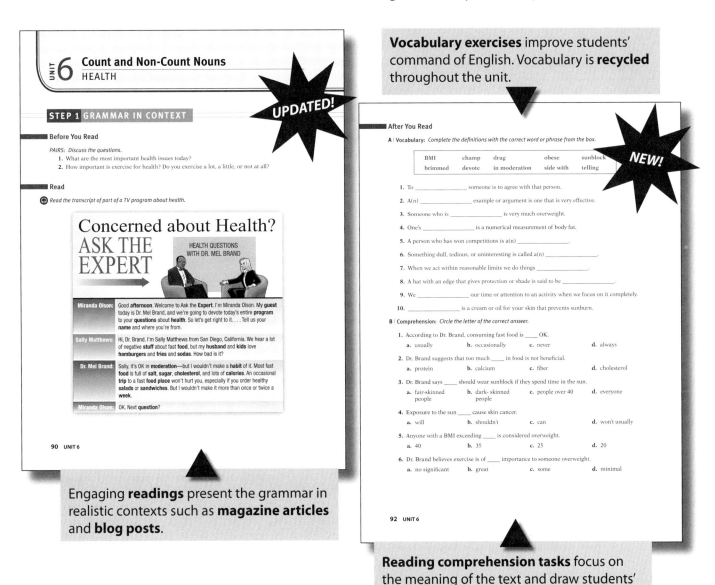

Engaging **readings** present the grammar in realistic contexts such as **magazine articles** and **blog posts**.

Reading comprehension tasks focus on the meaning of the text and draw students' attention to the target structure.

This section gives students a comprehensive and explicit overview of the grammar with detailed **Grammar Charts** and **Grammar Notes** that present the form, meaning, and use of the structure(s).

Grammar Charts present the structure in a clear, easy-to-read format.

Grammar Notes give concise, simple **explanations** and **examples** to ensure students' understanding.

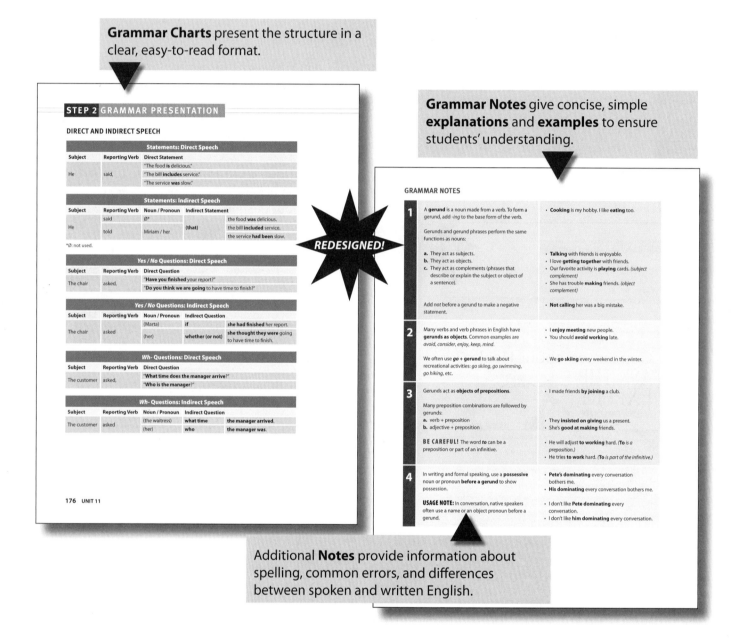

Additional **Notes** provide information about spelling, common errors, and differences between spoken and written English.

Controlled practice activities in this section lead students to master form, meaning, and use of the target grammar.

STEP 3 FOCUSED PRACTICE

EXERCISE 1: Discover the Grammar

A | *Read the sentences. Underline each noun clause and identify it as* **S** *(used as a subject),* **O** *(used as an object), or* **C** *(used as a complement).*

_____ 1. Moe was sure that the mansion would be her favorite gift.

_____ 2. What wasn't so admirable was their rivalry.

_____ 3. All I know is that the chicken you gave me was delicious.

_____ 4. Their mother said there was nothing she needed.

B | *Look at the sentences. Underline the embedded question in each. For each embedded question, write the direct question it was derived from.*

1. Each brother constantly tried to figure out how he could outdo the other two.

   How can I outdo the other two?

2. Curly was wondering what he could do to top his brothers.

3. At first he wondered if he could afford it.

4. I don't know if you believed me.

5. I don't know what you mean.

EXERCISE 2: Embedded Questions *(Grammar Notes 4–7)*

Based on the exchanges in the chart, complete the story with embedded **yes / no** *and* **wh**-*questions. Put the verbs in the simple past or the past perfect.*

1. **A:** Excuse me. How far is the nearest town?   **B:** I don't know.
2. **A:** Well, what's the name of the nearest town?   **B:** I'm not sure.
3. **A:** Can I borrow your cell phone?   **B:** What's a cell phone?

Discover the Grammar activities develop students' recognition and understanding of the target structure before they are asked to produce it.

A **variety of exercise types** engage students and guide them from recognition and understanding to accurate production of the grammar structures.

An **Editing** exercise ends every Focused Practice section and teaches students to find and correct typical mistakes.

EXERCISE 5: Editing

Read the letter. It has eight mistakes in the use of direct and indirect speech. The first mistake is already corrected. Find and correct seven more.

> November 20
>
> Dear Emily,
>
> I just wanted to fill you in on Tim's school adventures. About two months ago Melanie said she ~~feels~~ felt we should switch Tim to the public school. He'd been in a private school for several months, as you know. I asked her why did she think that, and she said, "He's miserable where he is, and the quality of education is poor. He says he doesn't really have any friends." I couldn't help but agree. She said she thought we can move him to the local high school, which has a good academic reputation. I told that I agreed but that we should ask Tim. The next morning we asked Tim if he wanted to stay at the private school. I was surprised at how strong his response was. He said me that he hated the school and didn't want to go there any longer. So we changed him. He's been at the new school for a month now, and he's doing well. Whenever I ask him does he have his homework done, he says, "Dad, I've already finished it." He's made several new friends. Every now and then he asks us why didn't we let him change sooner. He says people are treating him as an individual now. I'm just glad we moved him when we did.
>
> Not much else is new. Oh, yes—I do need to ask are you coming for the holidays. Write soon and let us know. Or call.
>
> Love,
>
> Charles

STEP 4 COMMUNICATION PRACTICE

This section provides practice with the structure in **listening** and **pronunciation** exercises as well as in communicative, open-ended **speaking** and **writing** activities that move students toward fluency.

Listening activities allow students to hear the grammar in natural contexts and to practice a range of listening skills.

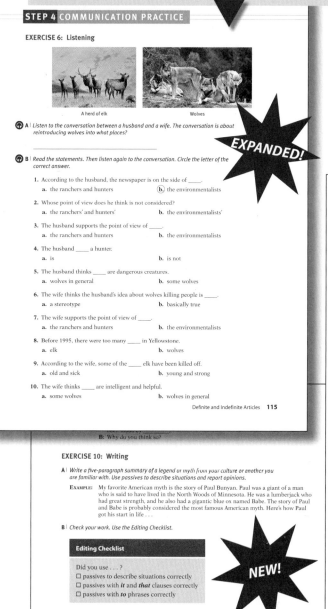

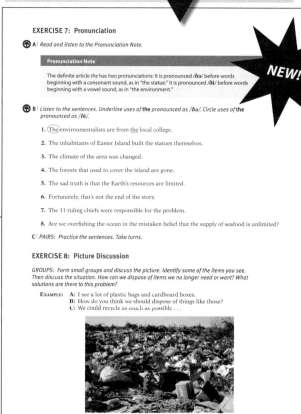

Pronunciation Notes and **exercises** improve students' spoken fluency and accuracy.

Writing activities encourage students to produce meaningful writing that integrates the grammar structure.

An **Editing Checklist** teaches students to correct their mistakes and revise their work.

Speaking activities help students synthesize the grammar through discussions, debates, games, and problem-solving tasks, developing their fluency.

Unit Reviews give students the opportunity to check their understanding of the target structure. **Answers** at the back of the book allow students to monitor their own progress.

UNIT 5 Review

Check your answers on page UR-1.
Do you need to review anything?

NEW!

A | *Circle the correct word or phrase to complete each sentence.*

1. That <u>must / may</u> be the answer to the mystery. All evidence points to it.
2. Ellen <u>might / will</u> be here later, but I don't know for sure.
3. A monk <u>must / might</u> have made the trip, but the evidence isn't conclusive.
4. It <u>couldn't / shouldn't</u> have been Newfoundland, which is too far north.
5. We <u>should / may</u> find out what really happened later today. Louis says he knows.
6. You <u>may not / ought not to</u> have trouble solving the problem—you're good at math.
7. They <u>had to / might</u> have been home—I heard their music.
8. She <u>might be / 's got to be</u> the one who took it. No one else had access to it.
9. They <u>had to be / must have been</u> away last week. Their car was gone.
10. There <u>must / might</u> be a key around here somewhere. Dad said he had one.

B | *In the blank after each sentence, write a modal or modal-like expression of certainty with a meaning similar to the underlined phrase.*

1. <u>It's possible that Jeremy</u> had to work late. _____
2. <u>It's very likely that Mari</u> missed her flight. _____
3. <u>It's impossible that they</u> heard the news. _____
4. <u>It's likely that we'll</u> know the answer soon. _____
5. <u>You had the opportunity to get</u> a scholarship. _____

C | *Circle the letter of the one underlined word or phrase in each sentence that is not correct.*

1. <u>Might</u> she <u>have forgotten</u>, or <u>could she had</u> <u>had to</u> work? A B C D
      A   B   C   D
2. I <u>think</u> Ed <u>isn't</u> here because he <u>should</u> <u>be</u> sick.
      A   B   C   D
3. Al <u>can't get</u> here by 7:00, but he <u>shouldn't</u> <u>make</u> it b...
      A   C   D
4. I suppose they <u>couldn't</u> <u>be working</u> late at the office...
                      A   B
   <u>didn't mention</u> it, and neither <u>did</u> Mary.
      C   D
5. I'm sorry; I <u>could had</u> called to say <u>I'd be</u> late, but I...
                  A   B   C

84 Unit 5 Review: Modals to Express Degrees of Certainty

Extended writing tasks help students integrate the grammar structure as they follow the steps of the **writing process.**

PART II

From Grammar to Writing
TOPIC SENTENCES

An important way to strengthen your writing is to provide a **topic sentence** for each paragraph. A topic sentence is a general sentence that covers the paragraph's content. All the supporting examples and details of the paragraph must fit logically under this sentence, which usually comes first.

EXAMPLE: **For me, a dog is a better pet than a cat.** When I come home from work, for example, my dog comes to meet me at the door. He is always glad to see me. My cat, on the other hand, couldn't care less whether I'm at home or not, as long as I keep filling her food dish. Another good thing about a dog is that you can teach him tricks. Cats, however, can't be bothered to learn anything new. The best thing about a dog, though, is that he's a great companion. I can take my dog on hikes and walks. He goes everywhere with me. As we all know, you can't take a cat for a walk.

The topic sentence for this paragraph tells the reader what to expect in the paragraph: some reasons why the writer considers a dog a superior pet.

1 | *Each of the word groups is a fragment but is also a potential topic sentence. Make necessary additions to each.*

EXAMPLE: Reasons why the legal driving age should be raised. (not an independent clause)
Correction: There are several reasons why the legal driving age should be raised.

1. A city where exciting and mysterious things happen.
   _____

2. Reasons why college isn't for everybody.
   _____

3. Wild animals not making good pets.
   _____

4. Regular exercise and its benefits.
   _____

2 | *Look at the following paragraphs containing supporting details but no topic sentences. For each set of details, write an appropriate topic sentence.*

1. _____
   a. For one thing, there's almost always a traffic jam I get stuck in, and I'm often late to work.
   b. Also, there's not always a parking place when I do get to work.
   c. Worst of all, I'm spending more money on gas and car maintenance than I would if I took public transportation.

(continued on next page)

From Grammar to Writing **85**

The *Focus on Grammar* Unit   **xiii**

SCOPE AND SEQUENCE

UNIT	READING	WRITING	LISTENING
1 page 2 **Grammar:** Present Time **Theme:** The Digital World	An article: *Connected!*	Two or three paragraphs about electronic devices in your life	A conversation about identity theft
2 page 15 **Grammar:** Past Time **Theme:** Marriage	An article: *A Marriage Made on the Internet?*	Two or three paragraphs about a situation that turned out unexpectedly	A broadcast about an unusual wedding
3 page 32 **Grammar:** Future Time **Theme:** Travel	An article: *Getting the Most Out of It!*	Two or three paragraphs about a world traveler's opinions or on your dream vacation	A family conversation about what to do on a trip
PART I From Grammar to Writing, page 45 **The Sentence: Avoiding Sentence Fragments:** Write a composition about a travel experience.			
4 page 50 **Grammar:** Modals to Express Degrees of Necessity **Theme:** Cultural Differences	An article: *What We Should and Shouldn't Have Done*	Two or three paragraphs about a situation you should have handled differently	A conversation about a gift for a surprise party
5 page 69 **Grammar:** Modals to Express Degrees of Certainty **Theme:** Puzzles	An article: *Who Really Discovered America?*	Three or four paragraphs about a world mystery	A discussion about hearing one's recorded voice
PART II From Grammar to Writing, page 85 **Topic Sentences:** Write a composition about a cross-cultural experience.			
6 page 90 **Grammar:** Count and Non-Count Nouns **Theme:** Health	A transcript of a TV program: *Concerned about Health? Ask the Expert*	Three or four paragraphs about health issues	A conversation between a doctor and a patient about health needs

SPEAKING	PRONUNCIATION	VOCABULARY	
Group Discussion: Electronic devices which are important in your life *Class Discussion:* The dangers of texting while driving	Two pronunciations of the letters *ng*	24/7 contemplating digitally do without	profile staying on top of telecommute tends
Information Gap: A married couple who took risks and made changes *Picture Discussion:* A married couple's relationship *Group Discussion:* Changes in one another's lives	Contracting auxiliary verbs in past forms	came up with out of the blue pondered tie the knot	turned in turned out ultimately*
Picture Discussion: What you think will happen in the future *Group Discussion:* Opinions of a world traveler	Contracting auxiliary verbs in future forms	chart your own course excruciatingly hectic landmarks	maximize* mindset out of whack scrapbook
Information Gap: Cultural differences and travel problems *Discussion:* Correct behavior in your culture	Reduction of modals and modal-like auxiliaries	chuckle decline* gracious have someone over	perplexed pointer praise rectify
Pair Discussion: Possible solutions to various puzzling events *Group Discussion:* Explanations to the mystery of Atlantis	Reductions of *to* and *have* in modal constructions	artifacts cohorts contenders debris	monasteries monks potential* stems from
Discussion: Statements about personal experiences *Personal Inventory:* Responses to a survey about health	Reduction of *of*	BMI brimmed champ devote* drag	in moderation obese side with sunblock telling

* = AWL (Academic Word List) items

UNIT	READING	WRITING	LISTENING
7 page 105 **Grammar:** Definite and Indefinite Articles **Theme:** Environmental Concerns	An article: *The Real Mystery of Easter Island*	Three or four paragraphs about your opinions on an environmental issue	A conversation about wolves
8 page 120 **Grammar:** Quantifiers **Theme:** Money	An article: *What's Happening to Cash?*	Three or four paragraphs about an interesting experience with money	A conversation between diners about how to pay for their meal
9 page 134 **Grammar:** Modification of Nouns **Theme:** Expectations	An article: *The Expectation Syndrome: I Hope for It, but I Don't Expect It*	Three or four paragraphs about an unexpected outcome	A conversation on anxieties about public speaking
PART III From Grammar to Writing, page 150 **Agreement:** Write a composition about societal issues.			
10 page 156 **Grammar:** Noun Clauses: Subjects, Objects, and Complements **Theme:** Humor	A humorous story: *The Three Brothers*	Three to five paragraphs about a humorous incident	A conversation about a humorous incident
11 page 173 **Grammar:** Direct and Indirect Speech **Theme:** Communication and Misunderstanding	An interview: *Understanding Misunderstandings*	Three to five paragraphs about a news story that interested you	A presentation about avoiding verbal conflict
PART IV From Grammar to Writing, page 191 **Direct and Indirect Speech:** Write a composition about a humorous incident.			
12 page 196 **Grammar:** Adjective Clauses: Review and Expansion **Theme:** Personality Types	An article: *What Type Are You?*	Five or more paragraphs about the personality type that fits you	A telephone conversation between a college student and his parents

SPEAKING	PRONUNCIATION	VOCABULARY	
Picture Discussion: Solutions to the problem of disposing of unwanted items *Game:* Asking *who* and *what* questions	Two pronunciations of *the*	bark desolate drastically hauling	ostrich-like rivalry toppled over trunk
Game: World facts *Personal Inventory:* Your life now compared to your life five years ago	Unstressed vowels	correspondingly* crisp e.g. fiat i.e.	the jury is still out live beyond our means succeeding take plastic
Story Discussion: A famous Arabic story *Picture Discussion:* A famous disaster at sea	Pausing between modifiers in the same category	buff exploit* irony live up to marathon	otherworldly relinquish surge syndrome tedious
Pair Discussion: Airline humor *Class Discussion:* Presenting a joke or amusing story	Intonation in *wh-*, *yes/no*, and embedded questions	ecstatic exemplary in a dilemma inclination* on call	one-upmanship outdo supplant uniqueness*
Group Reporting: Game about miscommunication *Picture Discussion:* An auto accident	Blending of /t/ or /d/ plus /y/	bottom line chair civility distressed glared	minimize* rancor short-handed spin sugarcoat
Pair Discussion: Dealing with conflict *Class Activity:* Identifying classmates based on descriptions given by others	Pauses in identifying and nonidentifying adjective clauses	charismatic correlation embrace entrepreneurs	gravitate toward insight* spotlight without mincing words

* = AWL (Academic Word List) items

UNIT	READING	WRITING	LISTENING
13 page 211 **Grammar:** Adjective Clauses with Prepositions; Adjective Phrases **Theme:** Movies	Movie reviews: *Five to Revisit*	A movie review of three or more paragraphs	Weekly movie reviews by a TV film reviewer
PART V **From Grammar to Writing,** page 229 **Punctuating Adjective Clauses and Phrases:** Write a composition about a photograph.			
14 page 234 **Grammar:** The Passive: Review and Expansion **Theme:** Unsolved Mysteries	An article: *Did He Get Away with It?*	Five or more paragraphs about an unsolved mystery	A news bulletin about an accident
15 page 250 **Grammar:** The Passive to Describe Situations and to Report Opinions **Theme:** Legends and Myths	An article: *The Strangest of Peoples*	A five-paragraph summary of a legend or myth	A news bulletin about a natural disaster
PART VI **From Grammar to Writing,** page 266 **Parallel Structure: Nouns, Articles, and Voice:** Write a composition about an unsolved mystery or unusual experience.			
16 page 270 **Grammar:** Gerunds **Theme:** Friendship	An article: *Friends*	Five or more paragraphs about a friend who fits a particular category	A telephone conversation about a club
17 page 285 **Grammar:** Infinitives **Theme:** Procrastination	An article: *Seize the Day*	Three or more paragraphs about a time you put off doing something that needed to be done	A news bulletin about a prison escape
PART VII **From Grammar to Writing,** page 303 **Parallel Structure: Gerunds and Infinitives:** Write a composition about a task you have difficulty accomplishing.			
18 page 308 **Grammar:** Adverbs: Sentence, Focus, and Negative **Theme:** Controversial Issues	A transcript of a radio call-in show: *Time to Sound Off*	Five paragraphs on a controversial topic	A radio call-in show about military service

SPEAKING	PRONUNCIATION	VOCABULARY	
Information Gap: Movie review: *A Beautiful Mind* *Group Discussion:* The current movie rating system *Picture Discussion:* The behavior of moviegoers	Vowel sound changes in words with the same spellings but different meanings	compilation* engrossing estranged incumbent on me	polarized spice up transcend vanquishing
Information Gap: Guessing a mystery object based on clues *Survey and Discussion:* Crime and punishment	*Has been* and *is being* in passive constructions	accomplice alias divulged gear get away with	hijacked inadvertently remains rotting
Game: People and places *Picture Discussion:* Famous people	The vowel sounds /ei/ and /ɛ/	bewitch font lacerates potions	repulsive rituals shrine supernatural
Personal Inventory: Life events *Group Discussion:* What you value in friendships	Pronunciation of nouns and verbs with the same spellings	catching up on coincide* context* counterpart	meander naive spare your feelings vulnerable
Personal Inventory: Personal beliefs and experiences *Group Discussion:* Famous sayings	The vowel sounds /æ/, /ɑ/, and /ʌ/	connotation flunk learned longhand	ring a bell scenario* tough nut to crack wretched
Personal Inventory: Personal beliefs and experiences *Pros and Cons:* Brainstorming ideas about controversial topics *Debate:* Debating a controversial topic	Sentence stress and meaning	compulsory controversial* fuzzy shed some light on	spirited stereotype uncensored willingly

* = AWL (Academic Word List) items

UNIT	READING	WRITING	LISTENING
19 page 323 **Grammar:** Adverb Clauses **Theme:** Sports	An editorial: *Are Sports Still Sporting?*	Three or four paragraphs about a sports topic	An interview with a sports star
20 page 340 **Grammar:** Adverb and Adverbial Phrases **Theme:** Compassion	An article: *Compassion*	Three or four paragraphs about a compassionate act you have witnessed	A news broadcast on world events
21 page 358 **Grammar:** Connectors **Theme:** Memory	An article: *Try to Remember*	Three or four paragraphs about a significant memory you have	An excerpt from a memory-training workshop
PART VIII **From Grammar to Writing,** page 374 **Using Transitions:** Write a composition that expresses a strong opinion.			
22 page 378 **Grammar:** Conditionals; Other Ways to Express Unreality **Theme:** Intuition	A story: *Intuition*	Four or five paragraphs about a time when you ignored your intuition	A conversation about a student's moral quandary
23 page 396 **Grammar:** More Conditions; The Subjunctive **Theme:** Advice	Letters to an advice columnist and responses: *Ask Rosa*	Four or five paragraphs about a time when you took good advice and another when you took bad advice	A conversation advising a friend about her daughter's demands
PART IX **From Grammar to Writing,** page 414 **Avoiding Run-On Sentences and Comma Splices:** Write a composition about an intuitive experience.			

SPEAKING	PRONUNCIATION	VOCABULARY	
Personal Inventory: Future possibilities *Picture Discussion:* Sports and violence	Placement of dependent adverb clauses and pauses in speaking	also-ran awry inevitable* lurking	partisanship prevalence stamina venues
Personal Inventory: Personal beliefs and expressions *Group Discussion:* Animal emotions	Vowel changes and stress shift in words of the same family	bandanna a blow was struck corneas dawned on decrepit	elude floored oozing petty weighed
Game: Connecting ideas *Picture Discussion:* A famous painting about memory	Pronunciation of clauses connected by conjunctions and those connected by transitions	core* glucose lobes mitigate	peg recollect tap vivid
Conditional Game: People and things *Personal Inventory:* Personal hopes and wishes *Group Discussion:* Story outcome	Contractions of the auxiliaries *would* and *had*	beastly bureau fluttered hailing inkling	mutilated sweltering token weirdo
Personal Inventory: Personal beliefs and experiences *Group Discussion:* Moral and political issues *Picture Discussion:* Advice about visiting another country	Silent consonants that are sometimes pronounced	at the end of my rope doormat intransigent lighten up neatnik	overbearing pigsty right the ship semblance slob

* = AWL (Academic Word List) items

ABOUT THE AUTHOR / ACKNOWLEDGMENTS

Jay Maurer has taught English in binational centers, colleges, and universities in Spain, Portugal, Mexico, the Somali Republic, and the United States; and intensive English at Columbia University's American Language Program. In addition, he has been a teacher of college composition, literature, and speech at Santa Fe Community College and Northern New Mexico Community College. He is the co-author with Penny LaPorte of the three-level *Structure Practice in Context* series; co-author with Irene Schoenberg of the five-level *True Colors* series and the *True Voices* video series; co-author with Irene Schoenberg of *Focus on Grammar 1*; and author of *Focus on Grammar 5*, editions 1 through 4. Currently he lives and writes in Arizona and Washington State. *Focus on Grammar 5: An Integrated Skills Approach*, Fourth Edition, has grown out of the author's experiences as a practicing teacher of both ESL and college writing.

Writing the fourth edition of *Focus on Grammar 5* has been even more interesting and rewarding than doing the first three editions. I'm indebted to many people who helped me in different ways. Specifically, though, I want to express my appreciation and gratitude to:

- My students over the years.
- **Marjorie Fuchs**, **Margaret Bonner**, and **Irene Schoenberg**—the other members of the FOG author team—for their support and encouragement.
- That genius, whoever he or she is, who created the joke about the parrot that has been floating around in cyberspace for a considerable time now. The same to the unknown authors of the bumper stickers.
- **Lise Minovitz** for her many well-taken comments about the manuscript, particularly in the early stages of the revision.
- **Amy Shearon** of Rice University for her careful review of the third edition and her many perceptive suggestions for improvement.
- **Debbie Sistino** for her vision and her excellent direction of the entire project. Thank you very much.

Above all I am grateful to:

- **John Barnes**, my editor, for his patience, his excellent eye for detail, his perceptive understanding of what works well in the classroom, and his overall vision. He has been instrumental in making this a better book.
- My wife **Priscilla** for her love, wonderful support, and assistance with the manuscript.
- My best friend.

REVIEWERS

We are grateful to the following reviewers for their many helpful comments:

Aida Aganagic, Seneca College, Toronto, Canada; **Aftab Ahmed**, American University of Sharjah, Sharjah, United Arab Emirates; **Todd Allen**, English Language Institute, Gainesville, FL; **Anthony Anderson**, University of Texas, Austin, TX; **Anna K. Andrade**, ASA Institute, New York, NY; **Bayda Asbridge**, Worcester State College, Worcester, MA; **Raquel Ashkenasi**, American Language Institute, La Jolla, CA; **James Bakker**, Mt. San Antonio College, Walnut, CA; **Kate Baldrige-Hale**, Harper College, Palatine, IL; **Leticia S. Banks**, ALCI-SDUSM, San Marcos, CA; **Aegina Barnes**, York College CUNY, Forest Hills, NY; **Sarah Barnhardt**, Community College of Baltimore County, Reisterstown, MD; **Kimberly Becker**, Nashville State Community College, Nashville, TN; **Holly Bell**, California State University, San Marcos, CA; **Anne Bliss**, University of Colorado, Boulder, CO; **Diana Booth**, Elgin Community College, Elgin, IL; **Barbara Boyer**, South Plainfield High School, South Plainfield, NJ; **Janna Brink**, Mt. San Antonio College, Walnut, CA; **AJ Brown**, Portland State University, Portland, OR; **Amanda Burgoyne**, Worcester State College, Worcester, MA; **Brenda Burlingame**, Independence High School, Charlotte, NC; **Sandra Byrd**, Shelby County High School and Kentucky State University, Shelbyville, KY; **Edward Carlstedt**, American University of Sharjah, Sharjah, United Arab Emirates; **Sean Cochran**, American Language Institute, Fullerton, CA; **Yanely Cordero**, Miami Dade College, Miami, FL; **Lin Cui**, William Rainey Harper College, Palatine, IL; **Sheila Detweiler**, College Lake County, Libertyville, IL; **Ann Duncan**, University of Texas, Austin, TX; **Debra Edell**, Merrill Middle School, Denver, CO; **Virginia Edwards**, Chandler-Gilbert Community College, Chandler, AZ; **Kenneth Fackler**, University of Tennessee, Martin, TN; **Jennifer Farnell**, American Language Program, Stamford, CT; **Allen P. Feiste**, Suwon University, Hwaseong, South Korea; **Mina Fowler**, Mt. San Antonio Community College, Rancho Cucamonga, CA; **Rosemary Franklin**, University of Cincinnati, Cincinnati, OH; **Christiane Galvani**, Texas Southern University, Sugar Land, TX; **Chester Gates**, Community College of Baltimore County, Baltimore, MD; **Luka Gavrilovic**, Quest Language Studies, Toronto, Canada; **Sally Gearhart**, Santa Rosa Community College, Santa Rosa, CA; **Shannon Gerrity**, James Lick Middle School, San Francisco, CA; **Jeanette Gerrity Gomez**, Prince George's Community College, Largo, MD; **Carlos Gonzalez**, Miami Dade College, Miami, FL; **Therese Gormley Hirmer**, University of Guelph, Guelph, Canada; **Sudeepa Gulati**, Long Beach City College, Long Beach, CA; **Anthony Halderman**, Cuesta College, San Luis Obispo, CA; **Ann A. Hall**, University of Texas, Austin, TX; **Cora Higgins**, Boston Academy of English, Boston, MA; **Michelle Hilton**, South Lane School District, Cottage Grove, OR; **Nicole Hines**, Troy University, Atlanta, GA; **Rosemary Hiruma**, American Language Institute, Long Beach, CA; **Harriet Hoffman**, University of Texas, Austin, TX; **Leah Holck**, Michigan State University, East Lansing, MI; **Christy Hunt**, English for Internationals, Roswell, GA; **Osmany Hurtado**, Miami Dade College, Miami, FL; **Isabel Innocenti**, Miami Dade College, Miami, FL; **Donna Janian**, Oxford Intensive School of English, Medford, MA; **Scott Jenison**, Antelope Valley College, Lancaster, CA; **Grace Kim**, Mt. San Antonio College, Diamond Bar, CA; **Brian King**, ELS Language Center, Chicago, IL; **Pam Kopitzke**, Modesto Junior College, Modesto, CA; **Elena Lattarulo**, American Language Institute, San Diego, CA; **Karen Lavaty**, Mt. San Antonio College, Glendora, CA; **JJ Lee-Gilbert**, Menlo-Atherton High School, Foster City, CA; **Ruth Luman**, Modesto Junior College, Modesto, CA; **Yvette Lyons**, Tarrant County College, Fort Worth, TX; **Janet Magnoni**, Diablo Valley College, Pleasant Hill, CA; **Meg Maher**, YWCA Princeton, Princeton, NJ; **Carmen Marquez-Rivera**, Curie Metropolitan High School, Chicago, IL; **Meredith Massey**, Prince George's Community College, Hyattsville, MD; **Linda Maynard**, Coastline Community College, Westminster, CA; **Eve Mazereeuw**, University of Guelph, Guelph, Canada; **Susanne McLaughlin**, Roosevelt University, Chicago, IL; **Madeline Medeiros**, Cuesta College, San Luis Obispo, CA; **Gioconda Melendez**, Miami Dade College, Miami, FL; **Marcia Menaker**, Passaic County Community College, Morris Plains, NJ; **Seabrook Mendoza**, Cal State San Marcos University, Wildomar, CA; **Anadalia Mendoza**, Felix Varela Senior High School, Miami, FL; **Charmaine Mergulhao**, Quest Language Studies, Toronto, Canada; **Dana Miho**, Mt. San Antonio College, San Jacinto, CA; **Sonia Nelson**, Centennial Middle School, Portland, OR; **Manuel Niebla**, Miami Dade College, Miami, FL; **Alice Nitta**, Leeward Community College, Pearl City, HI; **Gabriela Oliva**, Quest Language Studies, Toronto, Canada; **Sara Packer**, Portland State University, Portland, OR; **Lesley Painter**, New School, New York, NY; **Carlos Paz-Perez**, Miami Dade College, Miami, FL; **Ileana Perez**, Miami Dade College, Miami, FL; **Barbara Pogue**, Essex County College, Newark, NJ; **Phillips Potash**, University of Texas, Austin, TX; **Jada Pothina**, University of Texas, Austin, TX; **Ewa Pratt**, Des Moines Area Community College, Des Moines, IA; **Pedro Prentt**, Hudson County Community College, Jersey City, NJ; **Maida Purdy**, Miami Dade College, Miami, FL; **Dolores Quiles**, SUNY Ulster, Stone Ridge, NY; **Mark Rau**, American River College, Sacramento, CA; **Lynne Raxlen**, Seneca College, Toronto, Canada; **Lauren Rein**, English for Internationals, Sandy Springs, GA; **Diana Rivers**, NOCCCD, Cypress, CA; **Silvia Rodriguez**, Santa Ana College, Mission Viejo, CA; **Rolando Romero**, Miami Dade College, Miami, FL; **Pedro Rosabal**, Miami Dade College, Miami, FL; **Natalie Rublik**, University of Quebec, Chicoutimi, Quebec, Canada; **Matilde Sanchez**, Oxnard College, Oxnard, CA; **Therese Sarkis-Kruse**, Wilson Commencement, Rochester, NY; **Mike Sfiropoulos**, Palm Beach Community College, Boynton Beach, FL; **Amy Shearon**, Rice University, Houston, TX; **Sara Shore**, Modesto Junior College, Modesto, CA; **Patricia Silva**, Richard Daley College, Chicago, IL; **Stephanie Solomon**, Seattle Central Community College, Vashon, WA; **Roberta Steinberg**, Mount Ida College, Newton, MA; **Teresa Szymula**, Curie Metropolitan High School, Chicago, IL; **Hui-Lien Tang**, Jasper High School, Plano, TX; **Christine Tierney**, Houston Community College, Sugar Land, TX; **Ileana Torres**, Miami Dade College, Miami, FL; **Michelle Van Slyke**, Western Washington University, Bellingham, WA; **Melissa Villamil**, Houston Community College, Sugar Land, TX; **Elizabeth Wagenheim**, Prince George's Community College, Lago, MD; **Mark Wagner**, Worcester State College, Worcester, MA; **Angela Waigand**, American University of Sharjah, Sharjah, United Arab Emirates; **Merari Weber**, Metropolitan Skills Center, Los Angeles, CA; **Sonia Wei**, Seneca College, Toronto, Canada; and **Vicki Woodward**, Indiana University, Bloomington, IN.

ADJECTIVE CLAUSES

UNIT	GRAMMAR FOCUS	THEME
12	Adjective Clauses: Review and Expansion	Personality Types
13	Adjective Clauses with Prepositions; Adjective Phrases	Movies

Adjective Clauses: Review and Expansion

PERSONALITY TYPES

STEP 1 GRAMMAR IN CONTEXT

Before You Read

PAIRS: Discuss the questions.

1. Complete the sentence with the one adjective that best describes your personality: "I am a person who is _____."
2. Is it helpful to classify people into personality types or to place yourself in a personality category? Why or why not?

Read

Read the article about personality types.

WHAT TYPE ARE YOU?

Stella

Imagine you're at a party **where you know several people well**. The hosts have a new party game **that involves comparing each person to a flower**. Which flower would you choose for each person and which flower for yourself? Are you the kind of person **who resembles a daisy**, open to the world most of the time? Or are you more like a morning glory, **which opens up only at special moments**?

This may sound like just an amusing activity, but there is a science of personality

WHAT TYPE ARE YOU?

Rick

identification. Many personality tests and categories have been devised in the last century. Take a look at the following descriptions. Try to place yourself and people **you know** into one or more of the categories. You may learn something about your co-workers, friends, loved ones, and yourself. Bear in mind, though, that these are only broad outlines. Most people don't fit perfectly into a single category.

Extrovert or introvert? This category concerns the way **that people are energized**. An extrovert is basically a person **whose energies are activated by being with others**. An introvert is essentially a person **who is energized by being alone**. Stella is a good example of an extrovert. She's the kind of person **whom others consider shy**, but there's no correlation between shyness and either introversion or extroversion. At a party, Stella starts to open up and get energized once she meets people **who make her feel comfortable**. Her friend Rick is the opposite. He isn't shy, but after he's been at a party for a while, he's tired and ready to go home. He finds the conversation interesting enough but is just as likely to be imagining a time **when he is hiking alone in the mountains**.

Type A? Type A's are "drivers," competitive individuals **who have a no-nonsense approach to life**. They're the kind of people **who tell you exactly what they think without mincing words**. They embrace risk and change and often turn out to be entrepreneurs. Nancy, **who started her own greeting card business three years ago**, is

the perfect example. However, Nancy is impatient with detail and routine, **which is why she has hired Paul and Mandy to manage her business**.

Type B? Type B's are socializers. They're extroverts, the kind of people **who love the spotlight**. They love to entertain people. They often gravitate toward jobs in sales or marketing or as performers on radio and TV. Nancy's husband Jack, **whom most people consider a charismatic person**, is a good example. He's the host of a two-hour talk radio show.

Type C? Type C's are lovers of detail. They tend to be individuals **who become accountants, programmers, or engineers**. Type C's are sensitive, **which can translate into trouble communicating with others**. Paul, an accountant, is an example. He's the type of person **who loves the details that Nancy hates**.

Type D? Type D people are those **who like routine and tend not to enjoy adventure**. Not surprisingly, they usually resist change. They like to be told what to do. They're often compassionate. Mandy, **who loves her office job**, wouldn't be happy as the boss, but she appreciates working for Nancy.

In the end we're left with this question: What good is classifying people? It certainly doesn't give us any magical powers or tools for relationships. But it can give us insight. It can help us understand others better and perhaps minimize conflict. Best of all, it can help us understand ourselves.

After You Read

A | Vocabulary: *Match the blue words and phrases on the left with their meanings on the right.*

_____ **1.** There's no **correlation** between shyness and either introversion or extroversion.

_____ **2.** They tell you exactly what they think **without mincing words**.

_____ **3.** They **embrace** risk and change and often turn out to be entrepreneurs.

_____ **4.** They embrace risk and change and often turn out to be **entrepreneurs**.

_____ **5.** Type B's love the **spotlight**.

_____ **6.** They often **gravitate toward** jobs in sales or marketing.

_____ **7.** Most people consider Jack a **charismatic** person.

_____ **8.** Learning to classify people can give us **insight**.

a. move or are drawn to

b. center of attention

c. having special charm or personal qualities to attract people

d. deep understanding

e. shared relationship

f. eagerly accept

g. people who own and run a business

h. speaking plainly and honestly of something unpleasant

B | Comprehension: *Circle **T (True)** or **F (False)**. Correct the false statements.*

1. Most people fit perfectly into a personality category.	T	F
2. An extrovert is a person who is energized by others.	T	F
3. An introvert is a person who is energized by being alone.	T	F
4. There's a correlation between shyness and introversion.	T	F
5. A Type A person likes change.	T	F
6. A Type B person is an introvert.	T	F
7. A Type C person sometimes has trouble communicating with others.	T	F
8. A Type D person does not like to be told what to do.	T	F

ADJECTIVE CLAUSES: REVIEW AND EXPANSION

Adjective Clauses: Placement

Main Clause		Adjective Clause	
	Noun / Pronoun	Relative Pronoun	
They met	a woman	**who**	**teaches psychology.**
I've read	everything	**that**	**discusses her work.**

Main . . .	Adjective Clause		. . . Clause
Noun / Pronoun	Relative Pronoun		
The woman	**who**	**teaches psychology**	is also a writer.
Everything	**that**	**discusses her work**	is very positive.

Relative Pronouns as Subjects: *Who, Which, That*

People			Things		
I have a friend	**who**	loves to talk.	This is a book	**which**	is useful.
I have friends	**that**	love to talk.	These are books	**that**	are useful.

Relative Pronouns as Objects: *Who(m), Which, That, Ø**

People			Things		
This is the doctor	who(m) **that** Ø	we consulted.	This is the test	which **that** Ø	he gave us.

*Ø = no pronoun

Whose + Noun to Indicate Possession

People	Things
She is the woman **whose son** is so famous.	It's the book **whose reviews** were so good.
She is the woman **whose son** I am tutoring.	It's the book **whose reviews** I have just read.

Where and *When* in Adjective Clauses

Where			*When*		
Place			Time		
I remember the café	**where**	we met.	I remember the day	(when) (that) Ø	we parted.

(continued on next page)

Adjective Clauses: Identifying or Nonidentifying

Adjective Clauses That Identify	Adjective Clauses That Do Not Identify
No Commas	**Commas**
The woman **who / that created the test** studied psychology. The test **which / that / Ø she created** describes personality types.	Sara Gomez, **who created the test**, studied psychology. The Gomez test, **which she created**, describes personality types.

GRAMMAR NOTES

1	A sentence with an **adjective clause** can be seen as a combination of two sentences.	*John is a man. + He works hard.* = • John is a man **who works hard**. *Mary is interesting. + I like her a lot.* = • Mary, **whom I like a lot**, is interesting.
2	An adjective clause is a **dependent clause**. It modifies a noun or a pronoun in a main clause.	• Frank, **who is an introvert**, spends a lot of time alone. • Let's do something **that is fun**.
	An adjective clause often begins with a **relative pronoun**: *who*, *whom*, *which*, or *that*. It can also begin with *whose*, *when*, or *where*. The word that begins an adjective clause usually comes directly after the noun or pronoun that the clause modifies.	• Toronto, **which is the largest city in Canada**, is a beautiful place.
	An adjective clause can occur after a main clause or inside a main clause.	• Harriet is a woman **whom I respect**. • The house **that we bought** is in the suburbs.
3	To refer to people, use *who* and *that* as the subjects of verbs in adjective clauses.	• The Ings are the **people who** bought the house. • Sam is the **man that** lives next door to me.
	To refer to things, use *which* and *that* as the subjects of verbs in adjective clauses.	• Math is the **subject which** is the easiest for me.
	USAGE NOTE: *That* is less formal than *who* or *which*.	• This is the **car that** is the nicest.
	The verb in an adjective clause agrees with the noun or pronoun that the clause modifies.	• There are many **people who have taken** this personality test. • This test is the **one that is** the best known.
	BE CAREFUL! Do not use a double subject in an adjective clause.	• Extroverts are people **who like to be with others**. Not: Extroverts are people who ~~they~~ like to be with others.

4 To refer to people, use **whom**, **who**, and **that** as the **objects** of verbs in adjective clauses. *Whom* is quite formal. *Who* and *that* are less formal and used in conversation and informal writing. *That* is the least formal.

- **Mr. Pitkin**, **whom** I mentioned yesterday, is my boss.
- Mr. Pitkin was the **person who** I mentioned.
- Mr. Pitkin was the **person that** I mentioned.

To refer to things, use **which** and **that** as the **objects** of verbs in adjective clauses. *Which* is a bit more formal.

- The **test which** I took was difficult.
- The **test that** I took was difficult.

In conversation and informal writing, you can sometimes omit the relative pronoun if it is an object. This is the most common spoken form. *(See Note 8 for more information on omitting relative pronouns.)*

- Mr. Pitkin is the man **I mentioned**.
- The test **I took** was difficult.

The verb in an adjective clause agrees with the subject of the clause, not with the object.

- The Wangs are the people **that Sally sees frequently**.
  NOT: The Wangs are the people that Sally ~~see~~ frequently.

5 Use **whose** to introduce an adjective clause that indicates **possession**. We use *whose* to replace *his / her / its / their* + noun. An adjective clause with *whose* can modify people or things.

Ken is the man + We met his wife. =
- Ken is the man **whose wife we met**.
It's a theory. + Its origins go back many years. =
- It's a theory **whose origins go back many years**.

BE CAREFUL! *Whose* cannot be omitted.

- Harvey, **whose house we're renting**, is a lawyer.
  NOT: Harvey, ~~house we're renting~~, is a lawyer.

6 You can use **where** to introduce an adjective clause that modifies a noun of **place**. *Where* replaces the word *there*.

This is the restaurant. + We ate there. =
- This is the restaurant **where we ate**.

BE CAREFUL! Use an adjective clause with **where** only if you can restate the location with the word **there**. Do not use an adjective clause with *where* if the location cannot be stated in this way.

- Chihuahua is the town **where I was born**. = Chihuahua is the town. I was born **there**.
  NOT: Rio de Janeiro is a city ~~where has beautiful scenery~~.
- Rio de Janeiro is a city **that has beautiful scenery**.

NOTE: *Where* can be replaced by *which* or *that* + a preposition, such as *in*, *at*, or *for*. In this type of adjective clause, *which / that* can be omitted.

- This is the building **where** she works.
- This is the building **(that)** she works **in**.

(continued on next page)

7	You can use **when** or **that** to begin an adjective clause that modifies a noun of **time**. You can omit *when* and *that* in this type of adjective clause. A sentence without *when* or *that* is informal.	• I can't think of a time **when / that I wasn't happy**. • I can't think of a time **I wasn't happy**.
8	An adjective clause that distinguishes one person or thing from another is called **identifying** or **essential**. The clause is not enclosed in commas.	• The man **who delivers the mail** is friendly.
	An adjective clause that adds extra information but does not distinguish one person or thing from another is called **nonidentifying** or nonessential. The clause is enclosed in commas.	• The man, **who delivers the mail**, is friendly.

BE CAREFUL!

a. You can omit relative pronouns only in identifying adjective clauses. You cannot omit the relative pronoun in a nonidentifying adjective clause.

- The man **you met on Friday** is Tarik.
- That's Tarik, **whom you met on Friday**.
  Not: That's Tarik, ~~you met on Friday~~.

b. Don't use **that** as a relative pronoun in a nonidentifying clause.

- The Gomez test, **which I took a long time ago**, has proved to be accurate.
  Not: The Gomez test, ~~that I took a long time ago~~, has proved to be accurate.

You can use **which** informally to refer to an entire previous idea.

- **Helen is hardworking, which** impresses me.

In formal writing and speech, use a noun at the beginning of a **that** or **which** clause.

- **Helen is hardworking, a characteristic that / which** impresses me.

STEP 3 FOCUSED PRACTICE

EXERCISE 1: Discover the Grammar

A | *Read these sentences based on the opening reading. Could the relative pronoun be replaced by the relative pronoun in parentheses without creating a different meaning or making an incorrect sentence? Write* **Y (Yes)** *or* **N (No)**.

_____Y____ **1.** Are you the kind of person **who** resembles a daisy? (that)

_____ **2.** Or are you more like a morning glory, **which** opens up only at special moments? (that)

_____ **3.** Stella gets energized once she meets people **who** make her feel comfortable. (whom)

_____ **4.** He is likely to be imagining a time **when** he was hiking alone in the mountains. (Ø)

_____ **5.** She's the kind of person **whom** others consider shy. (that)

_____ **6.** Nancy is impatient with detail and routine, **which** is why she has hired Paul and Mandy to manage her business. (that)

_____ **7.** Type B's are the kind of people **who** love the spotlight. (which)

_____ **8.** Mandy, **who** loves her office job, wouldn't be happy as the boss. (that)

B | _Read the sentences based on the opening reading. Underline the adjective clause in each sentence. Then identify the clause as identifying_ **(I)** _or nonidentifying_ **(NI)**.

__/__ **1.** Imagine you're at a party <u>where you know several people well</u>.

_____ **2.** Are you the kind of person who resembles a daisy?

_____ **3.** Try to place yourself and people you know into one or more categories.

_____ **4.** Nancy, who started her own greeting card business several years ago, is the perfect example.

_____ **5.** An introvert is a person whose energies are activated by being alone.

_____ **6.** Nancy is impatient with detail and routine, which is why she has hired Paul and Mandy to manage her business.

_____ **7.** Nancy's husband Jack, whom most people consider a charismatic person, is a good example.

_____ **8.** Type C's are sensitive, which can translate into trouble communicating with others.

_____ **9.** Type D people are those who like routine and tend not to enjoy adventure.

EXERCISE 2: Relative Pronouns

(Grammar Notes 3, 5–6, 8)

Circle the correct relative pronoun in each sentence. The sentences are connected together in a story.

1. I come from a family (that)/ whom has eight members.

2. I have three sisters and two brothers, <u>that / which</u> made things pretty crowded when we were growing up.

3. Our house, <u>which / that</u> is four stories high, has eight bedrooms.

4. The members of my family, <u>who / whom</u> are all interesting, fit nicely into the Type A to D categories.

5. My mother and father, <u>who / whom</u> both like to be with people a great deal, are extroverts.

6. My favorite brother, with <u>who / whom</u> I still spend a lot of time, is an introvert.

7. My other brother, <u>who / which</u> is a Type A, is a great guy but always has to be right.

8. My favorite sister, <u>who / whose</u> fiancé is the same age as I am, is a Type A.

9. Of my other two sisters, the one <u>Ø / which</u> I am closer to is a Type C.

10. I'm less close to the sister <u>who / Ø</u> is much older than I am. She's a Type D.

EXERCISE 3: Identifying / Nonidentifying Clauses

(Grammar Notes 3–8)

Combine each pair of sentences into one sentence with an adjective clause, using the relative pronoun in parentheses. Use the first sentence in each pair as the main clause. Add commas where necessary. The sentences are connected as a story.

1. The company makes computers. I work for the company. (that)

   The company that I work for makes computers.

2. The company has existed for 15 years. It is named Excelsior Computer. (which)

   _____

3. The building is located downtown. We do most of our work in the building. (where)

   _____

4. The office has been remodeled. I work in the office. (that)

   _____

5. Darren Corgatelli is the boss. His wife is my aunt. (whose)

   _____

6. Darren is an excellent boss. I've known Darren since I was a child. (whom)

   _____

7. Sarah Corgatelli keeps the company running smoothly. She is Darren's wife. (who)

   _____

8. I joined the company in 1995. I graduated from college then. (when)

   _____

9. I really admire my colleagues. Their advice has been invaluable. (whose)

   _____

10. Part of my job is telemarketing. I like telemarketing the least. (which)

   _____

Read two reports by an attorney. Complete the spoken report with informal adjective clauses, omitting relative pronouns if possible and using contractions. Complete the written report with formal adjective clauses. Do not omit relative pronouns and do not use contractions. Put all verbs in the correct forms.

Spoken Report

Our client is a guy _____*who's been in trouble*_____ for minor offenses, but I don't
　　　　　　　　　　　1. (have / be / in trouble)

think he's a murderer, _____ I feel comfortable defending
　　　　　　　　　　　　　　　2. (be / why)

him. He did time in the penitentiary from 2008 to 2010, and according to all the

reports he was a person _____. Since he got out of jail
　　　　　　　　　　　　3. (the other prisoners / respected)

in 2010, he's had a good employment record with Textrix, an electronics company

_____. The psychological reports on him show that when he
4. (he / have / be working for)

was in prison he was a person _____ well-balanced and even-
　　　　　　　　　　　　　　5. (the psychiatrists / consider)

tempered, _____ I don't think he's guilty.
　　　　　6. (be / the reason)

⚖ Eager, Barnes, and Kirby
　Attorneys at Law
　555 North Liberty
　Boston MA 02110

Formal Written Report

　Our client is a man _____ for minor offenses, but I
　　　　　　　　　　7. (have / be / in trouble)

do not believe that he is a murderer, _____
　　　　　　　　　　　　　　　　8. (an opinion / make me)

comfortable defending him. He served time in the penitentiary from 2008 to 2010, and

according to all the reports he was a person _____ .
　　　　　　　　　　　　　　　　　9. (the other prisoners / respect)

Since he was released from prison in 2010, he has had a good employment record with

Textrix, an electronics company _____ . His
　　　　　　　　　　　　　10. (he / have / be working for)

psychological profile suggests that when he was in prison he was a person

_____ well balanced and even-tempered,
11. (the psychiatrists / consider)

_____ believe that he is not guilty.
12. (evidence / make me)

EXERCISE 5: Editing

Read the letter from a college student to her parents. There are eight mistakes in the use of adjective clauses. The first mistake is already corrected. Find and correct seven more.

September 28

Dear Mom and Dad,

Well, the first week of college has been tough, but it's turned out OK. My advisor, who ~~she~~ is also from Winnipeg, told me about growing up there, so we had something when we could talk about. Since I haven't decided on a major, she had me take one of those tests show you what you're most interested in. She also had me do one of those personality inventories that they tell you what kind of person you are. According to these tests, I'm a person whom is classified as an extrovert. I also found out that I'm most interested in things involve being on the stage and performing in some way, that doesn't surprise me a bit. I always liked being in school plays. Remember? I signed up for two drama courses. Classes start on Wednesday, and I'm getting to know the other people in the dormitory which I live. It's pretty exciting being here.

Not much else right now. I'll call in a week or so.

Love,

Alice

STEP 4 COMMUNICATION PRACTICE

EXERCISE 6: Listening

A | *Listen to a telephone conversation that Al, a new college student, had with his parents. What doesn't Al like about one of his roommates?*

B | *Read the pairs of sentences. Then listen again to the conversation. Circle the letter of the sentence that correctly describes what you heard.*

1. **a.** Al likes his dormitory.
   b. Al doesn't like his dormitory.

2. **a.** The dormitory has one supervisor.
   b. The dormitory has more than one supervisor.

3. **a.** Both of Al's roommates are from Minnesota.
   b. One of Al's roommates is from Minnesota.

4. **a.** Al has one English class.
   b. Al has more than one English class.

5. **a.** Al has one history class.
   b. Al has more than one history class.

6. **a.** Al's writing class is going to be easy.
   b. Al's math class is going to be easy.

7. **a.** There is one group of girls living in the dormitory.
   b. There is more than one group of girls living in the dormitory.

8. **a.** The girls live on the same side of the building as Al.
   b. The girls live on the other side of the building from Al.

9. **a.** Al has one advisor.
   b. Al has more than one advisor.

EXERCISE 7: Pronunciation

A | *Read and listen to the Pronunciation Note.*

Pronunciation Note

Notice the difference in pronunciation between sentences with identifying adjective clauses and those with nonidentifying adjective clauses. Identifying clauses have no pauses before and after them. Nonidentifying clauses *do* have pauses before and after them.

Examples: The woman **who is wearing a red skirt and a green blouse** is my friend's mother.
(no pauses—the clause is used to identify one particular woman)

The woman, **who is wearing a red skirt and a green blouse**, is my friend's mother.
(pauses—the clause does not identify one particular woman)

B | *Listen to the sentences. Place commas in sentences with nonidentifying clauses. Do not place commas in sentences with identifying clauses. Then circle the phrase that explains the meaning of the sentence.*

1. The man, who lives down the street from me, is a friend of my father.
   (one man)   more than one man

2. The man who lives down the street from me is a friend of my father.
   one man   more than one man

3. The tie which has a stain on it needs to be dry-cleaned.
   one tie   more than one tie

4. The tie which has a stain on it needs to be dry-cleaned.
   one tie   more than one tie

5. The teacher who handed out the awards is really a well-known scientist.
   one teacher   more than one teacher

6. The teacher who handed out the awards is really a well-known scientist.
   one teacher   more than one teacher

7. The student who lives close to the campus has low gasoline bills.
   one student   more than one student

8. The student who lives close to the campus has low gasoline bills.
   one student   more than one student

9. The garden which Mary planted is the most beautiful one of all.
   one garden   more than one garden

10. The garden which Mary planted is the most beautiful one of all.
    one garden   more than one garden

C | *PAIRS: Practice the sentences. Take turns. Your partner indicates which sentences you say.*

EXERCISE 8: Pair Discussion

A | *PAIRS: How can you deal with someone you are not getting along with? Describe a conflict situation that you have had. How did you handle it? Were you successful?*

B | *Share your conclusions with the class.*

> **EXAMPLE:**   **A:** How do you deal with a person you don't get along with?
> **B:** Well, when there's a problem with someone that I can't solve, I . . .

EXERCISE 9: Class Activity

A | *The instructor gives each student in the class the name of another student. Each student writes two sentences about his or her student. One sentence must contain an identifying adjective clause; the other must contain a nonidentifying adjective clause. Make the sentences challenging.*

> EXAMPLES: The student **I am writing about** is sitting in the second row.
> Mr. / Ms. X, **who is wearing blue**, works at a store.

B | *CLASS: Read each sentence aloud. The class tries to identify the student being talked about.*

EXERCISE 10: Writing

A | *Consider the personality categories that have been mentioned in this unit and choose the one that fits you best. Write five or more paragraphs explaining your choice. Include several examples from your experience. Use adjective clauses in your composition.*

> EXAMPLE: No single personality type applies perfectly to a person, but for me one comes closer than all the others. The personality category that fits me most closely is Type B. First, Type B's are social people who are basically extroverts. I think this category fits me quite well. Here's why . . .

B | *Check your work. Use the Editing Checklist.*

Editing Checklist

Did you use . . . ?
☐ adjective clauses correctly
☐ *who(m)*, *which*, and *that* correctly
☐ *whose*, *where*, and *when* correctly

Check your answers on page UR-2.

Do you need to review anything?

A | Circle the correct word or phrase to complete each sentence.

1. The lady who / which is my teacher is the third from the right.

2. Hong Kong is the city that / where I was born.

3. Elena, that / whom you met at the conference, left you a phone message.

4. The man whose / which car we borrowed is my father's boss.

5. Franco Gomez is energetic, that / which is why we should hire him.

6. I can't remember a time where / when he wasn't helpful.

7. Lions are animals that Lea see / sees often at the zoo.

8. Chuy is a person who / who he prefers to be alone.

B | Correct the mistakes in the underlined phrases.

1. The man whom lives next door is wearing a coat. _____

2. The book, Sara bought, was written by Jorge Amado. _____

3. The woman who dog is barking is very wealthy. _____

4. The man we met him is in the second row. _____

5. Barranquilla is the city which I was born. _____

6. I'm thinking of the time which we spoke. _____

7. Ms. Voicu who is a student is from Romania. _____

8. Sally, who's parents work here, lives alone. _____

C | Circle the letter of the one underlined word or phrase in each sentence that is not correct.

1. Al, whom is a freshman, likes the people he is rooming with. **A B C D**
      A   B   C   D

2. Ari, an extrovert loves working with others but who can also work alone, **A B C D**
           A   B
   shone in her last job, which is why she's the one we should hire.
                         C   D

3. Jaime, who is with a company that stresses teamwork, is someone **A B C D**
        A   B
   who values the people with he works.
     C   D

4. Police in Miami are investigating a crime happened last night. **A B C D**
          A   B   C   D

Adjective Clauses with Prepositions; Adjective Phrases

MOVIES

STEP 1 GRAMMAR IN CONTEXT

Before You Read

PAIRS: Discuss the questions.

1. Do you like movies? What do you look for in a movie? Do you see movies primarily for entertainment, or do you want a film to be something more?
2. Which kind of movie do you like better—one in which you already know what is going to happen or one in which you don't know what is going to happen?

Read

Read the movie reviews.

At the Movies

FIVE TO REVISIT

by Dartagnan Fletcher

Here we are at the end of another 10 years. I guess it's incumbent on me as a film critic to come up with a compilation of "The Best Movies of the Decade." The trouble is, I've seen a lot of movies since 2000, **many of which are outstanding in their own way**. To narrow down my list I'll start with five pictures **that anyone interested in cinema should revisit—or see for the first time**.

★ First: *Julie and Julia*. Anyone **having even the slightest interest in food** should see this one. Julie, a young woman **caught in a dead-end job**, decides to spice up her life by cooking all

Invictus

524 recipes in a famous cookbook and writing a blog about it. That didn't sound like a very exciting plot, but I was astonished at how enjoyable and hilarious the movie turned out to be. This film, **starring Meryl Streep and Amy Adams**, is about finding what you really want to do in life.

★ Second: *Invictus* takes place in South Africa in 1994, when Nelson Mandela becomes the leader of the first post-apartheid government. The country is racially polarized, but Mandela insists that blacks and whites reconcile. Mandela reaches out to François Pienaar, the captain of the mostly-white national

(continued on next page)

rugby team, **with whom he develops an enduring friendship**. **Criticized by some for his efforts**, Mandela persists in his vision of bringing blacks and whites together for the good of the nation. The picture stars Morgan Freeman and Matt Damon as Mandela and Pienaar, **both of whom play their roles to near perfection**. Clint Eastwood, **whose films I'm always impressed with**, directed with great skill.

Avatar

★ Third: Science fiction films, **a compelling example of which is** *Avatar*, continue to be popular. The movie, **set on a planetary moon called Pandora**, is a good-guys-versus-bad-guys story **in which the inhabitants of Pandora end up vanquishing a band of exploiters from Earth**. *Avatar*, **directed by James Cameron of *Titanic* fame**, is one of the most beautiful pictures ever made, with special effects **rivaled by those of few other films**.

★ Fourth: *Babel* is an engrossing story about the need for people to communicate. It shows the interconnectedness of events through three sets of characters **whose lives intersect**. An American couple, **played by Brad Pitt and Cate Blanchett**, are traveling in Morocco when the wife is wounded by a stray bullet. The bullet comes from a gun **left in Morocco** by a Japanese man **who'd been on safari**. The Japanese man has a daughter **he's estranged from**. Meanwhile, the American couple's Mexican housekeeper, **to whom they've entrusted their children**, takes the kids to her son's wedding in Mexico, where unfortunate events occur. This film is complicated but well worth your attention.

★ Fifth: *Slumdog Millionaire*, my favorite among favorites, is the story of Jamal, Salim, and Latika, three orphans from the slums of Mumbai **who manage to transcend their environment**. Jamal, **now 18**, is a contestant on India's version of *Who Wants to Be a Millionaire?* **About to answer the grand prize question**, Jamal is arrested and charged with cheating.

Slumdog Millionaire

After all, how could a "slumdog" really be this knowledgeable? In a series of flashbacks, Jamal recounts events in his life **illustrating how he knew the answers to the questions**. In the process he finds the lovely Latika, **from whom he's become separated**. The film, **featuring Dev Patel and Freida Pinto as hero and heroine**, is one of the most original pictures in a long time.

After You Read

A | **Vocabulary:** *Match the blue words and phrases on the left with their meanings on the right.*

_____ **1.** It's **incumbent on me** to come up with a "best movie" compilation.

_____ **2.** It's incumbent on me to come up with a "best movie" **compilation**.

_____ **3.** Julie decides to **spice up** her life.

_____ **4.** South Africa was racially **polarized**.

_____ **5.** The inhabitants of Pandora end up **vanquishing** a group of exploiters.

_____ **6.** *Babel* is an **engrossing** story about the need for people to communicate.

_____ **7.** The Japanese man has a daughter he's **estranged** from.

_____ **8.** The three orphans manage to **transcend** their environment.

a. divided into opposing groups

b. defeating

c. alienated

d. list

e. fascinating

f. make more interesting

g. my responsibility

h. rise above

B | **Comprehension:** *Refer to the reading and complete each sentence with a single word.*

1. The author of the article is a movie _____.

2. *Julie and Julia* is about the activity of _____.

3. Nelson Mandela was the leader of the first South African _____ after the end of apartheid.

4. Mandela insisted that blacks and whites _____.

5. In *Avatar,* the natives of Pandora defeat some _____ from Earth.

6. The film *Babel* illustrates the _____ of human events.

7. The action of *Slumdog Millionaire* takes place in the country of _____.

8. The three main characters of *Slumdog Millionaire* are able to rise above the limitations of their _____.

ADJECTIVE CLAUSES WITH PREPOSITIONS, QUANTIFIERS, OR NOUNS; ADJECTIVE PHRASES

Main Clause	Adjective Clause with Preposition			
People / Things	**Preposition**	**Relative Pronoun**		**Preposition**
He's the actor	to	whom	she was talking.	
		who(m) that Ø*	she was talking	to.
It's the studio	for	which	he works.	
		which that Ø	he works	for.
That's the director		whose	movies I told you	about.
That's the movie			director I spoke	of.

*Ø = no pronoun

Main Clause	Adjective Clause with Quantifier			
People / Things	**Quantifier**	*Of*	**Relative Pronoun**	
I have many friends,	all most a number		whom	are actors.
I was in a lot of movies,	some a few several	of	which	were successes.
That's the director,	a couple both		whose	movies are classics.
That's the movie,	two			actors got awards.

Main Clause	Adjective Clause with Noun		
Things	**Noun**	*Of Which*	
She makes comedies,	an example	of which	is *Julie and Julia*.
I love that series,	an episode		she directed.

Reducing Adjective Clauses to Adjective Phrases

	Adjective Clause		Adjective Phrase
He's the actor	**who's from** the film school.	He's the actor	**from** the film school.
I saw the film	**which is based** on that book.	I saw the film	**based** on that book.
That's the man	**who was in charge** of lighting.	That's the man	**in charge** of lighting.
I read the scripts	**that are on my desk**.	I read the scripts	**on my desk**.

Changing Adjective Clauses to Adjective Phrases

	Adjective Clause		Adjective Phrase
He's the actor	**who plays** the king.	He's the actor	**playing** the king.
Babel is a picture	**which stars** Brad Pitt.	*Babel* is a picture	**starring** Brad Pitt.
It's a love story	**that takes** place in Rome.	It's a love story	**taking** place in Rome.

GRAMMAR NOTES

1

The relative pronouns **who(m)**, **that**, **which**, and **whose** after a noun can be used as **objects of prepositions** in adjective clauses.

- Bill is the man **to whom** I spoke.
- That's the film **to which** he referred.

Sentences with the preposition at the beginning of the clause are formal; sentences with the preposition at the end of the clause are informal.

- She's the director **to whom** I wrote.
- She's the director **whom** I wrote **to**.

NOTE: A preposition can come at the beginning of the clause before *who(m)*, *which*, and *whose*. It cannot come at the beginning in a clause with *that*.

- It is the studio **for which** he works.
  Not: It is the studio ~~for that~~ he works.

We can omit the relative pronouns *who(m)*, *that*, and *which* after a preposition. When we do this, the preposition moves to the end of the clause.

- He has a daughter **he's estranged from**.
- That's the screenwriter **I read about**.

BE CAREFUL! *Whose* cannot be omitted.

- He's the director **whose films I go to**.
  Not: He's the director ~~films I go to~~.

Remember that there are two types of adjective clauses: identifying (essential) and nonidentifying (nonessential).

- The film **to which I'm referring** is *Avatar*. *(identifying)*
- *Avatar*, **to which I'm referring**, is exciting. *(nonidentifying)*

2

Some adjective clauses have the pattern **quantifier + *of* + relative pronoun**.

- The film has many stars, **few of whom** I recognized.
- He made eight films, **all of which** I like.

Quantifiers occur only in clauses with **whom**, **which**, and **whose**. These clauses may refer to **people** or **things**. These clauses are formal.

If a clause with a quantifier occurs within the main clause, it is enclosed in commas. If it occurs **after** the main clause, a comma precedes it.

- Her books, **most of which I've read**, are popular.
- I like her books, **most of which I've read**.

(continued on next page)

3	Some adjective clauses have the pattern **noun + of which**. These clauses refer only to **things**. If a clause with a noun + *of which* occurs within the main clause, it is enclosed in commas. If it occurs **after** the main clause, a comma precedes it.	• Musicals, **an example of which** is *Mamma Mia*, are still popular. NOT: Actors, ~~an example of which is Johnny Depp,~~ earn a lot of money. • Strikes, **occurrences of which may delay filming**, are uncommon. • She has reviewed films, an **example of which is** *Shrek*.
4	We sometimes **shorten adjective clauses** to **adjective phrases** with the same meaning. Remember that a clause is a group of words that has a subject and a verb. A phrase is a group of words that doesn't have both a subject and a verb.	• Anyone **who is interested in cinema** should see this film. *(adjective clause)* • Anyone **interested in cinema** should see this film. *(adjective phrase)*
5	To shorten an adjective clause with a *be* verb, **reduce** the clause to an adjective phrase by deleting the relative pronoun and the *be* verb. **BE CAREFUL!** Adjective clauses with *be* verbs can be reduced only when *who*, *which*, or *that* is the subject pronoun of the clause. If an adjective clause needs commas, the corresponding phrase also needs commas.	• *Slumdog Millionaire*, **which was directed by Danny Boyle**, won many awards. • *Slumdog Millionaire*, **directed by Danny Boyle**, won many awards. • I met George Clooney, **whose latest film is a hit**. NOT: I met George Clooney, ~~latest film is a hit.~~ • Penélope Cruz starred in *Vicky Cristina Barcelona*, **which was released in 2008**. • Penélope Cruz starred in *Vicky Cristina Barcelona*, **released in 2008**.
6	If there is no *be* verb in the adjective clause, it is often possible to **change** the clause to an adjective phrase. Do this by deleting the relative pronoun and changing the verb to its *-ing* form. You can do this only when *who*, *which*, or *that* is the subject pronoun of the clause.	• *Avatar*, **which stars Sam Worthington**, is the top-earning film. • *Avatar*, **starring Sam Worthington**, is the top-earning film. • I like any movie **that features Helen Mirren**. • I like any movie **featuring Helen Mirren**.

EXERCISE 1: Discover the Grammar

A | *Look at the sentences based on the opening reading. Underline the adjective clauses containing prepositions. Circle the noun(s) referred to in the adjective clause and draw a line between the noun(s) and the clause.*

1. I've seen a lot of movies since 2000, many of which are outstanding in their own way.

2. Mandela reaches out to François Pienaar, with whom he develops an enduring friendship.

3. The picture stars Morgan Freeman and Matt Damon, both of whom play their roles to near perfection.

4. Clint Eastwood, whose films I always go to, directed with great skill.

5. Science fiction films, a compelling example of which is *Avatar*, continue to be popular.

6. The movie is a story in which the Pandorans vanquish some exploiters from Earth.

7. The American couple's Mexican housekeeper, to whom they've entrusted their children, takes the kids to her son's wedding in Mexico.

8. In the process he finds the lovely Latika, from whom he's become separated.

B | *Look at the underlined adjective phrases. Make each phrase a clause by adding a relative pronoun and a verb or new verb form.*

1. Anyone interested in cinema should revisit these films.

   Anyone who is interested in cinema should revisit these films.

2. Julie is a young woman caught in a dead-end job.

   _____

3. This film, starring Meryl Streep and Amy Adams, is about finding what you really want to do in life.

   _____

4. The movie, set on a planetary moon called Pandora, is a good-guys-versus-bad-guys story.

   _____

5. *Avatar*, directed by James Cameron of *Titanic* fame, is one of the most beautiful pictures ever made.

   _____

(continued on next page)

6. The movie has special effects <u>rivaled by those of few other films</u>.

_____

7. The bullet comes from a gun <u>left in Morocco by a Japanese man</u>.

_____

8. The film, <u>featuring Dev Patel and Freida Pinto as hero and heroine</u>, is one of the most original pictures in a long time.

_____

EXERCISE 2: Adjective Clauses with Quantifiers

(Grammar Note 2)

Complete the following statements about movies using adjective clauses with the pattern quantifier + preposition + relative pronoun.

1. Animated productions, _____ _most of which are loved by children_ _____, continue to
            (most / be / loved by children)
increase in popularity.

2. _Titanic_ and _Avatar,_ _____, are critical and
                    (both / be / directed by James Cameron)
commercial successes.

3. Roberto Benigni, Pedro Almodóvar, and Lina Wertmüller,

_____, are becoming better known in the
    (all / be / highly regarded European directors)
United States.

4. _Star Wars, The Empire Strikes Back,_ and _Return of the Jedi,_

_____, are the middle three films in a planned
    (all / have / earn a great deal of money)
nine-part series.

5. Sean Connery, Roger Moore, and Daniel Craig,

_____, are from Great Britain, while Pierce
    (all / have / play the role of James Bond)
Brosnan is from Ireland.

6. Nicole Kidman and Ewan McGregor, _____,
                                (neither / be / known as a singer)
surprised everyone with their singing in _Moulin Rouge._

EXERCISE 3: Adjective Phrases

(Grammar Notes 5–6)

Combine each pair of sentences into one sentence with an adjective phrase. The adjective phrase comes from the first sentence, except in item 4, where it comes from the second sentence.

1. *E.T.* was directed by Steven Spielberg. It was the top-earning film until it was passed by *Titanic*.

   E.T., directed by Steven Spielberg, was the top-earning film until it was passed by Titanic.

2. *Spider-Man* is based on the popular comic book. It is one of the highest-earning movies of all time.

   _____

   _____

3. *The Pirates of the Caribbean* films star Johnny Depp. They are all very popular.

   _____

   _____

4. Clint Eastwood has directed many big movies. These include *Million Dollar Baby, Gran Torino,* and *Invictus*.

   _____

   _____

5. The Harry Potter novels were written by J. K. Rowling. They have translated well to the screen.

   _____

   _____

EXERCISE 4: Clause to Sentence

(Grammar Notes 2–3, 5–6)

Each sentence is about types of films and contains an adjective clause or phrase. Imagine that each was formed from an original pair of sentences. Write the original pairs.

1. Comedies, examples of which are *Legally Blonde, Julie and Julia,* and *Marley and Me,* have continued to be popular and successful.

   Comedies have continued to be popular and successful. Examples of these are Legally Blonde, Julie and Julia, and Marley and Me.

2. Many science fiction films have been financially successful, including *Spider-Man, Jurassic Park,* and *Avatar*.

   _____

   _____

(continued on next page)

3. The top-earning animated films, both of which I've seen, are *Finding Nemo* and *Shrek 2*.

_____

_____

4. *The Hurt Locker*, featuring lesser-known actors, was the best picture of 2009.

_____

_____

5. *Beverly Hills Chihuahua* stars Drew Barrymore and Andy Garcia, both of whom I respect.

_____

_____

EXERCISE 5: Personal Inventory   *(Grammar Notes 2–3, 5–6)*

Use the items from the box to describe movies you have seen or that you know about. Write a sentence with each item.

directed by	featuring	(*quantifier*) + of which
examples of which	including	starring

EXAMPLES: I've seen a lot of Arnold Schwarzenegger's movies, **including** *Terminator I, II,* and *III;* and *True Lies.*
Dances with Wolves and *Unforgiven,* **both of which I've seen**, made westerns more popular.

1. _____

2. _____

3. _____

4. _____

5. _____

6. _____

EXERCISE 6: Editing

Read the letter. There are six mistakes in the use of adjective clauses and phrases. The first mistake is already corrected. Find and correct five more. Delete verbs or change pronouns where necessary, but do not change punctuation or add relative pronouns.

July 28

Dear Brent,

    Sarah and I are having a great time in Los Angeles. We spent the first day at the beach in Venice and saw where <u>The Sting</u> was filmed—you know, that famous movie ~~starred~~ *starring* Paul Newman and Robert Redford? Yesterday we went to Universal Studios and learned about all the cinematic tricks, most of that I wasn't aware of. Amazing! The funny thing is that even though you know the illusion presented on the screen is just an illusion, you still believe it's real when you see the movie. Then we took the tram tour around the premises and saw several actors working, some of which I recognized. I felt like jumping off the tram and shouting, "Would everyone famous please give me your autograph?" In the evening we went to a party at the home of one of Sarah's friends, many of them are connected with the movie business. I had a really interesting conversation with a fellow working in the industry who claims that a lot of movies making these days are modeled conceptually after amusement park rides. Just like the rides, the movies start slowly and easily, then they have a lot of twists and turns are calculated to scare you to death, and they end happily. Maybe <u>Pirates of the Caribbean</u> is an example. Pretty fascinating, huh? What next?

    Sorry to spend so much time talking about movies, but you know what an addict I am. Anyway, I'll let you know my arrival time, which I'm not sure of yet, so that you can pick me up at the airport.

                                        Love you lots,

                                        Amanda

EXERCISE 7: Listening

🎧 **A** | *Listen to the film reviewer give her weekly review. Of the five movies, which is her all-time favorite?*

_____

🎧 **B** | *Read the sentences. Then listen to excerpts from the review. Write **T (True)** or **F (False)** to indicate if each item correctly restates the sentence that you hear.*

___T___ **1.** The film festival can be seen this holiday weekend.

_____ **2.** None of these great movies has been shown in more than a decade.

_____ **3.** *A Beautiful Mind* is about a character created by director Ron Howard.

_____ **4.** Jennifer Connelly won an Oscar for her portrayal of Nash's wife.

_____ **5.** *Rashomon* is probably the most famous modern film from China.

_____ **6.** *Rashomon* is about the way people view truth.

_____ **7.** *Chicago* has only one main star.

_____ **8.** Michael J. Fox was responsible for launching *Back to the Future*.

_____ **9.** All who regard themselves as serious movie buffs must see *Casablanca*.

_____ **10.** The reviewer says black-and-white movies are not pretty.

EXERCISE 8: Pronunciation

🎧 **A** | *Read and listen to the Pronunciation Note.*

> **Pronunciation Note**
>
> A number of words in English change their vowel sound but not the spelling of that vowel when the word changes form or use. For sounds and examples, refer to Appendix 25 on page A-11.
>
> **EXAMPLES:** I **read** the newspaper every day. (present form) /i/ vowel
> I **read** the newspaper yesterday evening. (past form) /ɛ/ vowel
> John is a great **athlete**. /i/ vowel
> He's always participated in **athletics**. /ɛ/ vowel

🎧 **B** | *Listen to the sentences. Circle the pronunciation of the boldfaced vowel in each word.*

1. a. He is the h**e**ro. /ɪ/ or /ɛ/

   b. She is the h**e**roine. /ɪ/ or /ɛ/

2. a. It's a n**a**tional problem. /eɪ/ or /æ/

   b. It's for the good of the n**a**tion. /eɪ/ or /æ/

3. a. It's located in **Sou**th Africa.   /aʊ/ or /ʌ/

   b. It's in a **sou**thern city.   /aʊ/ or /ʌ/

4. a. Their actions were atr**o**cious.   /oʊ/ or /ɑ/

   b. They committed atr**o**cities.   /oʊ/ or /ɑ/

5. a. The ch**i**ldren are safe.   /aɪ/ or /ɪ/

   b. A ch**i**ld must be protected.   /aɪ/ or /ɪ/

C | *PAIRS: Practice the sentences.*

EXERCISE 9: Information Gap

PAIRS: Each of you will read a version of a review of the film A Beautiful Mind. *Each version is missing some information. Take turns asking your partner questions to get the missing information.*

Student A, read the review of A Beautiful Mind. *Ask questions and fill in the missing information. Then answer Student B's questions.*

Student B, turn to the Information Gap on page 227 and follow the instructions there.

    EXAMPLE: **A:** What is the movie inspired by?
                B: It is inspired by . . . What was Nash's occupation?
                A: Nash was . . .

A Beautiful Mind
(2002) C-135 m.

Rating: ★★★   **Director:** Ron Howard
Starring: Russell Crowe, Jennifer Connelly, Ed Harris, Paul Bettany, Christopher Plummer, Adam Goldberg, Judd Hirsch, Josh Lucas, Anthony Rapp, Austin Pendleton

An unusual story inspired by _____ in the life of John Nash, a brilliant West Virginia mathematician who flowers at Princeton in the late 1940s and goes to work at _____. But his marriage and sanity are put to a painful test. _____ is amazing—and completely unexpected. Crowe is excellent as usual, and the film offers an overdue showcase for _____ as the student who becomes his wife. Oscar winner for Best Picture, Director, Supporting Actress (Connelly), and Adapted Screenplay (Akiva Goldsman). PG-13.

EXERCISE 10: Group Discussion

*Look at the chart describing the current movie rating system. Then complete the questionnaire for yourself; circle **yes** or **no**. Discuss your answers with a partner. Then discuss your answers with the class as a whole.*

EXAMPLE:　**A:** I think many movies are too violent today.
　　　　　　B: I disagree. Sometimes violence is necessary for the director to make the point.

Movie Ratings	Description
G	Suitable for general audiences, all ages.
PG	Parental guidance is suggested; some material may not be appropriate for children.
PG-13	Parents strongly cautioned; some material may not be appropriate for children under 13.
R	Restricted; anyone under 17 must be accompanied by a parent or adult guardian.
NC-17	No one under 17 is admitted.

Movies and Rating Systems		
Movie rating systems are a good idea.	yes	no
Rating systems are enforced in my area.	yes	no
If I want to see a movie, I don't pay attention to the rating.	yes	no
Many movies today are too violent.	yes	no
Movie rating systems should be made stronger.	yes	no

EXERCISE 11: Picture Discussion

A | *PAIRS: Discuss the picture, using adjective clauses or phrases whenever possible.*

> **EXAMPLE:** **A:** In the theater there are a lot of people trying to concentrate on the movie.
> **B:** One man, annoying the people near him, is talking on his cell phone.

B | *CLASS: What is proper behavior at movie theaters? Discuss these points with the class as a whole:*

- Should cell phones be allowed in movie theaters?
- Should moviegoers have to pick up their own trash?
- Should small children be allowed at movies?
- Should people be allowed to talk during showings of movies?

> **EXAMPLE:** **A:** I don't think cell phones should be allowed in movie theaters.
> **B:** Why not?
> **A:** It's inconsiderate to other people because . . .

EXERCISE 12: Writing

A | *Write your own movie review in three or more paragraphs. Choose a film that you liked or disliked, but try to be objective in your review. Read your review to the class, and answer any questions your classmates might ask about the movie. Use adjective clauses with prepositions and adjective phrases as appropriate.*

> **EXAMPLE:**   One of the best movies I've seen recently is *Super Size Me,* directed by Morgan Spurlock. Spurlock, fascinated by the recent court case in which two American women sued McDonald's for serving food that was less than healthy, decided to find out whether or not fast food is really unhealthy. His plan was simple: eat nothing but McDonald's food for a month. The film is about his month-long adventure. It's humorous and interesting, and . . .

B | *Check your work. Use the Editing Checklist.*

Editing Checklist

Did you use . . . ?
- ☐ adjective clauses with prepositions correctly
- ☐ adjective clauses with quantifiers correctly
- ☐ adjective clauses with nouns correctly
- ☐ adjective phrases correctly

Student B, read the review of A Beautiful Mind. *Answer Student A's questions. Then ask your own questions and fill in the missing information.*

EXAMPLE: **A:** What is the movie inspired by?
B: It is inspired by incidents in the life of John Nash. What was Nash's occupation?
A: Nash was . . .

A Beautiful Mind

(2002) C-135 m.

Rating: ★★★   **Director:** Ron Howard
Starring: Russell Crowe, Jennifer Connelly, Ed Harris, Paul Bettany, Christopher Plummer, Adam Goldberg, Judd Hirsch, Josh Lucas, Anthony Rapp, Austin Pendleton

An unusual story inspired by incidents in the life of John Nash, a brilliant West

Virginia _____ who flowers at Princeton in the late 1940s and

goes to work at M.I.T. But his _____ are put to a painful test.

The central story twist is amazing—and completely unexpected.

_____ is excellent as usual, and the film offers an overdue showcase

for Connelly as the student who becomes _____. Oscar winner

for Best Picture, Director, Supporting Actress (Connelly), and Adapted Screenplay

(Akiva Goldsman). PG-13.

Check your answers on page UR-2.
Do you need to review anything?

A | Circle the correct pronoun in each adjective clause.

1. *The Wizard of Oz, Dumbo,* and *Fantasia,* all of <u>whom / which</u> I've seen, are classics.

2. Pedro Almodóvar, <u>which / whose</u> films I enjoy, is a well-known Spanish director.

3. Streep and Adams, both of <u>who / whom</u> are prominent actresses, star in *Julie and Julia.*

4. *Avatar* and *2012,* neither of <u>them / which</u> I've seen yet, are science fiction movies.

5. Cruz and Hayek, both of <u>which / whom</u> are Spanish-speaking, are prominent actresses.

6. Anyone <u>interested / interesting</u> in film history should attend the lecture.

7. *Invictus,* <u>which was / that was</u> directed by Clint Eastwood, is a powerful film.

8. I try to see any movie <u>stars / starring</u> Jackie Chan.

B | Correct the mistakes in the underlined words or phrases.

1. He has directed five films, all of <u>them</u> I like.   _____

2. I'm taking two new courses, neither of <u>them</u> is interesting.   _____

3. I made two friends, both of <u>them</u> are teachers, this week.   _____

4. We saw great films, examples of <u>them</u> are *Tron* and *Up.*   _____

5. Several actors, one of <u>which</u> I've met, are in town.   _____

6. The novel is about a young man <u>which</u> is caught in a dead-end job.   _____

7. Emiko was the employee <u>whom</u> was in charge of bookkeeping.   _____

8. Boyle has won many awards, one of <u>that</u> was an Oscar.   _____

C | Circle the letter of the one underlined word or phrase in each sentence that is not correct.

1. The films <u>all</u> <u>starred</u> Depp, <u>that</u> <u>readily</u> explains their success.   **A B C D**
       A   B   C   D

2. Anyone <u>interested</u> in film <u>must</u> see *The Fighter,* <u>that</u> <u>opens</u> today.   **A B C D**
       A   B   C   D

3. Strikes, <u>occurrences</u> <u>of</u> <u>them</u> can delay <u>filming</u>, are uncommon.   **A B C D**
       A   B   C   D

4. The writer <u>to whom</u> I referred is Saki, <u>most</u> of <u>which</u> works I've read.   **A B C D**
       A   B   C   D

From Grammar to Writing
PUNCTUATING ADJECTIVE CLAUSES AND PHRASES

You can strengthen your writing by judiciously using adjective clauses and phrases and by punctuating them correctly. Remember that the two types of adjective clauses and phrases are **identifying** and **nonidentifying**. Identifying adjective clauses give information essential for distinguishing one person or thing from another. Nonidentifying clauses give additional (= nonessential) information that doesn't identify. Only nonidentifying clauses are set off by commas.

> **EXAMPLES:** I saw three movies last week. The movie **that I liked best** was *Salt. (essential—says which movie I'm commenting on)*
> *Salt,* **which stars Angelina Jolie**, is a spy movie. *(nonessential—adds information)*

Adjective phrases perform the same identifying and nonidentifying functions. Only nonidentifying phrases are set off by commas.

> **EXAMPLES:** A movie **directed by George Lucas** is likely to be a blockbuster. *(essential—says which type of movie is likely to be a blockbuster)*
> *Avatar,* **directed by James Cameron**, has awesome special effects. *(nonessential—adds extra information about* Avatar.*)*

1 | *Punctuate the pairs of sentences containing adjective clauses and phrases. One sentence or phrase in each pair is identifying, and the other is nonidentifying.*

1. **a.** College students who live close to campuses spend less money on gas.

   b. College students who are expected to study hard have to become responsible for themselves.

2. **a.** People who are the only animals with a capacity for creative language have highly developed brains.

   b. People who live in glass houses shouldn't throw stones.

3. **a.** The car which was invented in the late 19th century has revolutionized modern life.

   b. The car that I would really like to buy is the one in the far corner of the lot.

4. **a.** Science fiction movies which have become extremely popular in the last two decades often earn hundreds of millions of dollars for their studios.

   b. The science fiction movies that have earned the most money collectively are the *Star Wars* films.

5. **a.** The panda that was given to the National Zoo died recently.

   b. The panda which is native only to China is on the Endangered Species List.

(continued on next page)

6. **a.** A film directed by Steven Spielberg is likely to be a blockbuster.

   b. *A Beautiful Mind* directed by Ron Howard won the Academy Award for best picture.

7. **a.** Many Canadians including Donald Sutherland and Michael J. Fox are major international film stars.

   b. A film directed by Pedro Almodóvar is likely to be a financial success.

2 | *Complete the punctuation of this letter containing adjective clauses and phrases.*

September 30

Dear Mom and Dad,

Thanks again for bringing me down here to the university last weekend. Classes didn't start until Wednesday, so I had a few days to get adjusted. I'm signed up for five courses: zoology, calculus, English, and two history classes. It's a heavy load, but they're all courses that will count for my degree. The zoology class which meets at 8:00 every morning is going to be my hardest subject. The history class that I have in the morning is on Western civilization; the one that I have in the afternoon is on early U.S. history. Calculus which I have at noon every day looks like it's going to be relatively easy. Besides zoology, the other class that's going to be hard is English which we have to write one composition a week for.

I like all of my roommates but one. There are four of us in our suite including two girls from Texas and a girl from Manitoba. Here's a picture of us. Sally who is from San Antonio is great; I feel like I've known her all my life. She's the one on the left. I also really like Anne the girl from Manitoba. She's the one on the right. But Heather the other girl from Texas is kind of a pain. She's the one next to me in the middle. Heather is one of those people who never tell you what's bothering them and then get hostile. All in all, though, it looks like it's going to be a great year. I'll write again in a week or so.

Love,

Vicky

3 | *Before you write . . .*

1. A well-known proverb in English says, "A picture is worth a thousand words." While this may be an overstatement, we can learn a great deal from close examination of a picture, and we can use that information to make our writing interesting. Find a photograph (in a magazine, book, or your own personal collection) that interests you and bring it to class.

2. Describe your picture to a partner. Listen to your partner's description.

3. Ask and answer questions about your and your partner's picture. Why is the picture significant to you? What about it interests or touches you?

4 | *Write a draft of a two- or three-paragraph composition about your picture. Follow the model. Remember to include information that your partner asked about. Use identifying and nonidentifying adjective clauses and phrases in your composition.*

The people and things or places in the picture:

_____

_____

_____

_____

My experience with the people, things, or places in the picture:

_____

_____

_____

_____

What specifically interests or touches me about the picture:

_____

_____

_____

_____

5 | *Exchange compositions with a different partner. Complete the chart.*

---

1. The writer used identifying and nonidentifying adjective clauses and phrases. **Yes** ☐ **No** ☐

2. What I liked in the composition:

_____

_____

_____

3. Questions I'd like the writer to answer about the composition:

Who _____?

What _____?

When _____?

Where _____?

Why _____?

How _____?

(Your own question) _____?

---

6 | *Work with your partner. Discuss each other's chart from Exercise 5. Then rewrite your own compositions and make any necessary changes.*

PASSIVE VOICE

The Passive: Review and Expansion
UNSOLVED MYSTERIES

STEP 1 GRAMMAR IN CONTEXT

Before You Read

PAIRS: Discuss the questions.

1. Many people find unsolved mysteries fascinating. Do you enjoy hearing about them? If so, why? Do you know of any unsolved mysteries?

2. Some people think there is a need for mystery in life, for things to remain unexplained. Do you agree or disagree?

3. Why do people sometimes sympathize with criminals and want them to get away with their crimes?

Read

Read the news article about an unsolved mystery.

Did He Get Away With It?

Some crimes never **get solved**, and the case of Dan Cooper is one that **hasn't been**. Late in November of 1971, on a short flight between Portland and Seattle, a flight attendant **was handed** a note by a mysterious middle-aged man dressed in a dark suit. Leaning close to her, he said, "Miss, you'd better look at that note. I have a bomb." He then opened his briefcase so that she could see several red cylinders and a lot of wires. The man, who used the alias "Dan Cooper," was demanding $200,000, four parachutes, and a plane to fly him to Mexico.

The plane proceeded to Seattle with none of the other passengers even aware it **was being hijacked**. They got off the plane, and "Cooper" got what he was demanding: $200,000, all in $20 bills that **had been photocopied** by FBI agents so they **could** easily **be identified**. Then the plane **was refueled** and took off for Mexico.

A few minutes later, Cooper ordered the flight attendant to go to the cockpit and stay there. As she was leaving, she noticed him trying to tie something around his waist—presumably the bag of money. Then he opened the plane's rear stairway and jumped out of the plane. The crew felt pressure bumps that **were** probably **caused** by Cooper's jump. The air temperature was seven degrees below zero. Cooper was wearing no survival gear and only light, casual shoes.

Did He Get Away With It?

Cooper **has not been seen** or **heard from** since that night. Who was he? Did he get away with his plan? Or **was** he **killed** trying to commit the perfect crime?

Authorities speculate that Cooper landed near Ariel, a small town near the Columbia River north of Portland. Only one real clue **has been discovered**. In 1980, an eight-year-old boy inadvertently dug up $5,880 of Cooper's money near a riverbank. It was only a few inches below the surface of the earth, but it had decayed so much that only the picture and the serial numbers on the bills were visible. Rotting rubber bands **were found** along with the money, indicating that the cash **must have been deposited** there before the bands fell apart. Since then, the area **has been searched** thoroughly, but no trace of Cooper **has been found**.

What really happened? Many investigators believe that Cooper **had to have been killed** by the combination of the weather conditions and the impact of his fall, but if so, why **have** none of his remains ever **been discovered**? **Is** more information **known** than **has been divulged**? Is Cooper's body in some remote part of the wilderness area into which he jumped, or is he living a luxurious life under an alias somewhere? Did he **have** the $5,880 **buried** by an accomplice to throw the authorities off the track? Or did he bury it himself?

Cooper has become a legend. His story **has been told** in books and articles and even a movie. In Ariel the hijacking **is** still **celebrated** every year. Bar owner Dona Elliot says, "He did get away with it . . . so far." Others don't think so. Jerry Thomas, a retired soldier who has been working independently on the case, thinks that Cooper didn't survive the fall and his body **will** eventually **be found**. "I know there is something out here," he says. "There has to be."

As of 2011, none of the missing money **had been recovered**. The mystery goes on.

After You Read

A | Vocabulary: *Circle the letter of the best meaning for the blue words and phrases from the reading.*

1. The man, who used the **alias** "Dan Cooper," was demanding $200,000.

   a. nickname   **b.** false name   **c.** surname   **d.** title

2. None of the other passengers were aware that the plane was being **hijacked**.

   a. destroyed   **b.** affected   **c.** forcibly taken over   **d.** terrorized

3. Cooper was wearing no survival **gear** and only light, casual shoes.

   a. equipment   **b.** trousers   **c.** mechanical device   **d.** overcoat

4. An eight-year-old boy **inadvertently** dug up $5,880 of Cooper's money.

   a. by careful planning   **b.** by luck   **c.** by great effort   **d.** by accident

5. **Rotting** rubber bands were found along with the money.

   a. Decaying   **b.** Elastic   **c.** Ancient   **d.** Manufactured

6. Why have none of Cooper's **remains** ever been discovered?

   a. messages   **b.** body parts   **c.** DNA samples   **d.** clothes

7. Is more information known than has been **divulged**?

   a. proved   **b.** suggested   **c.** revealed   **d.** claimed

8. Did Cooper have the money buried by an **accomplice**?

   a. consultant   **b.** gang member   **c.** relative   **d.** helper in wrongdoing

9. Bar owner Dona Elliot believes that Cooper did **get away with** the crime.

   a. escape capture for   **b.** commit   **c.** pay for   **d.** plan

B | Comprehension: *Circle **T** (True) or **F** (False). Correct the false statements.*

1. The flight Cooper hijacked originated in Seattle.	T	F
2. Dan Cooper claimed to have a bomb.	T	F
3. The money Cooper received was in bills of different denominations.	T	F
4. The passengers were aware of what Cooper was doing.	T	F
5. A portion of Cooper's money was discovered by authorities.	T	F
6. Cooper was killed by the combination of the impact of his fall and the weather conditions.	T	F
7. Cooper may have buried the money dug up by the boy.	T	F
8. Most people think Cooper got away with the crime.	T	F

THE PASSIVE: REVIEW AND EXPANSION

Active Sentences			Passive Sentences		
Subject	**Verb**	**Object**	**Subject**	***Be* + Past Participle**	**(*By* + Agent)**
Cooper	**hijacked**	the plane.	The plane	**was hijacked**	by Cooper.
Someone	**found**	the bills.	The bills	**were found**.	

Passive Verb Forms

		Be (not)	Past Participle	
SIMPLE PRESENT		**is (not)**		
PRESENT PROGRESSIVE		**is (not) being**		
SIMPLE PAST		**was (not)**		
PAST PROGRESSIVE	The crime	**was (not) being**	**investigated**	(by the new team).
FUTURE		**will (not) be** **is (not) going to be**		
PRESENT PERFECT		**has (not) been**		
PAST PERFECT		**had (not) been**		
FUTURE PERFECT		**will (not) have been**		

The Passive with Modals

	Modals	*Be / Have Been*	Past Participle	
The case	**can (not)** **may (not)** **might (not)** **should (not)** **ought (not) to** **must (not)** **had better (not)**	**be**	**reopened**	in the future.
	could (not) **might (not)** **must (not)** **should (not)** **ought (not) to**	**have been**		years ago.

The Passive Causative

Subject	***Have / Get***	**Object**	**Past Participle**	**(*By* + Agent)**
We	**had**	the evidence	**checked**	by experts.
She	**has had**	the note	**analyzed**.	
They	**got**	the report	**printed**	by professionals.
He	**is going to get**	a copy	**made**.	

GRAMMAR NOTES

1

A sentence in the **passive voice** has a corresponding sentence in the **active voice**. The object in the active sentence becomes the subject in the passive sentence. We can say that the subject of a passive sentence is acted upon.

The subject of the active sentence becomes the agent (preceded by the preposition *by*) in the passive sentence, or disappears.

BE CAREFUL! Only transitive verbs, those that can be followed by an object, can be made passive. Intransitive verbs (those that cannot be followed by an object) cannot be made passive.

OBJECT
- The police never **catch some criminals**.

SUBJECT
- **Some criminals** are never caught.

SUBJECT
- **Someone took** the money.

AGENT
- The money **was taken (by someone)**.

- No one **has seen** Cooper since 1971.
- Cooper **has not been seen** since 1971.
- Several people **died** in the accident.
  Not: Several people ~~were~~ died in the accident.

2

Passive sentences are formed with *be* + past participle. They occur in present, past, and future forms.

To make a negative passive sentence, place *not* after the first verb.

Use the present progressive and past progressive passives to describe actions in progress (= not finished) at a certain time.

- Police officers **are** well **trained**.
- The suspect **was arrested** yesterday.
- He **will be held** in the local jail.

- Cooper **has not been caught**.

- The suspect **is being held** in prison.
- The robbery occurred while the money **was being taken** to a bank.

3

Use the **passive** voice
a. when you don't know who performed the action or when it is not important to say who performed it

b. when you want to avoid mentioning the agent

c. when you want to focus on the receiver or the result of an action instead of the agent

- The money **was stolen**.
- The plane **was refueled**.

- A criminal **is** sometimes **regarded** as a hero.
  (*We don't want to say who regards him as a hero.*)

RECEIVER   RESULT   AGENT
- The thief **was caught** by the detective.

4

Use the **passive with a *by* phrase**
a. to introduce new information about the agent

b. to credit someone who did something

c. when the agent is surprising

You can omit the *by* phrase in passive sentences if you feel it is unnecessary or undesirable to mention the agent.

- The money was stolen **by a person who has a criminal record**.

- The bills were photocopied **by FBI agents**.

- The money was found **by a little boy**.

- Why **hasn't** this crime **been solved**?

5

Most commonly, the direct object of an active sentence is the subject of the corresponding passive sentence.

DIRECT OBJECT
- The police **arrested** the suspect.

SUBJECT
- The suspect **was arrested** by the police.

However, an indirect object is sometimes the subject of a passive sentence.

INDIRECT OBJECT
- The F.B.I. **gave** Cooper the money.

SUBJECT
- **Cooper was given** the money by the F.B.I.

6

We often use **modals** and modal-like auxiliaries in the passive. To form the present passive with a modal, use the modal + *be* + past participle. To form the past passive with a modal, use the modal + *have been* + past participle.

- The criminal **should be arrested**.
- He **could have been arrested** before this.

Use *have (got) to*, *had better*, *had to*, *must*, *ought to*, and *should* in passive sentences to express advisability, obligation, and necessity.

- The charges **had to be dropped**.
- Criminal suspects **must be charged**.

Use *can* and *could* to express present and past ability.

- Suspects **can't be kept** in jail.
- The thief **could have been caught**.

Use *will* and *be going to* to talk about future events.

- This prisoner **will be tried**.
- The suspects **are going to be released**.

Use *can't*, *could*, *may*, and *might* to talk about future possibility and impossibility.

- The mystery **may** never **be solved**.
- He **can't be released** from jail.

7

The **passive** can also be formed with **get**. The passive with *get* is more informal than the passive with *be*. It is conversational and characteristic of informal writing.

- Will that criminal ever **get caught**?
- Our team **got beaten** in the soccer game.

BE CAREFUL! Although the *be* passive is used both with action and non-action verbs, the *get* passive is used only with action verbs.

- More research **is needed** about the causes of crime.
  Not: More research ~~gets needed~~ about the causes of crime.

8

Have and *get* + object + past participle are used to form the **passive causative**. There is usually little difference in meaning between the causative with *have* and with *get*.

- You should **have** your car **serviced**.
- I just **got** my best suit **dry-cleaned**.

The passive causative is used in the past, present, and future and with modals.

- We **had** the windows **washed**.
- I **get** my car **tuned up** twice a year.
- She**'s going to get** her hair **cut**.

(continued on next page)

9 Use the **passive causative** to talk about services or activities that people arrange for someone else to do.

- The detective **had** the evidence **analyzed**.
- Sometimes criminals **get** their hair **dyed** or **shaved**.

The passive causative can occur with a *by* phrase, but this phrase is often omitted. Use the *by* phrase only when it is necessary to mention the agent.

- I **got** my photos **developed** at the drugstore.
- We **had** our house **inspected by Jim**.

BE CAREFUL! Don't confuse the simple past causative with the past perfect.

- They **had** the grass **cut**. (*simple past causative—someone else cut the grass*)
- They **had cut** the grass. (*past perfect—they had done this before a specific time in the past*)

BE CAREFUL! Don't confuse the passive causative with the expression *to get something done* meaning *to finish something*.

- I **got** the work **done** by a mechanic. (*passive causative*)
- I **got** the work **done** by noon. (*I finished the work by 12 P.M.*)

STEP 3 FOCUSED PRACTICE

EXERCISE 1: Discover the Grammar

*Look at these sentences based on the opening reading. Underline the passive construction in each sentence. Then write **a, b,** or **c** above it to show why the passive is used.*

a = don't know who performed the action or not important to say

b = desire to avoid mentioning who performed the action

c = focus on the receiver or result of an action

1. Some crimes never get solved.

2. A flight attendant was handed a note by a mysterious middle-aged man.

3. None of the other passengers were even aware the plane was being hijacked.

4. The twenty-dollar bills had all been photocopied by FBI agents.

5. Only one real clue has been discovered.

6. Rotting rubber bands were found along with the money.

7. Many investigators believe Cooper had to have been killed in the jump.

8. Is there additional information that has not been divulged?

EXERCISE 2: Transitive / Intransitive

(Grammar Notes 1–2)

*Complete the sentences with the active or passive form of the verb in parentheses. Then identify the verbs as **T (Transitive)** or **I (Intransitive)**.*

___I___ **1.** Criminals often _____return_____ to the scene of a crime. (return)

_____ **2.** If they are not careful, they _____ (catch) by the authorities.

_____ **3.** Smart criminals _____ (disappear) entirely from the scene.

_____ **4.** They never _____ (go) back to the locale.

_____ **5.** Usually a smart criminal _____ (help) by one or more accomplices.

_____ **6.** The accomplices _____ (reward) by the intelligent criminal.

_____ **7.** Most criminals, however, aren't smart. They _____ (not realize) how resourceful the police are.

_____ **8.** Crime scenes _____ (watch) very closely by the police, but most criminals don't believe this.

EXERCISE 3: Progressive Passives

(Grammar Note 2)

Complete the TV news bulletin with present progressive and past progressive passives.

Here is breaking news from KKBO News Channel 6. Two suspects _____are being held_____

1. (hold)

in the county jail where they _____ about their role in a bank robbery

2. (question)

that took place this morning at the downtown branch of First International Bank. As the bank's

vault _____, the suspects, wearing masks and carrying guns, burst in

3. (open)

and demanded that an undisclosed amount of money be placed in a paper bag. They escaped with

the funds but were later caught after a customer who _____ noticed the

4. (help)

license plate number of the vehicle the suspects were driving and notified bank authorities. The

identities of the two suspects _____ until the initial investigation is

5. (withhold)

completed. Other bank customers _____ for additional information. This

6. (currently / interview)

is Ron Mason for KKBO News Channel 6. Stay tuned for further updates.

EXERCISE 4: Various Passives

(Grammar Notes 2, 6)

*Fill in the blanks in the article with passive constructions with **be** and the correct forms of the verbs in parentheses.*

Two Unsolved Mysteries Continue to Fascinate

So you think there are no more mysteries, that all mysteries ___*are solved*___ in

1. (solve)

time? Think again. The pages of history are full of mysteries that _____.

2. (not / crack)

Consider, for example, the case of the ship *Mary Celeste*. The ship had left New York for

Italy in 1872. Later it _____ floating east of the Azores. No one

3. (sight)

_____ on board, though everything _____ to

4. (find)   **5. (determine)**

be in order, and there was no indication why the *Mary Celeste* _____.

6. (abandon)

Apparently, in fact, tables ___*were*___ for afternoon tea. One theory speculates

7. (set)

that the ship ___*might have been threaten*___ by an explosion that _____

8. (might / threaten)   **9. (cause)**

by fumes from its cargo of alcohol. That theory, however, _____.

10. (not prove)

A second perplexing mystery is that of Amelia Earhart, the famous aviator who in the 1920s

and 1930s ___*was considered*___ the best example of an adventurous woman. Earhart

11. (consider)

flew across the Atlantic with two men in 1928 and set a record for a cross-Atlantic flight in 1932.

In 1937 she embarked on her most ambitious plan, a flight around the world. Earhart began her

flight in Miami in June and ___*was accompanied*___ only by Fred Noonan, her navigator.

12. (accompany)

They reached New Guinea and left for Howland in the South Pacific on July 1. After that, no

radio reports or messages of any kind ___*was*___. No remains of her plane

13. (receive)

_____ by naval investigators in the years since then. Did she simply attempt

14. (discover)

the impossible? _____ when her plane ran out of fuel and crashed? Or

15. (Could / she and Noonan / kill)

could something else have happened? No one really knows. For the time being, at least, the riddle of

the *Mary Celeste* and the fate of Amelia Earhart will have to remain mysterious. Some may think they

___*Should n't be solved*___ at all.

16. (should / not solve)

EXERCISE 5: Passive Causative

A | *Read the sentences. Then circle the letter of the choice that best explains the meaning of the sentence.*

Last week Detective Harry Sadler had an extremely busy schedule. . . .

1. On Monday morning, he had a tooth pulled before going to work.

   a. He pulled the tooth himself.   **(b.)** He arranged for someone to pull the tooth.

2. When he got to work, he had some crime notes typed up.

   a. He typed them himself.   **b.** Someone else typed them.

3. In the afternoon, he had to review another officer's report. He had finished it by 6:00 P.M.

   a. He finished it himself.   **b.** Someone else finished it.

4. On Tuesday and Wednesday, he had to write his own report on a case he had been working on. He got it done by the end of the day.

   a. He did it himself.   **b.** Someone else did it.

5. On Thursday, Harry got some crime pictures microfilmed.

   a. He microfilmed them himself.   **b.** Someone else microfilmed them.

6. On Friday, he worked until 5:30 P.M. and then went to an appointment. He'd had his income taxes done and needed to go over them.

   a. He did the taxes himself.   **b.** Someone else did the taxes.

B | *Complete the paragraph using the passive causative or active past perfect forms of the verbs in parentheses. Use verbs in the progressive where necessary.*

Yesterday was a typically unpredictable day in the life of detective Harry Sadler. Since

Harry hadn't been able to eat at home, he _got some breakfast brought_ to his office as
                                          1. (get / some breakfast / bring)

soon as he arrived. After breakfast he emailed some photos of a crime scene to the lab to

_____. He spent two hours going over files and then left for the
   2. (have / them / enlarge)

garage where he was _____. The mechanic said that he should also
                        3. (get / his car / tune up)

_____. Harry agreed and arranged to pick the car up later. At lunchtime
   4. (have / a tail light / replace)

he met with the members of his team. Time was short, so they _____
                                                                5. (get / lunch / deliver)

from a restaurant. They studied evidence they had _____ by the
                                                      6. (get / analyze)

crime lab. By 2:00 they _____. After the meeting Harry wrote a report
                           7. (have / complete / the work)

by hand. He _____ by 4:00; then he _____
               8. (have / finish / the report)   **9. (have / it / type)**

by his secretary. At 5:30 he left, picked up his car, and met his wife for dinner. They were

_____ and couldn't do any cooking. At 9:00 P.M. they got home. It's good
   10. (have / their kitchen / remodel)

that Harry loves his work because it was another long, tiring, but interesting day.

EXERCISE 6: Editing

Read this student essay about the crop circles in Great Britain and elsewhere. There are nine mistakes in the use of the passive. The first one is already corrected. Find and correct eight more.

The Crop Circles

In our day we believe in science and have the feeling that every question can be *explained* ~~explain~~ and every problem can be solved. But some of us want the opposite. We don't want everything to be explained. We like puzzles. We feel that mystery is needed in our lives.

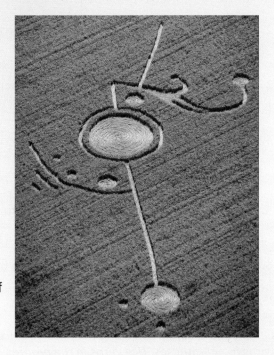

The mysterious crop circles that have been appeared around the world in the last 25 years or so are an example of this. These formations have reported in more than 20 countries, including the United States, Canada, and Australia. But most of them have been found in grain fields in southern England. These circles, which are large and flat, are caused by a force that flattens the grain but does not destroy it. They are still been made.

How have these circles been produced? By whom have they been made? Since the first discovery of the circles, many explanations have been proposed. According to some people, the circles have been made by spirit creatures such as fairies. Others say they have been caused by "Star Wars" experiments or are messages that have been leaving by extraterrestrials visiting our planet. Two British painters, David Chorley and Douglas Bower, say they were made the crop circles over a period of years as a joke. If this is true, however, how can we explain the crop circles in Australia and Canada and other places? They couldn't all have being made by Chorley and Bower, could they?

In 2002, director M. Night Shyamalan released his movie *Signs*, which is about the crop circle question. The movie shows clearly that the crop circles made by invading aliens from beyond our solar system. This is one interesting and enjoyable theory. More explanations like it get needed. What's fun is speculation. The mystery doesn't need to be solved.

EXERCISE 7: Listening

🎧 **A** | *Listen to the news bulletin. What kind of accident occurred this evening?*

_____

🎧 **B** | *Listen again. Answer each question with a complete sentence.*

1. What time did the accident occur?

   The accident occurred this evening at 8:45 p.m.
   _____

2. The boy was struck by what kind of car?

   _____

3. What was the boy doing when he was struck?

   _____

4. What happened to the car?

   _____

5. What kind of injuries did the boy sustain?

   _____

6. Where was the boy taken after the accident?

   _____

7. Where is the boy being cared for?

   _____

8. How is his condition described?

   _____

9. Anyone with information is asked to call what number?

   _____

10. What is being offered?

    _____

EXERCISE 8: Pronunciation

A | *Read and listen to the Pronunciation Note.*

> **Pronunciation Note**
>
> The phrase *has been* in a passive sentence means that the action has already been performed. The phrase *is being* in a passive sentence means that the action is happening now—still being performed.
>
> **EXAMPLES:** The suspect **has been** questioned. *(has already happened)*
> The suspect **is being** questioned. *(is happening now)*

B | *Listen to the sentences. Circle* **'s been (has been)** *or* **'s being (is being)** *depending on what you hear. Then circle* **already done** *or* **happening now.**

1. The prisoner 's been / ('s being) interrogated.   already done / (happening now)

2. The issue 's been / 's being discussed.   already done / happening now

3. Bob 's been / 's being promoted to police chief.   already done / happening now

4. The investigation 's been / 's being completed.   already done / happening now

5. The plane 's been / 's being hijacked.   already done / happening now

6. The boy 's been / 's being treated for injuries.   already done / happening now

7. The report 's been / 's being written.   already done / happening now

8. The mystery 's been / 's being solved.   already done / happening now

C | *PAIRS: Practice the sentences. Take turns.*

EXERCISE 9: Information Gap

PAIRS: Student A, read clues 1–4 to Student B. Student B will complete the clues. Switch roles after item 4. Then put the clues in the correct order and decide what the mystery object is.

Student B, turn to page 248 and follow the instructions there.

Student A's Clues

1. I was born, or maybe I should say I was created . . .
2. An all-night card game . . .
3. I was created by . . .
4. The "hero" type of me gets its name . . .

Student A's Completions

5. . . . have been known by my name since then.
6. . . . some slices of meat between two slices of bread.
7. . . . is shaped like a submarine.
8. . . . so he ordered a snack to be delivered to the gaming table.
9. . . . that I'm being eaten somewhere in the world this very minute.

EXERCISE 10: Survey and Discussion

A | *GROUPS: Within your group, conduct a survey of opinions on the questions. Write* **Y (Yes)** *or* **N (No)***. Then discuss the responses.*

_____ Should juveniles indicted for crimes ever be tried as adults?

_____ Should juveniles be incarcerated with hardened criminals?

_____ In general, are criminals today punished sufficiently for the crimes they commit?

_____ In general, is the criminal justice system in your country being improved?

_____ Should hit-and-run drivers be jailed?

B | *CLASS: Discuss the conclusions of all the groups.*

EXERCISE 11: Picture Discussion

A | *GROUPS: Look at the photos of a UFO and "an alien from a UFO crash" near Roswell, New Mexico, in 1947. Discuss the pictures using passive verb constructions where appropriate.*

• What do the pictures represent?

• Was there really a UFO crash in 1947?

• Was the incident covered up by the government, as some people say?

• How can UFOs be explained?

ExAMPLE: **A:** Do you think the Roswell alien story was covered up by the government?
 B: No, I don't.
 C: How else can it be explained?
 B: I think . . .

 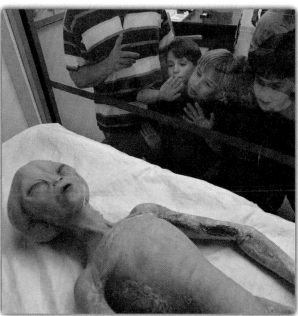

B | *CLASS: Share your conclusions with those of the other groups.*

EXERCISE 12: Writing

A | *Write a composition of five or more paragraphs describing an unsolved mystery. It could involve a crime, someone's disappearance, or some strange natural phenomenon. Describe what the mystery is and how it might have been caused. Offer some possible solutions to the mystery. Use passive constructions as appropriate.*

EXAMPLE: We've all heard about the Bermuda Triangle, an area in the Caribbean Sea where planes and ships supposedly get captured by unknown forces. One of the most famous mysteries of the Bermuda Triangle is the case of Flight 19, a U.S. military expedition that took off on December 5, 1945, to do navigational research. There were five planes, and all of them were piloted by skilled fliers . . .

B | *Check your work. Use the Editing Checklist.*

Editing Checklist

Did you use . . . ?
☐ passive verb forms correctly
☐ passives with modals correctly
☐ passive causatives correctly

INFORMATION GAP FOR STUDENT B

Choose one of phrases 1–4 to complete each clue that Student A reads. Switch roles after item 4. Then put the clues in the correct order and decide what the mystery object is.

Student B's Completions

1. . . . because of the hero-sized appetite that's needed to eat one.
2. . . . at 5:00 in the morning on August 6, 1762.
3. . . . was being played at a gaming table.
4. . . . an Englishman named John Montagu, the fourth earl of the place I was named after.

Student B's Clues

5. The snack ordered by my creator was composed of . . .
6. It's almost certain . . .
7. My creator was hungry but too busy to leave the game, . . .
8. Two slices of bread with a filling between them . . .
9. And the "submarine" type of me . . .

14 Review

UNIT

Check your answers on page UR-2.

Do you need to review anything?

A | *Circle the word or phrase that correctly completes each sentence.*

1. Right now a new hotel is constructed / ~~is being constructed~~ downtown.

2. Tadao ~~had his car serviced~~ / had serviced his car because he couldn't do it himself.

3. The thieves were caught / caught when they tried to spend stolen money.

4. The driver of the car died / was died in the accident.

5. Evidence shows that the theory has been / being disproved.

6. The children were been / being driven to school when the accident happened.

7. The work won't have been / been being finished by this weekend.

8. Without any help, I got the job done by noon / the job done by an assistant.

B | *Complete the sentences with the verb* report *in the indicated passive constructions.*

1. The news _are reported_ daily. (simple present)

2. The news _____ right now. (present progressive)

3. The news _____ twice today. (present perfect)

4. The news _____ an hour ago. (simple past)

5. The news _____ when the earthquake occurred. (past progressive)

6. The news _____ an hour before the earthquake occurred. (past perfect)

7. The news _____ at 5:00 P.M. (simple future)

8. The news _____ by 3:30 P.M. (future perfect)

C | *Circle the letter of the one underlined word or phrase in each sentence that is not correct.*

1. The Turkish city of Trabzon <u>has</u> just <u>being</u> <u>hit</u> <u>by</u> a tsunami.　　　　A **B** C D
   　　　　　　　　　　　　　A　　B　C D

2. The tsunami <u>got</u> <u>caused</u> <u>by</u> an earthquake <u>centered</u> in the Black Sea.　　**A** B C D
   　　　　　　A　　B　C　　　　　　　　D

3. Peace talks <u>were</u> <u>been</u> <u>held</u> last week <u>between</u> Tintoria and Illyria.　　A **B** C D
   　　　　　A　　B　C　　　　　D

4. The United Nations <u>had said</u>, "We <u>must</u> <u>get</u> these talks <u>start</u> again."　　A B C **D**
   　　　　　　　　A　　　　　B　C　　　　　D

Unit 14 Review: The Passive: Review and Expansion　**249**

The Passive to Describe Situations and to Report Opinions

LEGENDS AND MYTHS

STEP 1 GRAMMAR IN CONTEXT

Before You Read

PAIRS: Look at the picture on page 251 and discuss the questions.

1. What does the illustration show?
2. What is an aspect of your culture that might be hard for people of other cultures to understand? How would you explain it?

Read

Read the article about an unusual tribe of people.

THE STRANGEST OF PEOPLES

For decades anthropologists have studied strange and unusual peoples all over the world. One of the strangest is a group called the Nacirema, a prominent tribe living in North America.

The territory of the Nacirema **is located** between the Canadian Cree and the Tarahumara of Mexico. On the southeast their territory **is bordered** by the Caribbean. Relatively little **is known** of the origin of this people, though they **are said** to have come from somewhere in the East. In fact, the Nacirema **may be related** to certain European and African peoples.

Nacirema people spend a great deal of time on the appearance and health of their bodies. In Nacirema culture the body **is** generally **believed** to be ugly and likely to decay. The only way to prevent this decay is through participation in certain magical ceremonies. Every Nacirema house has a special shrine room dedicated to this purpose. Some Nacirema houses have more than one shrine room. In fact, it **is felt** in Nacirema culture that the more shrine rooms a family has, the richer it is.

What is in the shrine room? The focal point is a box built into the wall, inside which is a large collection of magical potions, medicines, and creams. Below the box is a small font from which water is obtained. Every day each member of the Nacirema family enters the shrine room, bows to the chest, and receives magic holy water from the fountain.

Several rituals in Nacirema culture are performed by one sex or the other, but not by both. Every morning, for example, a Nacirema man places a magic cream on his face and then scrapes and sometimes even lacerates his face with a sharp instrument. A similar ritual performed only by women involves the scraping of the legs and underarms.

In Nacirema culture, the mouth **is regarded as** a highly significant part of the body. The Nacirema are fascinated by the mouth and believe its condition has an important and supernatural effect on all social relationships. The daily body ritual

holes in the teeth, they are enlarged with these tools. Then a supernatural substance is placed in each hole. It **is said** that the purpose of this practice is to prevent decay in the teeth and to help Nacirema people to find spouses.

involves an activity which **would be considered** repulsive in some cultures. It **is reported** that the Nacirema actually insert into their mouths a stick on one end of which are plasticized hairs covered with a magical paste! They then move these sticks back and forth in their mouths in highly ritualized gestures.

Among the most important individuals in the culture are the "holy-mouth-people." Naciremans visit these practitioners once or twice a year. They possess excellent sharp instruments for performing their magic ceremonies. They place these instruments in the mouths of the Naciremans. If there are

Another significant person in Nacirema culture is the "listener," a witch doctor who **is thought** to have the power to get rid of the devils in the heads of people who have been bewitched. Naciremans believe parents often bewitch their own children, especially while teaching the secret toilet rituals, and the listeners must "unbewitch" them. It **is** also **believed** that the secret to getting rid of these devils is simply to talk about them, usually while reclining on a sofa.

Clearly, the Nacirema are a magic-inspired tribe. Much more research is needed in order to understand this strange people.

After You Read

A | Vocabulary: *Circle the letter of the best meaning for the blue words from the reading.*

1. Every Nacirema house has a special **shrine** room dedicated to this purpose.

   a. work   **b.** sleeping   **c.** worship   **d.** relaxation

2. Inside the box is a collection of **potions**, medicines, and creams.

   a. magical devices   **b.** magical foods   **c.** magical containers   **d.** magical creams or liquids

3. Below the box is a small **font**.

   a. water source   **b.** printing device   **c.** door   **d.** mirror

4. Several **rituals** in Nacirema culture are performed by one sex or the other.

   a. instructions   **b.** greetings   **c.** examinations   **d.** ceremonial acts

5. A Nacirema man scrapes and sometimes even **lacerates** his face daily.

   a. washes   **b.** cuts   **c.** decorates   **d.** takes care of

6. Then a **supernatural** substance is placed in each hole.

   a. having magical powers   **b.** highly effective   **c.** poisonous   **d.** very expensive

7. The daily ritual involves a practice that would be considered **repulsive** in some cultures.

   a. dangerous   **b.** barbaric   **c.** attractive   **d.** disgusting

8. Naciremans believe that parents often **bewitch** their own children.

   a. positively influence   **b.** ignore totally   **c.** magically control   **d.** treat unkindly

B | Comprehension: *Complete each statement with a single word.*

1. In reality, the Nacirema people are the _____.

2. The shrine room is the _____.

3. The font in the shrine room is the _____.

4. The activity of scraping the face, legs, or underarms is _____.

5. The stick that Naciremans insert in their mouths is a _____.

6. The holy-mouth-people are _____.

7. The listeners or witch doctors are in reality _____.

8. In reality, the devils in the heads of bewitched people are mental _____.

THE PASSIVE TO DESCRIBE SITUATIONS AND TO REPORT OPINIONS

Describing Situations or States (Stative Passive)

Active Sentences	Passive Sentences			
	Subject	*Be* + Past Participle	Prepositional Phrase	(*By* + Agent)
Ø*	The people	**are related**	(**to** each other).	Ø
	The country	**is composed**	**of** two regions.	
	The island	**is connected**	**to** the mainland.	
	The capital	**was located**	**in** the South.	

*Ø = These forms do not occur.

Reporting Opinions or Ideas

Active Sentences		
Subject	Verb	*That* Clause
Some anthropologists	**say** **think** **believe** **allege**	(**that**) the people came from the East.

Passive Sentences with *It* + *That* Clause			
It	*Be* + Past Participle	(*By* + Agent)	*That* Clause
It	**is said** **is thought** **is believed** **is alleged**	(by some anthropologists)	(**that**) the people came from the East.

Passive Sentences with *To* Phrase			
Subject	*Be* + Past Participle	(*By* + Agent)	*To* Phrase
The people	**are said** **are thought** **are believed** **are alleged**	(by some anthropologists)	**to** have come from the East.

GRAMMAR NOTES

1   Remember that the passive is used to describe situations in which the subject is acted upon. The passive is also used to describe situations or states. This use is called the **stative passive**.

- These peoples **are related** to each other.
- St. Louis **is located** on the Missouri River.

The stative passive is formed with *be* + past participle. Most stative passive sentences do not have a corresponding active sentence, and most do not contain a *by* phrase.

- Our two families **are related**.
  Not: Genealogists relate our two families.

A few stative passives do have a corresponding active sentence. These include passives formed with *connect* and *surround*.

- England and France **are connected by** the Chunnel.
- The Chunnel **connects** England and France.

2   We use the **stative passive** to describe situations or states. In stative passive sentences there is normally no action taking place.

- The United States **is composed** of 50 states.

In stative passive constructions, the past participle functions as an adjective. It is often followed by a prepositional phrase.

- Cuba **is located** in the Caribbean.

Stative passive sentences are often used in everyday English. Examples of stative passives: *be bordered by, be composed of, be connected to / with / by, be divided into / by, be found in, be located in / on, be made up of, be related to, be surrounded by.*

- Curitiba **is found** in southern Brazil.
- A peninsula **is surrounded** by water on three sides.

3   **Passives** are commonly used to report ideas, beliefs, and opinions. They often occur in the form *it* + *be* + past participle + *that* clause. Common examples of verbs used to form this type of passive are *allege, assume, believe, claim, say,* and *think.*

- **It is assumed that** this culture is very old.
- **It is said that** present-day Basques are descendants of Atlanteans.

Passive sentences of this type have corresponding active sentences.

- Scholars **assume that** this culture is very old.

BE CAREFUL! We use this structure only with verbs that can be followed by a *that* clause. *That* is optional and is frequently omitted in informal English. *Regard* cannot be followed by a *that* clause.

- It **is said (that)** these people came from Asia.
  Not: It is regarded (that) these people came from Asia.

These passive structures may take an optional *by* phrase.

- It **is claimed (by some scholars) that** Shakespeare didn't write all his plays.

4 **Passives** that report ideas, beliefs, and opinions also commonly occur in the form subject + *be* + past participle + *to* phrase. This type of sentence can be converted from an equivalent active sentence with a *that* clause. A *by* phrase is optional.

- Scholars **assume that the culture dates** from 5000 B.C.E.
- **The culture is assumed** (by scholars) **to date** from 5000 B.C.E.
- Bigfoot **is thought** to live in the Pacific Northwest.

The verb in the *to* phrase can be present or past.

- He is said **to be** the author.
- The Japanese are thought **to have visited** the New World before Columbus.

NOTE: *Consider* can take an infinitive but is often followed by just a noun phrase or an adjective. *Regard* is followed by *as* + a noun phrase.

- Native Americans **are considered (to be) the real discoverers**.
- Columbus **is regarded as the discoverer of America**.

5 **Passive sentences** with *that* clauses or infinitive phrases are often used in academic discourse and in reporting the news. They create an objective impression by distancing the author from the idea.

- **It is believed that** the Abominable Snowman actually exists.
- **The defendant is alleged to have committed** the crime.

Authors can create the greatest distance between themselves and an idea by starting a passive sentence with *It* + *be* + past participle + *that* clause. This type of sentence is formal.

- **It is thought that** the Vikings explored the New World long ago.

BE CAREFUL! This construction with *it* occurs only with verbs that can be followed by a clause beginning with *that*.

REFERENCE NOTES

For use of **infinitive phrases**, see Unit 17.
For a list of **verbs used in the passive followed by a *that* clause**, see Appendix 10 on page A-6.
For a list of common **stative passive verbs + prepositions**, see Appendix 11 on page A-6.

EXERCISE 1: Discover the Grammar

A | *Read the sentences based on the opening reading. Are the underlined passive structures stative passives (**S**) or opinion / belief passives (**O**)?*

___S___   **1.** The territory of the Nacirema <u>is located</u> roughly between that of the Tarahumara of Mexico and the Cree of Canada.

_____   **2.** On the southeast, their territory <u>is bordered</u> by the Caribbean.

_____   **3.** They <u>are said</u> to be from somewhere in the East.

_____   **4.** Actually, the Nacirema may <u>be related</u> to certain European and African peoples.

_____   **5.** In Nacirema culture, the body <u>is</u> generally <u>considered</u> ugly and likely to decay.

_____   **6.** It <u>is felt</u> that the more shrine rooms a family has, the higher its social status is.

_____   **7.** The mouth <u>is regarded as</u> a highly significant part of the body.

_____   **8.** The daily body ritual involves an activity which <u>would be considered</u> repulsive in some cultures.

_____   **9.** The "listener" <u>is thought</u> to have the power to get rid of the devils in the heads of bewitched people.

_____   **10.** In the shrine room, Naciremans <u>are surrounded</u> by a collection of potions, medications, and creams.

B | *Read the sentences from the opening reading. For each sentence, answer the questions* **yes** *or* **no***:*

    a. Could the sentence be rewritten with a *by* phrase?

    b. Could the sentence be rewritten in the active voice?

1. The territory of the Nacirema is located roughly between that of the Tarahumara of Mexico and that of the Cree of Canada.

    a. _____   **b.** _____

2. Actually, the Nacirema may be related to certain European and African peoples.

    a. _____   **b.** _____

3. The mouth is regarded as a highly significant part of the body.

    a. _____   **b.** _____

4. It is felt that the more shrine rooms a family has, the higher its social status is.

    a. _____   **b.** _____

EXERCISE 2: Stative Passives

(Grammar Notes 1–2)

Look at the map. Complete the sentences by writing the stative passive forms of the verbs from the box. Some of the verbs may be used more than once.

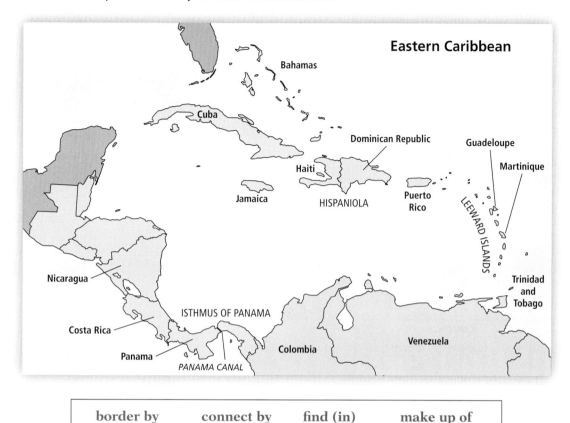

border by	connect by	find (in)	make up of
compose of	divide into	locate (in)	surround by

1. North and South America _are connected by_ the Isthmus of Panama.

2. The island nations of the region, of course, _____ the waters of the Caribbean.

3. The island of Hispaniola _____ two nations: Haiti and the Dominican Republic.

4. Cuba _____ about 90 miles south of Florida.

5. The nation of Trinidad and Tobago _____ two separate islands: Trinidad and Tobago.

6. On the north, Costa Rica _____ Nicaragua and on the south by Panama.

7. The nation of The Bahamas _____ many islands, some large and some small.

8. The nation of Panama _____ two parts by the Panama Canal.

9. Jamaica and Puerto Rico _____ west and east, respectively, of Hispaniola.

10. The French-speaking islands of Guadeloupe and Martinique _____ the eastern Caribbean, north of South America.

EXERCISE 3: Beliefs / Thoughts / Opinions   (Grammar Notes 4–5)

A | *Complete the sentences with a present or past passive form of the verbs in parentheses.*
Add **as** *or* **to** *as needed.*

1. In some circles, the Basques _____*are considered to be*_____ the descendants of the
(consider / be)

   Atlanteans.

2. For centuries before Copernicus, the Earth _____ the center of the
(think / be)

   universe.

3. Lee Harvey Oswald _____ the assassin of President John F. Kennedy,
(claim / be)

   but there are some who don't believe this.

4. Mother Teresa and Albert Schweitzer _____ great humanitarians.
(regard)

5. In the Middle Ages, fairies and other spirit creatures _____ real.
(believe / be)

6. Since the 19th century, George Washington and Abraham Lincoln

   _____ the greatest American presidents by many.
(consider)

7. Bigfoot, supposedly a large, mysterious forest creature, _____ in the
(say / live)

   Pacific Northwest.

8. In the 15th century and afterwards, King Richard III of England

   _____ a monstrous king. Today he has a better reputation.
(regard)

9. Today William Shakespeare _____ the author of the plays credited
(assume / be)

   to him, but some have suggested he couldn't have written them all.

10. From time to time, certain people _____ criminals, but they are
(allege / be)

    later proved innocent by DNA evidence.

B | *Rewrite sentences 2, 3, 5, 7, 9, and 10 using a passive sentence with **it** + **be** + past participle + **that** clause.*

2. _For centuries before Copernicus, it was thought that the Earth was the center of the universe._

3. _____

5. _____

7. _____

9. _____

10. _____

EXERCISE 4: Personal Inventory

(Grammar Note 4)

Use each of the items from the box to write passive sentences showing beliefs, opinions, or facts about people or things in your country.

allege to be	believe to be	consider	say to be
assume to be	claim to be	regard as	think to be

EXAMPLE: Jorge Amado **is considered** one of the greatest Brazilian writers.

1. _____

2. _____

3. _____

4. _____

5. _____

6. _____

7. _____

8. _____

EXERCISE 5: Editing

Read this student essay about a creature that may or may not be real. There are eight mistakes in passive constructions. The first one is already corrected. Find and correct seven more.

The Snowman

Every area of the world has its own legends, and Asia is no different. One of the most famous Asian legends is about the Abominable Snowman, also called the yeti, of the Himalayas. Is the yeti just a legend that is ~~believe~~ *believed* because people want things to be real, or does he really exist?

The yeti thought to be a huge creature—perhaps as tall as 8 feet. His body is supposed to be covered with long, brown hair. He says to have a pointed head and a hairless face that looks something like a man's. It is claimed that he lives near Mount Everest, the highest mountain in the world, which locates on the border of Nepal and Tibet.

Sightings of the yeti have been reported for centuries, but the yeti was made known to the rest of the world only in 1921. In that year, members of an expedition to climb Mount Everest saw very large tracks in the snow that looked like prints of human feet. No conclusive evidence of the yeti's existence was found during that expedition, but interest was stimulated. Other expeditions were undertaken. In 1951, explorer Eric Shipton led a search in which some gigantic, human-appearing tracks were found. Once again, the yeti himself was not seen. In 1969, Sir Edmund Hillary, who is regarded one of the greatest climbers ever, arranged another expedition, this time with the intention of not only seeing the yeti but also of capturing him. Once again, tracks were discovered, but that was all. Hillary eventually decided the footprints might simply considered normal animal tracks enlarged by the daytime melting of the snow. In 1964, Boris F. Porshev, a Russian scientist, said that he believed that the yeti actually existed. He theorized that the yeti is a surviving descendant of Neanderthal man, a creature who is believed to live from 200,000 to 25,000 years ago and is thought by some to be an ancestor of modern humans. Porshev has never actually been able to spot the yeti, however.

The mystery continues. Does the yeti really exist, or do people just want to believe he exists? It seems to me that there must be more to this mystery than just melted tracks. Centuries of reports by Himalayan trail guides must mean something. Besides, other yeti-type creatures have reported—most notably, Bigfoot in North America. Time will tell, but maybe we shouldn't be so quick to dismiss the Abominable Snowman as nothing more than an entertaining story.

EXERCISE 6: Listening

A | *Listen to the news bulletin. What is the locale?*

_____

B | *Listen again and check (✓)* **True** *or* **False.**

	True	False
1. The earthquakes are said to have registered a nine on the Richter scale.	☑	☐
2. The epicenter of the quakes was located in the Pacific Ocean.	☐	☐
3. The exact number of drowned people is known.	☐	☐
4. Coastal areas were hit by a tsunami.	☐	☐
5. It is thought that severe flooding has occurred inland.	☐	☐
6. The president was vacationing at his seaside retreat.	☐	☐
7. So far, no looting has been reported.	☐	☐
8. The president hopes citizens of the country will stay calm and law-abiding.	☐	☐
9. The citizens should go to low areas.	☐	☐

EXERCISE 7: Pronunciation

A | *Read and listen to the Pronunciation Note.*

Pronunciation Note

The vowel sound /eɪ/ is a tense vowel in which the lips are spread wide.

The vowel sound /ɛ/ is a lax vowel in which the lips are not spread wide.

EXAMPLES: Don't s**ay** that. /eɪ/ *(tense)*
She s**ai**d that. /ɛ/ *(lax)*
How do you spell ***mate***? *(tense)*
How do you spell ***met***? *(lax)*

| Listen to the sentences. Circle the /eɪ/ sounds. Underline the /ɛ/ sounds. Note: Consider only stressed syllables in the boldfaced words.

1. She **said** a lot of **clever** things in the **paper** she wrote.

2. The people **spend** a **great** deal of time on the appearance and **health** of their bodies.

3. The **president says** that a **great** tragedy has struck the **nation**.

4. It is **alleged** that **they came** from the East.

5. It is **said** that **strange** creatures like the **yeti may** actually **exist**.

6. **Every day** each **member** of the family **enters** the room.

7. The countries of **Haiti** and the Dominican Republic are located on the **same** island.

8. **Betty's letter** arrived on **Wednesday** afternoon.

C | PAIRS: Practice the sentences. Take turns.

EXERCISE 8: Game

CLASS: Form two teams. Each team uses its prompts to construct six passive voice questions about people and places mentioned in this unit. Then each team creates two questions of its own, for a total of eight questions. The other team answers each question in a complete sentence. Add definite articles and put verbs in the past where necessary. For answers, see page G-AK3.

EXAMPLE: continents / connect by / Isthmus of Panama

      A: Which continents are connected by the Isthmus of Panama?
      B: North and South America are connected by the Isthmus of Panama.

Team A's Prompts
1. island / compose of / nations of Haiti, Dominican Republic
2. Central American country / border by / Panama, Nicaragua
3. people / consider by some / be / descendants of Atlanteans
4. legendary creature / think / live / Himalayas
5. individual / claim / be / assassin / U.S. President John F. Kennedy
6. individuals / regard / great humanitarians
7. _____
8. _____

Team B's Prompts
1. Caribbean nation / compose of / many islands
2. Caribbean nation / locate / about 90 miles south of Florida
3. forest creature / say / live / Pacific Northwest
4. lost continent / think / be located / Atlantic Ocean
5. planet / think / be / center of the universe / before Copernicus
6. presidents / regard by many / greatest American presidents
7. _____
8. _____

EXERCISE 9: Picture Discussion

A | *GROUPS: Look at the pictures. In small groups, talk about each of the people in the photos, using passive constructions.*

> **EXAMPLE:** Albert Einstein is considered one of the greatest scientists of all time.

Albert Einstein

Mother Teresa

Queen Elizabeth I

Vincent van Gogh

B | *Discuss the quality of the individuals' contributions to culture. Who has made the most significant contributions? Share your conclusions with the class.*

> EXAMPLE: **A:** We believe the most significant contribution to world culture has been made by _____.
>
> **B:** Why do you think so?

EXERCISE 10: Writing

A | *Write a five-paragraph summary of a legend or myth from your culture or another you are familiar with. Use passives to describe situations and report opinions.*

> EXAMPLE: My favorite American myth is the story of Paul Bunyan. Paul was a giant of a man who is said to have lived in the North Woods of Minnesota. He was a lumberjack who had great strength, and he also had a gigantic blue ox named Babe. The story of Paul and Babe is probably considered the most famous American myth. Here's how Paul got his start in life . . .

B | *Check your work. Use the Editing Checklist.*

Editing Checklist

Did you use . . . ?
- [ ] passives to describe situations correctly
- [ ] passives with *it* and ***that*** clauses correctly
- [ ] passives with ***to*** phrases correctly

A | *Circle the word or phrase that correctly completes each sentence.*

1. Spain <u>bordered by / is bordered by</u> Portugal to the west and France to the north.

2. Europeans and Africans are regarded <u>as / that</u> the ancestors of the Nacirema.

3. It <u>claims / is claimed</u> that the nation of Atlantis actually existed.

4. The body <u>is believed to be / is considered that it is</u> ugly in Nacirema culture.

5. Gebru and I are related <u>to / by</u> marriage.

6. The capital <u>locates in / is located in</u> the center of the nation.

7. Bigfoot <u>is thought to / thinks to</u> live in the forests of the Pacific Northwest.

8. The Basques <u>allege / are alleged</u> to have come from Atlantis.

B | *Correct the mistakes in the underlined words.*

1. Denmark is bordered <u>of</u> Germany on the south. _____

2. The yeti <u>says</u> to live in the Himalayas. _____

3. An island is an area of land that <u>surrounds</u> on all sides by water. _____

4. The Nacirema <u>allege</u> to be related to Europeans and Africans. _____

5. Ilya and Irina <u>believe</u> to come from Ukraine. _____

6. It is <u>claiming</u> by some that Homer was not one single person. _____

7. Indonesia is composed <u>from</u> many islands, some large and some small. _____

8. Mother Teresa <u>regards</u> as a great humanitarian. _____

C | *Circle the letter of the one underlined word or phrase in each sentence that is not correct.*

1. <u>It</u> <u>is</u> <u>regarded</u> <u>that</u> Native Americans came originally from Asia.
   A B   C   D   **A B C D**

2. <u>It</u> <u>says</u> <u>by scholars</u> that Basque <u>is unrelated</u> to other languages.
   A B   C   D   **A B C D**

3. The yeti <u>claimed</u> <u>by witnesses</u> <u>to be</u> <u>covered</u> with long brown hair.
            A   B   C   D   **A B C D**

4. The culture <u>is</u> <u>assumed</u> <u>by experts</u> <u>date</u> from the year 3000 B.C.E.
             A   B   C   D   **A B C D**

From Grammar to Writing
PARALLEL STRUCTURE: NOUNS, ARTICLES, AND VOICE

Parallel structure (also called **parallelism**) is an important feature of English that makes our speaking, and especially our writing, easier to understand. You will strengthen your writing by making sure that appropriate items are in parallel structure. To do this, put all **items in a series** in the same grammatical form.

EXAMPLES: Over the weekend I **bought a new car**, **painted the living room**, and **planted a garden**. *(All three verbs in the predicate are in the simple past and in the active voice.)*

The prisoner was **arrested**, **taken** to the police station, **booked**, and **fingerprinted**. *(All four verbs are in the simple past and in the passive voice.)*

On her shopping trip, Mrs. Figueroa bought **a book**, **a dress**, and **a CD**. *(All three count nouns are preceded by the indefinite article.)*

We will concentrate in this Part on parallel structure with nouns and articles and with active or passive voice. See Part VII **From Grammar to Writing**, pages 303–306, for a discussion of parallel structure with gerunds and infinitives.

1 | *Read the text and correct the four mistakes in parallel structure with nouns and articles.*

> Rolleen Laing poured herself a second cup of coffee as she ate her breakfast, which consisted of a fried egg, orange, and a piece of dry toast. She was 62 years old and had been successful as a university professor, writer of detective fiction, and an amateur detective. Just then the telephone rang. It was Harry Sadler, a local police detective. Ever since Rolleen had helped Harry crack a murder case several years previously, she had been called in as an unofficial consultant on several cases. She had helped Harry solve cases involving a hit-and-run victim, a murdered TV executive, and, most recently, koala stolen from the city zoo.
>
> "Hi, Rolleen. This is Harry. You're needed on another case. It's a robbery this time. Some thieves broke into the art museum and stole a van Gogh, a Picasso, Gauguin, and a Matisse. Meet me at the museum at 10:00, OK?"

On the evening of August 6, 1930, Judge Joseph Force Crater, a wealthy, successful, and good-looking New Yorker, disappeared without a trace. Earlier in the evening he had been seen with friends at a Manhattan restaurant, and they observed him departing. At 9:10 P.M. he walked out the door of the restaurant and hailed a taxi. He was soon driven away. No one ever saw or heard from him again. It was 10 days before he was even reported missing. On August 16, his wife called his courthouse, the secretary was asked of his whereabouts, and learned that he was probably off on political business. This news reassured Mrs. Crater somewhat, but when he still hadn't turned up by August 26, a group of his fellow judges started an investigation. A grand jury was convened, but its members could not come to any conclusion as to what had happened to Judge Crater. They theorized that the judge might have developed amnesia, might have run away voluntarily, or been a crime victim. His wife disagreed with the first two possibilities, holding that he had been murdered by someone in the Tammany Hall organization, the political machine that controlled New York City at the time. The mystery remains unsolved to this day. Crater could have been killed by a Tammany Hall agent, a girlfriend could have murdered him, or kidnapped by an organized crime group. He might, in fact, have suffered from amnesia, or his own disappearance might have been planned by him. Reports of Judge Crater sightings have continued to surface over the last several decades.

3 | *Before you write . . .*

1. Most of us are intrigued by unsolved mysteries and by unusual experiences. Think of an unsolved mystery that you are aware of or an unusual or mysterious experience that you have had.
2. Describe your mystery or unusual experience to a partner. Listen to your partner's description.
3. Ask and answer questions about your and your partner's topic. Why is the topic significant to you? What about it interests or touches you?

4 | *Write a draft of a composition about your unsolved mystery or unusual experience. Follow the model. Remember to include information that your partner asked about. Use at least one sentence containing passive voice verbs in parallel structure. Also include at least one sentence containing a series of nouns in parallel structure.*

The events of the mystery or unusual experience:

_____

_____

_____

_____

What specifically interests or touches me about the mystery or experience:

_____

_____

_____

_____

5 | *Exchange compositions with a different partner. Complete the chart.*

1. The writer used parallel series of passive voice verbs and of nouns and articles.   **Yes** ☐ **No** ☐

2. What I liked in the composition:

_____

_____

_____

3. Questions I'd like the writer to answer about the composition:

Who _____?

What _____?

When _____?

Where _____?

Why _____?

How _____?

(Your own question) _____?

6 | *Work with your partner. Discuss each other's chart from Exercise 5. Then rewrite your own composition and make any necessary changes.*

GERUNDS AND INFINITIVES

UNIT	GRAMMAR FOCUS	THEME
16	Gerunds	Friendship
17	Infinitives	Procrastination

Gerunds
FRIENDSHIP

Before You Read

PAIRS: Discuss the questions.

1. What do you value in friendships?
2. Are all of your friends the same type of friend (for example, long-term friends, special-interest friends), or are some different types of friends?

Read

Read the article about types of friends.

POPULAR PSYCHOLOGY

FRIENDS

by Jim Garcia

I was having difficulty **finding** a subject for this month's column until I remembered a childhood rhyme that went like this: "True friends are diamonds, precious and rare; false friends are oak leaves that fall anywhere." But are friendships really that black and white? This was my childhood concept, but I suspect my perception was pretty naive. I've long since stopped **thinking** in these terms. Some friends are true and others false, but there are many different types of "true" friends. In fact, I can recognize at least six types:

Type 1: Convenience Friends

These are the friends we make when our schedules and activities coincide. Years ago I played on a soccer team. I didn't have a way of **getting** to the practices and tried **taking** the bus, but it always got me there late.

Then I learned that Andrés, a team member, lived near me. He had a car, and it was convenient for him to pick me up. We became friends by **riding** with each other and developed a good relationship. We didn't get together outside the soccer context, though.

Type 2: Special-interest friends

My brother, whose passion is **kayaking**, belongs to a kayaking club. He's made several good buddies at meetings and on river trips. They have great times, and **living** through dangerous experiences has made them close. Once the trips are over, though, they don't socialize with each other. Their special interest, kayaking, is the only thing that holds them together.

Type 3: Long-term friends

I have several of these, but my best long-time friend is a guy named Al. We've known each other since we were 12, and our friendship links our past to our present. We

FRIENDS

can go months without **contacting** each other, but whenever we do make contact it seems like we were together yesterday. We enjoy just **catching up on** each other's activities. We'd like to spend more time together, but it doesn't seem to matter if we don't.

Type 4: Cross-generational friends

We most often seek friends in our own age group, but cross-generational friendships are worth **pursuing**. My friend Bill is an example. He's about 25 years older than I am—a kind of father figure. He's more than that, though. Actually, Bill was my teacher in a university writing class. I was having trouble **figuring** out my career, but Bill supported my **becoming** a writer, and that's what I did. After the class was over, we became friends.

Type 5: Part-of-a-couple friends

My wife Amanda and Bill's wife Gretta are good examples of this common type of friendship. When our partner has a friend in another couple, we have to go through the often difficult process of **getting** to know the "other person" in that couple. People may feel they have little or nothing in common with their counterpart and may even rebel against **socializing** with a "friend" they didn't choose. Fortunately, Amanda and Gretta have become good friends on their own through their common interest in **collecting** rare books.

Type 6: "Best" friends

To me a best friend is a person with whom we don't have a problem **being** honest or vulnerable. It's someone who will never desert you, who keeps no record of wrongs, who doesn't spare your feelings or avoid **telling** you what you need to hear. I have two best friends. One is Ken, whom I met in the military. Our **having gone** through difficult experiences has bonded us for life. The other is Amanda. We love **having** long conversations that can meander everywhere and nowhere. Sometimes we talk for hours. We both love **being listened to**. Other times we like **being** together without **saying** much of anything. I would have a hard time **living** without my two "best" friends, but it's awfully important to have the others too.

A **Vocabulary:** *Match the blue words and phrases on the left with their meanings on the right.*

_____ 1. I now see that my perceiving friendship in this way was **naive**.

_____ 2. These are the friends we make when our schedules and activities **coincide**.

_____ 3. We didn't get together outside the soccer **context**, though.

_____ 4. We enjoy just **catching up on** each other's activities.

_____ 5. People may feel they have little or nothing in common with their **counterpart**.

_____ 6. A best friend is a person with whom we don't have a problem being honest or **vulnerable**.

_____ 7. It's someone who doesn't **spare your feelings**.

_____ 8. We love having conversations that can **meander** everywhere and nowhere.

a. person having a parallel position

b. move without a goal in mind

c. undefended

d. having or showing no experience

e. getting up to date with

f. happen at the same time

g. conditions in which something occurs

h. avoid hurting someone's ego

B **Comprehension:** *Refer to the reading and complete each sentence with a single word.*

1. _____ friends are those you make when your schedules and activities coincide.

2. The author's brother met a lot of friends through _____, his special interest.

3. The author and his long-term friend Al can go months without _____ each other.

4. A cross-generational friend is someone from a different _____ group.

5. The author's cross-generational friend Bill supported his becoming a _____.

6. A spouse may object to _____ with a friend he or she didn't choose.

7. A best friend is someone with whom you can easily be _____ or vulnerable.

8. The author and his wife both place great importance on being _____ to.

GERUNDS

Gerund as Subject

Gerund (Subject)	Verb	Object
Kayaking	involves	some risks.
Swimming	builds	endurance.
Not inviting him	will cause	resentment.

Gerund as Object

Subject	Verb	Gerund (Object)
They	enjoy	**kayaking.**
I	went	**swimming.**
We	don't advise	**not inviting** him.

Gerund as Subject Complement

Subject	Verb	Gerund (Subject Complement)
My sport	is	**skiing.**
His problem	is	**not exercising.**

Gerund as Object Complement

Subject	Verb	Object	Gerund (Object Complement)
He	spends	time	**reading.**
She	found	him	**not working.**

Gerund as Object of a Preposition

	Preposition	Gerund	
She insists	**on**	**going out**	every weekend.
He's accustomed	**to**	**giving**	parties.
They have a reason	**for**	**not inviting**	Michael.

Possessive + Gerund

	Possessive	Gerund	
Bob and Helen worry about	**Emily's** / **her** / **the children's** / **their**	**having**	so few friends.

Active and Passive Gerunds

	Active Gerunds	Passive Gerunds
SIMPLE	**Inviting** them to her wedding was a nice gesture on her part.	**Being invited** to her wedding was a great surprise to them.
PAST	**Having invited** them to her wedding made her feel good.	**Having been invited** to her wedding is a fond memory for them.

GRAMMAR NOTES

1	A **gerund** is a noun made from a verb. To form a gerund, add *-ing* to the base form of the verb.	• **Cooking** is my hobby. I like **eating** too.
	Gerunds and gerund phrases perform the same functions as nouns:	
	a. They act as subjects. **b.** They act as objects. **c.** They act as complements (phrases that describe or explain the subject or object of a sentence).	• **Talking** with friends is enjoyable. • I love **getting together** with friends. • Our favorite activity is **playing** cards. *(subject complement)* • She has trouble **making** friends. *(object complement)*
	Add *not* before a gerund to make a negative statement.	• **Not calling** her was a big mistake.

2	Many verbs and verb phrases in English have **gerunds as objects**. Common examples are *avoid, consider, enjoy, keep, mind*.	• I **enjoy meeting** new people. • You should **avoid working** late.
	We often use **go + gerund** to talk about recreational activities: *go skiing, go swimming, go hiking,* etc.	• We **go skiing** every weekend in the winter.

3	Gerunds act as **objects of prepositions**.	• I made friends **by joining** a club.
	Many preposition combinations are followed by gerunds: **a.** verb + preposition **b.** adjective + preposition	• They **insisted on giving** us a present. • She's **good at making** friends.
	BE CAREFUL! The word *to* can be a preposition or part of an infinitive.	• He will adjust **to working** hard. *(**To** is a preposition.)* • He tries **to work** hard. *(**To** is part of the infinitive.)*

4	In writing and formal speaking, use a **possessive** noun or pronoun **before a gerund** to show possession.	• **Pete's dominating** every conversation bothers me. • **His dominating** every conversation bothers me.
	USAGE NOTE: In conversation, native speakers often use a name or an object pronoun before a gerund.	• I don't like **Pete dominating** every conversation. • I don't like **him dominating** every conversation.

5 Gerunds can occur in simple or past form. We can use a **simple gerund** (without a past participle) to make a generalization.

- **Making** friends is a natural thing to do.

We can use a **past gerund** (*having* + past participle) to show an action that occurred before the action of the main verb in the sentence.

- **Having met** Jane in my first week of college **helped** me throughout my college career.

NOTE: We use a past gerund to emphasize the difference in time between two actions. The simple gerund is also correct in many situations.

- **Having gone** to college is one of the best things **I've ever done**.
  OR
- **Going** to college is one of the best things **I've ever done**.

Gerunds can occur in **passive** form. In the present, use *being* + past participle. In the past, use *having been* + past participle.

- She hates **being ignored**.
- She's still angry at **having been ignored**.

BE CAREFUL! Many words in English end in *-ing*. Do not confuse gerunds with verbs in the progressive form or with present participles used as adjectives or in adverb phrases.

- I've been **making** friends at work. (*progressive form*)
- Mary is enrolled in a **cooking** class. (*as adjective*)
- **Walking** on the beach, I wondered why she was angry at me. (*adverb phrase*)

REFERENCE NOTES
For a list of common **verbs followed by gerunds**, see Appendix 12 on page A-6.
For a list of common **adjective + preposition combinations followed by gerunds**, see Appendix 16 on page A-8.

STEP 3 FOCUSED PRACTICE

EXERCISE 1: Discover the Grammar

A | *Read the sentences. Is the gerund used as a subject (**S**), an object (**O**), an object of a preposition (**OP**), or a subject or object complement (**C**)?*

   _C_   **1.** I was having difficulty finding a subject.

         2. I remembered learning a rhyme.

         3. I didn't have a way of getting to the practices.

         4. My brother's passion is kayaking.

         5. We can go months without contacting each other.

         6. I was having trouble figuring out my career.

         7. Bill supported my becoming a writer.

         8. I would have a hard time living without my two "best" friends.

B | *Are the* -ing *words in the sentences gerunds? Write* **Y (Yes)** *or* **N (No).**

_____Y____ **1.** I've long since stopped thinking of friendship in these terms.

_____ **2.** These are the friends we make by engaging in some specific activity.

_____ **3.** He belongs to a kayaking club.

_____ **4.** We enjoy just catching up on each other's activities.

_____ **5.** Cross-generational friendships are worth pursuing.

_____ **6.** He was my teacher in a writing class.

_____ **7.** They have become good friends on their own through their common interest in collecting rare books.

_____ **8.** I would have a hard time being single again.

EXERCISE 2: Simple Gerunds

(Grammar Notes 1–4)

A | *Brian Hansen is constantly tired and dissatisfied. He has gone to a doctor to see if there is anything physically wrong with him. Complete the conversation with gerunds. Make the gerunds negative if necessary.*

DOCTOR: Well, Brian, what seems to be the problem?

BRIAN: I'm tired all the time. Some nights when I come home from work I'm so exhausted I don't

feel like _____*doing*_____ anything but collapsing on the sofa and _____
               1. (do)   **2. (vegetate)**

in front of the TV. Is there anything physically wrong with me?

DOCTOR: No, I've looked at your test results, and you're healthy. How long have you been feeling

like this?

BRIAN: Oh, two or three months, I guess. Long enough so that I've begun _____
                                                               3. (worry)

about _____ any energy. Basically I'm not doing anything besides punching
           4. (have)

a time clock.

DOCTOR: How much are you working?

BRIAN: Well, I'm putting in a lot of overtime—all in all, at least 60 hours a week, I'd say.

DOCTOR: Why are you doing this? Are you trying to make yourself sick?

BRIAN: Well, at this point, _____ overtime is out of the question. I've got a lot
                                 5. (work)

of bills to pay off. The other thing is that I only recently moved here, and I hardly

know anyone, so my focus is on _____ money for a while. I like
                                            6. (make)

_____ , and I really miss _____ close friends, but I don't know
  7. (socialize)   **8. (have)**

quite how to go about _____ new people.
                             9. (meet)

DOCTOR: You're not married, then?

BRIAN: No, not yet.

DOCTOR: Well, I think you need to stop _____ so much and start _____
10. (work)   11. (play)

a little—to put things in balance. I'd say you need a hobby—and some friends.

BRIAN: A hobby? You mean some boring thing like stamp _____?
12. (collect)

DOCTOR: No. That's an OK hobby if you like it, but there are more interesting ones.

BRIAN: Like what?

DOCTOR: Oh, maybe like karaoke. Do you like _____?
13. (sing)

BRIAN: I love music, but I don't have much of a voice. In my case, _____ is better
14. (sing)

than _____ off key.
15. (sing)

DOCTOR: Well, have you ever gone _____?
16. (orienteer)

BRIAN: What's that?

DOCTOR: It's a contest. People use a map and a compass and try to be the first person to find

locations of hidden clues.

BRIAN: Sounds interesting. Where can I find out more about it?

DOCTOR: I've got a friend who belongs to an orienteering club. I'll give you her number.

BRIAN: Super. Thanks.

B | *Complete the sentences with a possessive noun or pronoun and a gerund.*

1. I have two best friends, Bob and Mary. Bob is my co-worker. I'm grateful for

   _____*his giving*_____ me a ride to work every day.
   (he / give)

2. I'm new to the firm, so I also appreciate _____ me learn my job.
   (Bob / help)

3. _____ my work is hard to deal with, so Bob's encouragement is vital.
   (My boss / criticize)

4. Mary is my neighbor. _____ so close is wonderful.
   (She / live)

5. I especially appreciate _____ me on tough issues.
   (Mary / advise)

6. She knows how to deal with _____ discouraged.
   (I / become)

7. I couldn't ask for two better friends than Bob and Mary. I'm thankful for

   _____ there for me when I need them.
   (they / be)

8. _____ together frequently helps us stay close.
   (We / get)

EXERCISE 3: Simple / Past Gerunds

(Grammar Note 5)

Complete the sentences with simple gerunds or past gerunds with **having** + past participle.
Use a past gerund if it is possible to do so.

Martha, who is 20 years older than I am, is my best cross-generational friend. ___*Having met*___

1. (meet)

her when I was an unhappy college sophomore is one of the best things that has ever happened

to me. Martha and I have stayed friends. I look forward to _____ her whenever

2. (see)

our schedules permit. Our relationship hasn't always been smooth, though. Martha and I were

both in the same calculus class. I was having a lot of difficulty and was angry at myself for

_____ in a class I didn't need for my degree. It was too late to drop the class, however,

3. (enroll)

and since I was frustrated, I frequently got irritated with the teacher for _____ so

4. (assign)

much difficult homework every day. Martha stopped me one day after class. She said she was tired

of my continual _____ with the teacher. "You need to grow up," she said. I was

5. (argue)

offended at first, but the older I get the clearer it is to me that her _____ that is one

6. (say)

of the major events in my life. I had to change my negative attitude. I did need to grow up. A few

days later I asked Martha if she would mind _____ with me and _____

7. (study)   **8. (help)**

me with the homework. She agreed. With a lot of patient work, I succeeded in _____

9. (pass)

the course. Eventually we became great friends. I suspect that most of us know someone whose

_____ us what we needed to hear when we needed to hear it has made a difference in

10. (tell)

our life. Martha has certainly made a difference in mine.

EXERCISE 4: Active / Passive Gerunds

(Grammar Notes 2, 4)

A | *Write a question using a passive gerund and an active gerund.*

EXAMPLE: (like / awaken / by an alarm clock) (wake up / on your own)
Do you like **being awakened** by an alarm clock or **waking up** on your own?

1. (prefer / ask out on a date) (ask / someone / yourself)

   _____

2. (more interested in / entertain / yourself) (in / entertain / by others)

   _____

3. (prefer / prepare dinner / yourself) (invite / to dinner / by friends)

   _____

4. (like / tell / what to do) (give / orders)

   _____

5. (like / figure things out / yourself) (show / how to do things)

   _____

6. (prefer / give / advice by friends) (give / your friends / advice)

   _____

B | *PAIRS: Take turns asking and answering the questions.*

EXAMPLE: **A:** Do you like being awakened by an alarm clock or waking up on your own?
B: I like waking up on my own. I hate being awakened by an alarm clock. What about you?

EXERCISE 5: Editing

The letter has ten mistakes in the use of gerunds. The first mistake is already corrected. Find and correct nine more.

Dear Adam,

    I've been here for three days and am having a great time, but I can't help *wishing*
~~wish~~ you were here too. Tell your boss I'm really angry at him. His not let you

take any vacation time qualifies him for the Jerk-of-the-Year Award. (Just

kidding. Don't say that!)

    Believe it or not, the first night I missed hearing all the city noises, but I

haven't really had any trouble to get used to the peace and quiet since then.

Everything's so relaxed here—there's no rush around or write things down in your

Daily Planner. Get out of New York City was definitely what I needed, even if it's

only for two weeks. The ranch has lots of activities—horseback ride, river raft

on the Rio Grande, hiking in the wilderness—you name it. The ranch employees do

everything for you—being taken care of is nice for a change, and I love being

chauffeured around Santa Fe in the ranch limousine. Tonight a group of us are

going out to a country and western dance place called Rodeo Nites in Santa Fe, so

having taken those two-step dance lessons last summer will come in handy. It's

just too bad you couldn't come along so we could both have a good time. Tomorrow

we're all going to Taos Pueblo to watch some weaving being done and to see some

Native American dancing, which is great because I'm really interested in learn

more about Native American culture. And I'm looking forward to see *Carmen* at

the Santa Fe Opera on Saturday.

    I'll write again in a day or two. Miss you lots.

Love,

Louise

EXERCISE 6: Listening

A | *Brian Hansen and Jane Travanti are having a telephone conversation about the orienteering club Jane belongs to. Listen to the conversation. Answer both questions in a complete sentence.*

1. What is one requirement for participating in the club activities?

_____

2. What will Brian use to find Darcy's Coffee Shop if he has trouble locating it?

_____

B | *Listen again and check (✓)* **True** *or* **False**.

	True	False
1. Brian has tried orienteering before.	☐	☑
2. Dr. Stevens wants Brian to stop working.	☐	☐
3. Being experienced in orienteering is necessary to join Jane's club.	☐	☐
4. Jane's club tries to go orienteering at least twice a month.	☐	☐
5. In the summer, they get around by biking.	☐	☐
6. In the winter, they get around by cross-country skiing.	☐	☐
7. Brian has done cross-country skiing before.	☐	☐
8. Being single is a requirement for joining the club.	☐	☐
9. The club collects dues to pay for organizing their activities.	☐	☐
10. On the 15th, they'll get to the forest by carpooling.	☐	☐

EXERCISE 7: Pronunciation

A | *Read and listen to the Pronunciation Note.*

Pronunciation Note

We distinguish nouns and verbs that have the same spelling by modifying the stress. Nouns (and adjectives) have the stress on the first syllable. Verbs have it on the second syllable.

EXAMPLES: There are several interesting **ob**jects on the table. *(noun—stress on syllable 1)*
Mary ob**jects** to my working late hours. *(verb—stress on syllable 2)*

1. I predict that the **rebel** will **rebel** against the plan.

2. The **suspect** I **suspect** is the one on the far left.

3. The band is going to **record** a new **record** for their album.

4. A **desert** is a place that people **desert**.

5. The dictator is going to **subject** the **subject** to difficult questioning.

6. The students are going to **present** their teacher with a wonderful **present**.

C | *PAIRS: Practice the sentences.*

EXERCISE 8: Personal Inventory

A | *Using events in your own life, complete the sentences with gerunds or gerund phrases.*

   EXAMPLE: I especially enjoy **playing** board games with friends.

1. I especially enjoy _____.

2. I have stopped _____.

3. I've always avoided _____.

4. I have trouble _____.

5. I spend a lot of time _____.

6. I'm looking forward to _____.

7. I'm still not used to _____.

8. I strongly dislike _____.

9. On weekends I don't feel like _____.

10. If you visit my country, I recommend _____.

B | *PAIRS: Discuss your answers to the questions. Report interesting answers to the class.*

EXERCISE 9: Group Discussion

A | *What do you value in friendships? Add your own item to the chart. Then complete the chart for yourself by rating each item.*

3 = Very Important   2 = Somewhat Important   1 = Not Important
in a Friendship   in a Friendship   in a Friendship

	Rating
Giving each other presents	
Always being honest with one another	
Not hurting each other's feelings	
Giving help whenever it is asked for	
Lending money if it is asked for	

B | *SMALL GROUPS: Discuss your answers with three classmates. Report your overall results to the class.*

EXERCISE 10: Writing

A | *Look at the categories of friendship in the opening reading. Choose one of the categories and write five or more paragraphs about a friend of yours who fits into it. Use gerunds and gerund phrases in your composition.*

> EXAMPLE: I have a friend named Sarah who perfectly fits the category of long-time friend. Sarah and I met when we were in the fifth grade, when I had just moved to a new town and didn't know anyone. Ever since Sarah and I became friends, we've enjoyed sharing all kinds of experiences and can't go more than a month or so without contacting each other. Making friends wasn't that easy at first, however . . .

B | *Check your work. Use the Editing Checklist.*

Editing Checklist

Did you use . . . ?
- ☐ gerunds as subjects correctly
- ☐ gerunds as objects correctly
- ☐ gerunds as complements correctly
- ☐ gerunds with prepositions correctly

Check your answers on page UR-3.

Do you need to review anything?

A | *Circle the word or phrase that correctly completes each sentence.*

1. Thank you very much for <u>not to smoke / not smoking</u>.

2. We go <u>shopping / to have shopped</u> every Saturday.

3. I'm bothered by <u>Emiko's / Emiko is</u> talking so loudly.

4. <u>Me not giving / Not giving</u> myself enough time to get to work was a mistake.

5. Carlos is used <u>to have / to having</u> his family near him.

6. People with glaucoma have difficulty <u>to see / seeing</u>.

7. Most people dislike <u>being awakened / being awaken</u> by an alarm clock.

8. Pavlina was annoyed at <u>not having been invited / not to be invited</u>.

B | *Correct the mistakes in the underlined words or phrases.*

1. Max has trouble <u>to finish</u> his work on time.   _____

2. <u>Missing</u> my flight, I'll have to wait six hours for the next one.   _____

3. We were bothered by his <u>come</u> in without asking permission.   _____

4. Yoshi has stopped <u>to drive</u> to work and is now walking.   _____

5. Li hates <u>told</u> what to do; he prefers making his own decisions. _____

6. Going to the movie was a good idea; it's definitely worth <u>to see</u>. _____

7. We're excited about Walid's <u>having taking</u> the job.   _____

8. I suggest not <u>to mention</u> anything political to Dad.   _____

C | *Circle the letter of the one underlined word or phrase in each sentence that is not correct.*

1 <u>Mary's</u> <u>invite</u> <u>them</u> to the get-together was <u>surprising</u> to us.   **A B C D**
    A   B   C   D

2. <u>Be</u> <u>invited</u> <u>to</u> her get-together was <u>astonishing</u> to them.   **A B C D**
    A   B   C   D

3. Bob is <u>feeling</u> sad about <u>not</u> <u>have</u> <u>called</u> you when he was in town.   **A B C D**
          A   B C D

4. Emiko is <u>concerned about</u> her <u>children's</u> <u>not</u> <u>have</u> any friends.   **A B C D**
             A   B   C D

Infinitives
PROCRASTINATION

Before You Read

PAIRS: Discuss the questions.

1. What is procrastination?
2. What are the dangers of procrastination?
3. Do you ever procrastinate? If so, in what situations?

Read

Read the article about procrastination.

SEIZE THE DAY

by Jessica Taylor

Picture this scenario: It's Sunday evening. Steve's sister Alice has a term paper due tomorrow. It's written in longhand, but it has **to be typed**. Alice doesn't type well.

ALICE: Steve, can you type my paper? It's due tomorrow.

STEVE: Alice, my friends are coming in half an hour, and I'm trying **to finish** something. I can't stop **to type** your paper now.

ALICE: But, Steve, you **have to**. I can't do it myself. It'll take me all night.

STEVE: Why didn't you ask me before now?

ALICE: I **forgot to**. I really did plan **to ask**. Steve, you've got to do it, or I'll flunk. Please?

STEVE: No, Alice, there's not enough time **to do** it now. You go start typing.

PROCRASTINATION
"Never put off until tomorrow what you can do the day after tomorrow."

(continued on next page)

Does this situation ring a bell? It illustrates the problem of procrastination, which I asked psychiatrist Robert Stevens **to talk about**.

TAYLOR: I want **to ask** you if there's such a thing as a procrastination syndrome.

STEVENS: Well, I don't know if we can call it a syndrome, but for many people procrastination is a very serious problem.

TAYLOR: Can we start with a definition of procrastination?

STEVENS: Of course. **To procrastinate** is literally **to put** things **off** until tomorrow. It's a postponing of events until a later time. But unlike the word "postpone," which has a neutral sense, the word "procrastinate" has a negative connotation. There are sometimes good reasons **to postpone** things, but never **to procrastinate**. Procrastinating has the sense of avoidance.

TAYLOR: All right. Now what causes people **to procrastinate**? Supposedly it's laziness, isn't it?

STEVENS: That's a popular idea, but I'd have to say that laziness isn't the major cause. No, I think that fear is really the most important force that motivates people **to put** things **off**.

TAYLOR: Fear? Not laziness? Can you explain?

STEVENS: Well, it's like the expectation syndrome. People do what others expect in order **to live up to** their expectations. Procrastinators are afraid **to fail** or make mistakes, or maybe they don't want **to be rejected**. Interestingly, procrastination has nothing **to do** with education. Some of the most learned people are among the worst procrastinators.

TAYLOR: What would be an example of that?

STEVENS: Well, let's see . . . Suppose someone—a young woman we'll call Blanche— has been planning a party. She's mentioned the party to friends but has put off making any actual invitations. Either consciously or subconsciously, she expects **to fail**, so she delays calling people until the very last moment. Her friends expected her **to have called** them before now, and when she didn't they forgot about the event and made other plans. It's too short notice for most of them **to come**. Blanche's fear has caused things **to turn out** like this. She feels wretched about it, but she doesn't know how **to change**.

TAYLOR: Mmm-hmm. Well, what if a procrastinator would like **to change**? What would you advise that person **to do**?

STEVENS: Getting a procrastinator **to change** can be a tough nut **to crack**, but I recommend three principles for my clients. The first is never **to put off** until tomorrow what needs **to be done** today. **Not to avoid** painful or difficult things is the second. They're part of life. The third is contained in the Latin phrase *carpe diem*—"seize the day." I try **to consider** every experience an opportunity. I don't want people **to take** unnecessary or foolish risks, but I do advise them **not to put off** living. They may not get another chance.

TAYLOR: Well, Dr. Stevens, thanks for another stimulating discussion.

After You Read

A | **Vocabulary:** *Match the blue words and phrases on the left with their meanings on the right.*

_____ **1.** Picture this **scenario**.

_____ **2.** The paper is written in **longhand**.

_____ **3.** Steve, you've got to do it, or I'll **flunk**.

_____ **4.** Does this situation **ring a bell**?

_____ **5.** The word *procrastinate* has a negative **connotation**.

_____ **6.** Some of the most **learned** people are among the worst procrastinators.

_____ **7.** She feels **wretched** about her failure.

_____ **8.** Getting a procrastinator to change can be a **tough nut to crack**.

a. difficult problem to solve

b. fail

c. educated

d. terrible

e. description of a possible situation

f. not in a machine-produced form

g. remind one of something

h. meaning additional to the basic meaning

B | **Comprehension:** *Circle* **T (True)** *or* **F (False).** *Correct the false statements.*

1. Steve is not going to type Alice's term paper.	**T**	**F**
2. The word *postpone* has a positive sense.	**T**	**F**
3. To procrastinate is literally to put things off until tomorrow.	**T**	**F**
4. Dr. Stevens believes it is sometimes appropriate to procrastinate.	**T**	**F**
5. Dr. Stevens believes that fear is the major cause of procrastination.	**T**	**F**
6. According to Dr. Stevens, procrastinators are afraid to fail.	**T**	**F**
7. Dr. Stevens believes it is sometimes permissible to avoid difficult or painful things.	**T**	**F**
8. Dr. Stevens thinks it is good to consider every experience an opportunity.	**T**	**F**

INFINITIVES

Infinitive as Subject		
Infinitive (Subject)	**Verb**	**Object**
To procrastinate	causes	a lot of problems.
Not to go ahead	proved	a mistake.

Infinitive as Object		
Subject	**Verb**	**Infinitive (Object)**
Not everyone	wants	**to procrastinate.**
He	decided	**not to go ahead.**

Infinitive as Subject Complement			
Subject	**Verb**	**Infinitive (Subject Complement)**	
His job	is	**to motivate**	people.
Their real intention	is	**not to succeed.**	

It + Infinitive				
It	*Be*	**Adjective**	(*For / Of* + Noun / Pronoun)	**Infinitive**
It	is	foolish	(for Alice / her)	**to procrastinate.**
It	was	wrong	(of Hal / him)	**not to go ahead.**

Verbs Followed by Infinitives			
	Verb	**(Noun / Pronoun)**	**Infinitive**
They	**decided / hoped / neglected**, etc.	Ø*	
	convinced / told / urged, etc.	Steve / him	**to call.**
	expected / needed / wanted, etc.	(Steve / him)	

*Ø = not used

Adjectives Followed by Infinitives			
	Adjective	**Infinitive**	
Hal is	**reluctant**	**to complete**	his work on time.
He's	**careful**	**not to make**	mistakes.
They're	**happy**	**to hear**	the test has been postponed.

Nouns Followed by Infinitives			
	Noun	**Infinitive**	
He can always think of	**reasons**	**to put off**	studying.
It seems like	**the thing**	**to do.**	
She always shows	**reluctance**	**to finish**	a job.

Too / Enough with Infinitives

	Too + Adjective / Adverb	Infinitive	
The project is	**too** complicated	**to finish**	on time.
Alice types	**too** slowly	**to meet**	the deadline.
	Adjective / Adverb + Enough	Infinitive	
Steve is	intelligent **enough**	**to understand**	the situation.
He didn't call	quickly **enough**	**to get**	the job.
	Enough + Noun	Infinitive	
They have	**enough** intelligence	**to pass**	the test.
	intelligence **enough**		

Active and Passive Infinitives

	Active Infinitives	Passive Infinitives
SIMPLE PAST	She plans **to invite** them.	They expect **to be invited**.
	She was glad **to have invited** them.	They were happy **to have been invited**.

GRAMMAR NOTES

1

An **infinitive** is *to* plus the base form of a verb. Infinitives and infinitive phrases often perform the same functions as nouns.

a. They act as subjects.

NOTE: Using an infinitive as a subject is formal. *It* + an infinitive phrase is more common. We often add *for* + a noun or pronoun to say who or what does the action.

b. They act as objects.

c. They act as subject complements (phrases that describe or explain the subject of a sentence).

To make an infinitive negative, place *not* before *to*.

BE CAREFUL! Don't confuse *to* in an infinitive with *to* as a preposition. *To* in an infinitive is followed by the base form of the verb. *To* as a preposition is followed by a gerund, regular noun, or pronoun.

USAGE NOTE: To avoid repeating an infinitive just mentioned, replace the verb with *to*. This is called **ellipsis**.

- **To graduate** from college is important. I want **to do** that.

- **To finish** what you started is advisable.

- **It's** advisable **to finish** what you started.
- **It's** important **for a student to take** good notes in class.

- I'd like **to invite** you to dinner.

- A teacher's job is **to create** a desire to learn.

- I warned you **not to** put this off.

- I **plan to work** hard. *(infinitive)*
- I'm **used to working** hard. *(gerund)*

- Steve knew he had to go to work, but he didn't want **to**.

(continued on next page)

2 Certain **verbs** are followed only by **infinitives**.

- She **offered to help** me.
- He **learned to be** efficient.

Other verbs are followed by a required noun or pronoun + an infinitive.

- I **warned Stan to make** the payments.
  Noτ: I warned ~~to make the payments~~.

Still other verbs are followed by an optional noun or pronoun + an infinitive, depending on the meaning of the verb.

- We **expected to finish** on time.
- We **expected Jim to finish** on time.

3 Certain **adjectives** can be followed by **infinitives**. These adjectives usually describe people, not things. They often express feelings about the action described in the infinitive.

- George is **afraid to make** mistakes.
- Mary is **not willing to help** us.

Common adjectives followed by infinitives: *afraid, amazed, excited, fortunate, glad, happy, important, likely, proud, reluctant, sorry,* and *willing.*

4 A **noun** is often followed by an **infinitive**. When this occurs, the infinitive gives information about the noun.

- Cozumel is a good **place to spend** a vacation.
- Generosity is a good **trait to have**.

A noun + infinitive often expresses advisability or necessity.

- Starting immediately is the **thing to do**.

5 **BE CAREFUL!** Remember that some verbs can be followed only by infinitives, others only by gerunds, and others by either infinitives or gerunds. These verbs fall into four patterns:

a. Examples of verbs and verb phrases followed only by infinitives: *appear, decide, expect, hope, manage, need, pretend, seem, want, would like.*

- They **managed to find** new jobs.
- She **pretended to be** busy.

b. Examples of verbs and verb phrases followed only by gerunds: *avoid, be worth, can't help, consider, enjoy, feel like, have trouble, keep, mind, miss, spend (time).*

- We **considered hiring** him.
- I don't **feel like working** today.

c. Examples of verbs followed by infinitives or gerunds with no change in meaning: *begin, can't stand, continue, hate, like, love, prefer, start.*

- They **began to encourage** her.
- They **began encouraging** her.

d. Examples of verbs followed by infinitives or gerunds with a significant change in meaning: *forget, go on, quit, regret, remember, stop, try.*

- I **stopped / quit to go** to the movies. (= I stopped / quit another activity in order to go to the movies.)
- I **stopped / quit going** to the movies. (= I stopped / quit the activity of going to the movies.)

6 The words **too** and **enough** are often used before infinitives. *Too* is used in the pattern *too* + adjective / adverb + infinitive. It implies a negative result.

- We're **too tired to do** any work today.
- Sam started **too late to finish** on time.

Enough + infinitive is used after an adjective / adverb.

- Ken is **strong enough to lift** 175 pounds.
- Mia runs **fast enough to be** first.

Enough can be used before a noun + infinitive.

- There's not **enough money to pay** for the repairs.

Enough can also be used after a noun. This usage is formal.

- There is not **money enough to pay** for the repairs.

NOTE: Add *for* + **a noun or pronoun** to show who performs the action of the infinitive.

- There's not **enough money for Jane to pay** for the repairs.

7 Infinitives can occur in simple or past forms. We use a **simple infinitive** (without a past participle) to indicate an action in the same general time frame as the action in the main verb.

- I **expected** you **to call**.

We use a **past infinitive** (*to* + *have* + past participle) to show an action that occurred before the action of the main verb in the sentence.

- You **seem to have forgotten** the report that was due today.

Infinitives can occur in **passive** form. In the present, use *to* + *be* or *get* + past participle. In the past, use *to* + *have* + *been* + past participle. Use the past form to indicate an action that occurred before the action of the main verb.

- The work is supposed **to be finished** by tomorrow.
- The work was **to have been done** before now.

REFERENCE NOTES

For a list of **verbs followed directly by infinitives**, see Appendix 13 on page A-7.
For **verbs followed by gerunds or infinitives**, see Unit 16 and Appendices 14 and 15 on page A-7.
For a list of **verbs followed by noun / pronoun + infinitives**, see Appendix 17 on page A-8.
For a list of **adjectives followed by infinitives**, see Appendix 18 on page A-8.

EXERCISE 1: Discover the Grammar

A | *Read these sentences from the opening reading. Is each underlined infinitive or infinitive phrase used as a subject (**S**), an object (**O**), or a subject complement (**SC**)?*

<u> O </u> **1.** I really did plan <u>to ask</u>.

_____ **2.** I want <u>to ask</u> you if there's such a thing as . . .

_____ **3.** <u>To procrastinate</u> is literally to put things off until tomorrow.

_____ **4.** To procrastinate is literally <u>to put</u> things <u>off</u> until tomorrow.

_____ **5.** Maybe they don't want <u>to be rejected</u>.

_____ **6.** She expects <u>to fail</u>.

_____ **7.** The first is never <u>to put off</u> until tomorrow what needs to be done today.

_____ **8.** <u>Not to avoid</u> painful or difficult things is the second.

_____ **9.** I try <u>to consider</u> every experience as an opportunity.

B | *Read the pairs of sentences. According to the first sentence in each pair, is the second sentence true (**T**) or false (**F**)?*

1. "I can't stop to type your paper now."
The speaker is not able to stop what he is doing for the purpose of   **T**   **F**
typing the paper.

2. "I forgot to, Steve, but I really did plan to ask."
The speaker doesn't remember asking Steve.   **T**   **F**

3. "Maybe they don't want to be rejected."
Maybe they're worried about rejecting someone.   **T**   **F**

4. "Maybe they just don't want to be told *no*."
Maybe they always want to be given *yes* answers.   **T**   **F**

5. "Her friends no doubt expected her to have called them."
Her friends probably thought she was going to call them before now.   **T**   **F**

6. "The second piece of advice is not to avoid painful or difficult things."
The advice is to stay away from painful or difficult things.   **T**   **F**

EXERCISE 2: Verbs / Nouns / Infinitives   *(Grammar Notes 2–3)*

Complete the sentences with a verb + infinitive or verb + noun / pronoun + infinitive. Three constructions will contain adjectives as well. If necessary, refer to Appendices 13, 17, and 18 on pages A-7—A-8 for help in completing the exercise.

I'm basically a procrastinator. I've always _____*wanted to stop*_____ procrastinating
                                                    1. (want / stop)

but never knew how. It started when I was a teenager and I had trouble getting my schoolwork

done. My parents always _____ doing my assignments, but they
                                 2. (warn / not / put off)

_____ my own decisions. I guess they thought it _____
3. (want / make)   **4. (be important / experience)**

the consequences of one's actions, and they never _____ at any particular
5. (force / study)

time, so I didn't. I guess I _____ from high school. When I got to college,
6. (be fortunate / graduate)

I _____ my courses by doing things at the last minute or not doing
7. (expect / pass)

them at all. However, things were different there. There were a hundred students in my history

class, and the professor _____ a term paper. I put it off, of course, and
8. (require / write)

didn't even start it until the day it was due. When I tried to turn it in a week late, the professor

_____ it. That action _____ the course. I asked
9. (refuse / accept)   **10. (cause / fail)**

my counselor what to do, and she _____ the course and change my whole
11. (advise / retake)

attitude toward finishing necessary tasks. She _____ my assignments
12. (encourage / start)

without worrying about whether they were perfect. I took her advice and many painful months later,

conquered the procrastination demon.

EXERCISE 3: Past Infinitives

(Grammar Note 7)

Complete the account with past infinitives. One sentence will be in the passive.

My husband and I took a five-day trip out of town and left the kids in charge. On the morning we

were returning, we called our son and daughter. We expected them ____*to have cleaned*____
1. (clean)

the house because we were having dinner guests that evening. When I asked Jennifer about

this, she at first seemed _____ me and quickly changed the subject. I
2. (not / hear)

persisted in the question, and this time Jennifer pretended _____ what
3. (not / understand)

I'd said. "You mean the house needs to be clean tonight?" she said. "Yes," I said. "Did you clean

it?" "Well, sort of. Josh was supposed _____ some cleaning supplies, but
4. (get)

I can't find them anywhere. I did what I could, Mom." "Well, this is important, Jen. We expect you

_____ the cleaning by the time we get home," I said in my firmest voice.
5. (finish)

When we got home, the house appeared _____ by a tornado. The
6. (hit)

kids were nowhere to be found. Dirty dishes were everywhere. Jennifer and Josh appeared

_____ the animals, but they seemed _____
7. (feed)   **8. (not / do)**

anything else. Next time we won't leave things to the kids.

EXERCISE 4: Passive Infinitives

(Grammar Note 8)

A | *For each item, complete the question with a passive infinitive.*

1. On your second day of a new job, you are an hour late to work. (fire / by the company)

   Would you expect _to be fired by the company_____?

2. You have a flat tire on a busy freeway. (help / by a passing motorist)

   Would you expect _____?

3. You have put off paying your phone bill for more than two months. (your phone service / disconnect)

   Would you expect _____?

4. Your son or daughter has been stopped for speeding. (notify / by the police)

   Would you expect _____?

5. You are going 10 miles over the speed limit. (stop / by a police officer)

   Would you expect _____?

6. Your English term paper was due three days ago. (question / by your teacher)

   Would you expect _____?

B | *PAIRS: Take turns asking and answering the questions.*

> **EXAMPLE:**   **A:** On your second day of a new job, you are an hour late to work. Would you
> expect to be fired by the company?
> **B:** No, I wouldn't expect to be fired by the company. How about you?

EXERCISE 5: *Too / Enough / Infinitives*

(Grammar Note 6)

For each situation, write a sentence with **too** *or* **enough** *and an infinitive.*

1. It's 5:15. Jill's flight leaves at 5:45, and it takes 45 minutes to get to the airport. (enough)

   _Jill doesn't have enough time to get to the airport._____

2. Jack's 10-page report is due in an hour. He types only 25 words a minute. (too)

   _____

3. Marcy wants to buy her friend's used car, which costs $5,000. She has $4,000 in the bank and is able to save $400 a month. Her friend must sell the car within three months. (enough)

   _____

4. Eve invited guests to dinner. She waited until 6:15 to start preparing the meal. The guests are expected by 7:00. (too)

   _____

5. Sally's doctor advised her to eat three meals a day to stay healthy. To lose weight, Sally ate only one small meal a day. She became quite sick. (enough)

_____

6. Carlos is enrolled in an extremely difficult calculus class, but he is a very intelligent man and can pass the course if he applies himself. (enough)

_____

EXERCISE 6: Editing

Read the entry from Alice's journal. There are ten mistakes in the use of infinitives. The first mistake is already corrected. Find and correct nine more.

   I just had write tonight. Until now I've never had the courage do this, but now
I do. I've decided to have confronted Sarah about her irresponsibility. This is
something that has been bothering me for some time now, but somehow I've
always been reluctant force the issue. So here's the situation: Sarah invites
people to do things, but she doesn't follow through. Last week she asked my
fiancé, Al, and me have dinner, and she also invited our friends Mark and
Debbie. The four of us made plans go to her house on Friday evening. Something
told me I should call Sarah asking what we should bring, and it's a good thing I
did. Sarah said, "Dinner? I'm not having dinner tonight. I know I mentioned it as a
possibility, but I never settled it with you guys. You misunderstood me." Well, that's
just silly. She told us planning on it for Friday evening at 7 P.M. When I told the
others, they were furious. Al said, "I don't expect being treated like royalty. I do
expect to be treated with consideration." So tomorrow I'm going to call Sarah up
and make my point. I'm not going to allow her make my life miserable.

   Enough for now. Time for bed.

EXERCISE 7: Listening

A | *Listen to the news bulletin. How long a sentence did Charles Gallagher receive two years ago? Answer in a complete sentence.*

_____

B | *Read the questions. Listen again. Answer each question in a complete sentence.*

1. How many prisoners are reported to have escaped?

   Three prisoners are reported to have escaped.

2. How are they believed to have escaped?

   _____

3. By whom are they believed to have been helped?

   _____

4. When was the new security system supposed to have been installed?

   _____

5. What are the prisoners thought to have?

   _____

6. In what direction are they believed to be heading?

   _____

7. What are listeners warned not to do?

   _____

8. What are they asked to do if they have any information?

   _____

EXERCISE 8: Pronunciation

A | *Read and listen to the Pronunciation Note.*

Pronunciation Note

Note the pronunciation of these three vowel sounds in English: /æ/ as in *cat*, /ɑ/ as in *cot*, /ʌ/ as in *cut*.

EXAMPLES: How do you spell *hat*? /æ/
How do you spell *hot*? /ɑ/
How do you spell *hut*? /ʌ/

B | *Listen to the sentences. Listen again and repeat. Then write the symbol for the boldfaced vowel in the underlined word: /æ/, /ɑ/, /ʌ/.*

1. I can't <u>st**o**p</u> to type your paper now.   /ɑ/

2. There's not <u>en**ou**gh</u> time to do it now.   _____

3. I'll <u>fl**u**nk</u> if you don't do it.   _____

4. Steve, you <u>h**a**ve</u> to type my paper.   _____

5. It illustrates the problem of <u>procr**a**stination</u>.   _____

6. Some friends of mine are <u>c**o**ming</u> in half an hour.   _____

7. I <u>forg**o**t</u> to ask you.   _____

8. Procrastination is a very serious <u>pr**o**blem</u>.   _____

9. Procrastination has <u>n**o**thing</u> to do with education.   _____

10. The <u>L**a**tin</u> phrase *carpe diem* means "seize the day."   _____

11. The word procrastinate has a negative <u>c**o**nnotation</u>.   _____

12. <u>Th**a**nks</u> for another stimulating discussion.   _____

C | *PAIRS: Practice the sentences.*

EXERCISE 9: Personal Inventory

A | *Write sentences on these topics, based on your own experience. Use infinitive or gerund structures.*

1. something you stopped doing

   _____

2. an activity you stopped in order to do something else

   _____

3. something you remember doing

   _____

4. something you didn't remember to do

   _____

5. something you are reluctant to do

   _____

6. something you have always been afraid to do

   _____

7. something you feel is wrong for people to do

   _____

8. something you expected to have happened before now

   _____

9. a quality that you feel is important to have

   _____

10. something that you are happy to have experienced (use the past passive)

   _____

B | *SMALL GROUPS: Discuss your answers with others in your group. Report interesting examples to the class as a whole.*

EXERCISE 10: Group Discussion

A | *Put each saying in your own words, using infinitives.*

**EXAMPLE:**   "It is better to light one candle than to curse the darkness."
—*The motto of the Christophers*

It's better **to do** one small, positive thing than **to complain** about a problem and **do** nothing.

1. "To be or not to be, that is the question."—*William Shakespeare*

_____

2. "It is better to die on your feet than to live on your knees."—*attributed to Emiliano Zapata*

_____

3. "To err is human, to forgive divine."—*Alexander Pope*

_____

4. "It is better to seek than to find."—*source unknown*

_____

5. "It is better to have loved and lost than never to have loved at all."—*Alfred, Lord Tennyson*

_____

6. "It is better to arrive late than never to arrive at all."—*source unknown*

_____

B | *SMALL GROUPS: Discuss with others in your group the extent to which you believe the sayings are true. Use infinitives. Report interesting conclusions to the class.*

EXAMPLE: I basically agree that it is better to light one candle than to curse the darkness. Complaining about a difficult situation doesn't help to solve it.

EXERCISE 11: Picture Discussion

SMALL GROUPS: *Discuss the photo. What does it show about procrastination? Does it seem to say that procrastination is a bad thing, or perhaps partially a good thing? What would you advise the owner of this desk to do?*

    EXAMPLE: **A:** I would advise the owner of this desk to put the desk in order.

                       B: I disagree. I'd advise the owner to . . .

EXERCISE 12: Writing

A | *Most of us have procrastinated at one time or another. Write three or more paragraphs about a time when you put off doing something that needed to be done. Tell about the results. Speculate about the reasons for your procrastination and discuss the consequences. Use infinitives and infinitive phrases in your composition.*

EXAMPLE: I've had lots of experiences with putting off things that needed to be done, but one that sticks in my mind is about getting my car tuned up. I was scheduled to go on a cross-country trip, and I knew I needed to take my car in for a tune-up. One thing led to another, though, and I continued to procrastinate. Finally, the day of my departure arrived, and I hadn't had the tune-up done. I said to myself . . .

B | *Check your work. Use the Editing Checklist.*

Editing Checklist

Did you use . . . ?
- ☐ infinitives as subjects correctly
- ☐ infinitives as objects correctly
- ☐ infinitives as subject complements correctly
- ☐ verbs followed by infinitives correctly

A | *Circle the word or phrase that correctly completes each sentence.*

- **A:** What did Carlos decide <u>to do / doing</u> about his job?
  1.

  B: He quit <u>accepting / to accept</u> a position at Windale's.
  2.

- **A:** Did Ben ever manage <u>giving up / to give up</u> tobacco?
  3.

  B: Yes. He actually stopped <u>to smoke / smoking</u> two months ago.
  4.

- **A:** Did you remember <u>to have locked / to lock</u> the front door?
  5.

  B: I'm sure I <u>locked / locking</u> it when I left.
  6.

- **A:** Alicia is afraid <u>to confront / confronting</u> Jaime about the problem.
  7.

  B: That's because he hates <u>to be criticized / to be criticizing</u>.
  8.

B | *Correct the mistakes in the underlined words or phrases.*

1. That child is not <u>enough strong</u> to lift the box. _____

2. I <u>warned</u> not to procrastinate, but you did. _____

3. There are occasionally good reasons <u>postpone</u> things. _____

4. All term papers have to <u>typed</u>. _____

5. I'm lucky <u>to have</u> Vijay as a friend many years ago. _____

6. Jin-Su warned me <u>to get</u> involved in the argument. _____

7. Said never came; he seems <u>to forget</u> the meeting. _____

8. Berta was too tired <u>finishing</u> her assignment. _____

C | *Circle the letter of the one underlined word or phrase that is not correct.*

1. You <u>warned me</u> <u>not to put off</u> <u>doing</u> things, but I decided <u>do</u> just that. **A B C D**
       A   B   C   D

2. It was <u>important</u> <u>experience</u> freedom, so I <u>was allowed</u> <u>to choose</u>. **A B C D**
       A   B   C   D

3. The work was <u>have</u> <u>been done</u>, but that seems <u>not to</u> <u>have happened</u>. **A B C D**
           A   B   C   D

4. We'd told you <u>to clean up</u>, but the place <u>appeared</u> <u>to be</u> <u>hit</u> by a tornado. **A B C D**
           A   B   C   D

PART VII

From Grammar to Writing

PARALLEL STRUCTURE: GERUNDS AND INFINITIVES

Remember that in parallel structure, all items in a series are in the same grammatical form: singulars with singulars, plurals with plurals, actives with actives, passives with passives, and so forth. Parallelism makes our speaking and writing stronger and more communicative. Therefore, mixing gerunds and infinitives in the same series should always be avoided.

EXAMPLES: My summer hobbies are **hiking**, **boating**, and **swimming**. *(All three complements are gerunds.)*

I want to thank everyone for making this party a success. I especially appreciate **Sumi's inviting** the guests, **Rafal's cooking** the food, and **Jennifer's organizing** the whole thing. *(All three objects are gerund phrases.)*

When my friend Li started college, her goals were **to make** new friends and **to become** well educated. *(Both complements are infinitives.)*

A series of short infinitives or infinitive phrases may be presented with the word *to* before each item or before the first item only.

EXAMPLE: Helen loves **to read**, **(to) write**, and **(to) attend** the opera.

If a sentence is long, it is often best to include the word *to* before each infinitive phrase.

EXAMPLES: In his sensitivity training at work, Dan learned **to listen** carefully to other people, **to consider** their feelings, and **to imagine** himself in their situations.

Applicants to the university are expected **to have completed** a college preparatory program, **to have graduated** in the upper third of their high school class, and **to have participated** in extracurricular activities.

1 | *Each of the sentences contains an error involving parallelism with gerunds or infinitives. Correct the nonparallel items.*

1. Ramiro loves camping, to collect stamps, and surfing the Internet.

2. Lately I've been trying to stop speeding in traffic, to schedule too many activities, and rushing through each day like a crazy person.

3. To have a happier family life, we should all focus on eating meals together, on airing our problems and concerns, and on take time to talk to one another.

4. I'm advising you not to sell your property, take out a loan, and not to buy a new house right now.

(continued on next page)

5. Most presidents want to be reelected to a second term, taken seriously by other world leaders, and to be remembered fondly after they leave office.

6. To be hired in this firm, you are expected to have earned a bachelor's degree and having worked in a bank for at least two years.

2 | *Read the paragraph about speech anxiety. Correct the 10 mistakes in parallelism with gerunds and infinitives.*

What are you most afraid of? Are you worried about being cheated, to lose your job, or contracting a deadly disease? Well, if you're like the vast majority of Americans, you fear standing up, to face an audience, and to deliver a speech more than anything else. Surveys have found that anxiety about public speaking terrifies Americans more than dying does. Somehow, people expect to be laughed at, ridiculed, or to be scorned by an audience. Many college students fear public speaking so much that they put off taking a speech class or even to think about it until their last term before graduation. Speech instructors and others familiar with the principles of public speaking stress that the technique of desensitization works best for overcoming speech anxiety. This idea holds that people can get over their fear of speaking in public by enrolling in a course, to attend the class faithfully, and to force themselves to perform the speech activities. Once they have discovered that it is rare for people to die, making fools of themselves, or to be laughed at while making a speech, they're on their way to success. Consequently, their anxiety becomes a little less each time they get up and talk in public. It may take a while, but eventually they find themselves able to stand up willingly, speaking comfortably, and expressing themselves clearly.

3 | *Before you write . . .*

1. Most of us have things that are easy for us to do, but we also have a number of things we have difficulty doing. Think of something that is particularly difficult for you to do.
2. Describe your difficult task to a partner. Listen to your partner's description.
3. Ask and answer questions about your and your partner's topic. Why do you think the task is hard for you? What could you do to make the task easier to accomplish?

4 | *Write a draft of a composition about the task you have difficulty accomplishing. Follow the model. Remember to include information that your partner asked about. Use examples of parallel structure with gerunds and with infinitives.*

Details about my difficult task:

_____

_____

_____

_____

Why I think the task is difficult for me:

_____

_____

_____

_____

What I could do to make the task easier to accomplish:

_____

_____

_____

_____

5 | *Exchange compositions with a different partner. Complete the chart.*

---

1. The writer used parallel structures with gerunds and infinitives.   **Yes** ☐ **No** ☐

2. What I liked in the composition:

_____

_____

_____

3. Questions I'd like the writer to answer about the composition:

Who _____?

What _____?

When _____?

Where _____?

Why _____?

How _____?

(Your own question) _____?

---

6 | *Work with your partner. Discuss each other's chart from Exercise 5. Then rewrite your own composition and make any necessary changes.*

ADVERBS

Adverbs: Sentence, Focus, and Negative
CONTROVERSIAL ISSUES

STEP 1 GRAMMAR IN CONTEXT

Before You Read

PAIRS: Discuss the questions.

1. How do you feel about military service? Should it be required or voluntary?
2. What is your opinion of women in military service? Should women participate in combat?

Read

🎧 *Read the transcript of a radio call-in show.*

Time to Sound Off
Show #267

McGAFFEY: Good evening, and welcome to *Sound Off*, the international talk show where you express your uncensored opinions on today's controversial issues. I'm Mike McGaffey. Tonight's topics: Should military service be required or voluntary? Should women join the military, and if they do, should they fight in combat? Let's see if we can shed some light on these issues. Here's our first caller, Jerry Burns, from Kingston, Jamaica. Where do you stand, Jerry?

BURNS: Hi, Mike. **Basically**, I think military service should be voluntary. And I'm **definitely** against women in combat.

McGAFFEY: OK. Why should it be voluntary? Why shouldn't it be required of everyone?

BURNS: Because, **overall**, young people are not all the same. Some people have a military orientation. For them, military service is fine. Others aren't oriented that way. Compulsory military service interferes with their freedom, **essentially**.

McGAFFEY: But many argue that we all owe our country something. It protects us and gives us benefits. Shouldn't we give something in return?

BURNS: We should if we're motivated to. But it shouldn't be an obligation. And I'd go further: Military forces have done a lot of evil. Maybe we shouldn't **even** have them.

McGAFFEY: Hmm. I don't know, Jerry—I'm a pretty accepting guy, but **even** I find that suggestion extreme. But let's go to your second point. Why shouldn't women be in combat?

BURNS: Men and women are **clearly** different. Let's keep them that way. Women **just** aren't suited for combat. If women are in combat, they're **just** like men. **There** goes the difference.

McGAFFEY: Are you saying that **only** men are strong enough? That's an old stereotype, isn't it?

BURNS: I'm not saying that. I **just** don't think fighting is feminine.

McGAFFEY: Wow. All right, Jerry, very interesting. I expect we'll hear some pretty spirited responses to what you've said. Our next caller is Sarah Lopez from Toronto, Canada. Sarah, is Jerry on target, or is this just fuzzy thinking?

LOPEZ: Thanks, Mike. **Actually**, I couldn't disagree more with Jerry. It's not fuzzy thinking. He made his point clearly, but I **just** don't agree with him.

McGAFFEY: OK. So military service shouldn't be voluntary?

LOPEZ: No. If we're going to have it, it should be required.

McGAFFEY: Why?

LOPEZ: It's the only way to ensure fair treatment for all. People in the military make major sacrifices—sometimes they risk their lives. That kind of risk should be spread out evenly. **Actually**, I'd go further: I'd support required national service. It wouldn't have to be **only** military.

McGAFFEY: Expand a bit on that.

LOPEZ: There are lots of worthwhile things citizens can do for their country—like working in day-care centers, hospitals, or the Peace Corps. National service has been started in a few countries, and **hopefully** it will be adopted in a lot more.

McGAFFEY: All right. Now, Jerry opposes women in combat. What's your position? Should it be allowed?

LOPEZ: **Not only** should it be allowed, **but** it should **also** be promoted. I should know: I've been in the military for 18 months.

McGAFFEY: You have?

LOPEZ: Yes, and I totally disagree with the way Jerry characterizes women. **No way** is combat unfeminine!

McGAFFEY: Have you ever been in combat?

LOPEZ: No, but if I'm ever called to combat, I'll go willingly. Most women wouldn't agree with Jerry about maintaining the difference between the sexes. **Neither** do I.

McGAFFEY: OK, Sarah. Thanks. Let's see where we can go with this. Our next caller is from Singapore. **Here's** Lu Adijojo. Lu, what's your view?

Adverbs: Sentence, Focus, and Negative   **309**

After You Read

A | Vocabulary: *Circle the letter of the best meaning for the* blue *words and phrases from the reading.*

1. *Sound Off* is the international talk show where you express your **uncensored** opinions on today's controversial issues.

   a. unrestricted　　**b.** favorite　　**c.** emotional　　**d.** unpopular

2. *Sound Off* is the international talk show where you express your uncensored opinions on today's **controversial** issues.

   a. interesting　　**b.** exciting　　**c.** debatable　　**d.** terrible

3. Let's see if we can **shed some light on** these issues.

   a. criticize　　**b.** illuminate　　**c.** discuss　　**d.** disprove

4. **Compulsory** military service interferes with their freedom, essentially.

   a. Voluntary　　**b.** Required　　**c.** Difficult　　**d.** Unpleasant

5. That's an old **stereotype**, isn't it?

   a. standardized picture　　**b.** record　　**c.** first example　　**d.** lie

6. I expect we'll hear some pretty **spirited** responses to what you've said.

   a. angry　　**b.** thoughtful　　**c.** emotional　　**d.** religious

7. It's not **fuzzy** thinking.

   a. wrong　　**b.** unclear　　**c.** elementary　　**d.** ridiculous

8. And if I'm ever called to combat, I'll go **willingly**.

   a. without fear　　**b.** without pleasure　　**c.** without explanation　　**d.** without objection

B | Comprehension: *Refer to the reading and complete each statement with a single word.*

1. Jerry, the first caller, thinks military service should be _____.

2. Jerry is _____ women being in combat.

3. Jerry doesn't think fighting is _____.

4. Sarah, the second caller, thinks military service should be _____.

5. In her opinion, it's the only way to ensure _____ treatment for everyone.

6. Sarah does not believe combat is _____.

ADVERBS: SENTENCE, FOCUS, AND NEGATIVE

Sentence Adverbs: Placement	
BEGINNING	**Clearly**, these are bitter controversies.
MIDDLE	These are **clearly** bitter controversies.
END	These are bitter controversies, **clearly**.

Focus Adverbs: Placement and Meaning				
They	**just** don't	support what he says.		They think he's wrong.
	don't **just**			They agree with him 100 percent.
Even	he	can do	that.	Almost anyone can do that task.
She	can do	**even**	that.	It's amazing how many things she can do.
Only	men	can	attend.	Women can't.
Men	can	**only**		They can't do anything else.

Negative Adverbs: Placement and Inversion			
We	**rarely**	agree	on such things.
Rarely	do we		
I have	**seldom**	heard	that idea.
Seldom	have I		
They	**never**	disagreed	with him.
Never	did they	disagree	

GRAMMAR NOTES

1 Remember that adverbs modify verbs, adjectives, and other adverbs. Some adverbs also modify entire sentences. These are called **sentence adverbs** (also called viewpoint adverbs) because they express an opinion or view about an entire sentence. Common sentence adverbs are *actually, basically, certainly, clearly, definitely, essentially, fortunately, hopefully, obviously, overall, maybe, perhaps, possibly,* and *surely.*

- **Fortunately**, Bill's military service paid for his college education. (= *It is fortunate that Bill's military service paid for his college education.*)

Some adverbs can function either as sentence adverbs or as simple adverbs.

- **Clearly**, he is a very good speaker. *(sentence adverb that modifies the entire idea—it is clear that he is a very good speaker)*
- He speaks **clearly**. *(not a sentence adverb, but a simple adverb that modifies speaks)*

You can use sentence adverbs in various places in a sentence. If the adverb comes first or last in a sentence, separate it from the rest of the sentence by a comma. If the adverb comes elsewhere in the sentence, it usually comes after the verb *be* and before other verbs. Where *be* follows a modal verb, the adverb comes after the modal. In these cases, *be* is usually not enclosed in commas.

- **Basically**, I'm in favor of that.
- I'm in favor of that, **basically**.
- I'm **basically** in favor of that.
- I **basically** agree with the plan.

2 **Focus adverbs*** focus attention on a word or phrase. These adverbs usually precede the word or phrase focused on. Common focus adverbs are *even, just, only,* and *almost.*

- **Even I** believe that. *(focuses on I)*
- I believe **even that**. *(focuses on that)*

NOTE: Changing the position of a focus adverb often changes the meaning of the sentence.

- **Just teenagers** can attend the meetings. *(focuses on teenagers—they are the only ones allowed to attend)*
- Teenagers can **just attend** the meetings. *(focuses on attend—they're not allowed to participate in the other club activities)*

NOTE: In spoken English, the word you are focusing on is stressed.

- **Only** teenagers can attend.
- Teenagers can **only** attend.

*The author wishes to acknowledge L. G. Alexander regarding the term **focus adverb** (*Longman Advanced Grammar, Reference and Practice*, New York: Longman Publishing, 1993).

3 **Negative adverbs** include *hardly*, *in no way* (informal *no way*), *little*, *neither*, *never*, *not only*, *only*, *rarely*, and *seldom*. In sentences or clauses beginning with a negative adverb, put the verb or auxiliary before the subject to emphasize the negative meaning.

- **Women are** required to serve in the military **only** in Israel.
- **Only** in Israel **are women** drafted to serve in the military.
- **He is seldom** on time.
- **Seldom is he** on time.

If the verb is in the simple present or simple past (except for the verb *be*), use *do*, *does*, or *did* after an initial negative adverb.

- **Rarely do** women **make** a career of the military.

The negative adverb *not only* combines with *but also*.

- **Not only should we** allow that, **but** we should **also** encourage it.

If the verb is in perfect form, place the auxiliary before the subject.

- **Never had I** heard such a strange idea.

NOTE: Sentences beginning with *neither* are common in both formal and informal English. Sentences beginning with other negative adverbs usually sound more formal.

- My grandfather didn't join the military. **Neither** did my father.
- **Seldom** have women served in combat. *(more formal)*

4 *Here* and *there* are other adverbs that force inversion when they come at the beginning of a sentence.

- **Here is your money**.
- **There goes the bus**.

BE CAREFUL! In a sentence beginning with *here* or *there*, invert the subject and verb if the subject is a noun. Don't invert them if it is a pronoun.

- **Here comes the bus**.
- **Here it comes**.
  Not: Here ~~the bus comes~~.
  Not: Here ~~comes it~~.

REFERENCE NOTE
For a list of **sentence adverbs**, see Appendix 19 on page A-9.

EXERCISE 1: Discover the Grammar

*Find and underline the adverb in each sentence. Then identify the adverbs as sentence adverbs (**S**), negative adverbs (**N**), or focus adverbs (**F**).*

_F_ **1.** Sarah doesn't <u>just</u> support the idea of women in combat.

_____ **2.** Basically, I think service should be voluntary.

_____ **3.** Young people aren't all the same, obviously.

_____ **4.** I'm a pretty accepting guy, but even I find that suggestion extreme.

_____ **5.** Men and women are clearly different.

_____ **6.** Little do many people realize how dangerous military service can be.

_____ **7.** I just don't agree with the basic idea.

_____ **8.** In some countries women are only allowed to perform medical duties in the military.

_____ **9.** Not only should it be allowed, but it should also be promoted.

_____ **10.** In Switzerland only men are allowed to serve in combat.

EXERCISE 2: Sentence Adverbs
(Grammar Note 1)

Combine each pair of statements into one statement. Use the adverb form of the underlined word.

1. National service is beneficial. This is <u>obvious</u>.

   Obviously, national service is beneficial. / National service is obviously beneficial. /

   National service is beneficial, obviously.

2. Military service can be dangerous. That's <u>unfortunate</u>.

_____

3. I'm against the death penalty. The <u>essential</u> reason for this is that I consider it cruel and unusual punishment.

_____

4. There's a lot more violence in movies than in the past. This is <u>certain</u>.

_____

5. Nuclear weapons can be eliminated. I'm <u>hopeful</u> this will be the case.

_____

6. A vaccine against AIDS can be found. This is <u>perhaps</u> the case.

_____

7. The prime minister's position is wrong. It's <u>clear</u>.

_____

8. There's increasing opposition to people's owning SUVs. This is the <u>actual</u> situation.

_____

EXERCISE 3: Focus Adverbs

(Grammar Note 2)

Circle the letter of the choice with the correctly used focus adverb.

1. Bill believes that women should not fight. He feels _____ in noncombat roles.

   (a.) they should only serve   **b.** only they should serve

2. Carrie thinks women can do most jobs men can do, but she feels _____ in combat.

   a. men should serve only   **b.** only men should serve

3. Samantha is against gambling, but _____ the benefits of lotteries.

   a. even she can recognize   **b.** she can even recognize

4. I'm in favor of higher taxes. _____ taxing food and medicine.

   a. Even I'm in favor of   **b.** I'm even in favor of

5. My husband has some good reasons for supporting nuclear power. However, I _____ with his reasoning.

   a. don't just agree   **b.** just don't agree

6. My father _____ the military draft; he's a military recruiter.

   a. doesn't just support   **b.** just doesn't support

EXERCISE 4: Negative Adverbs

(Grammar Note 3)

Change one sentence in each pair. Use the negative adverb in parentheses.

1. I don't support the government's policy on taxation. My friends don't support the government's policy. (neither)

   I don't support the government's policy on taxation. Neither do my friends.

2. There are many women in the military worldwide. Women fight alongside men in combat. (rarely)

_____

3. Some uninformed people oppose the military. Military service is useless. (in no way)

_____

(continued on next page)

4. Violence won't ever be completely eliminated. Poverty won't be completely eliminated. (neither)

_____

5. We need to stop global warming. We also need to find new energy sources. (not only)

_____

6. I bought an SUV. It had occurred to me that SUVs could harm the environment, but I learned they could. (Never)

_____

EXERCISE 5: Negative / Focus Adverbs

(Grammar Notes 2–3)

Study the chart. Complete the sentences with the adverbs **even, just, only in,** *or* **not only . . . but also** *and a form of the verbs in parentheses.*

Country	Has a military	Has required military service	Allows women to serve in the military	Drafts women to serve in the military	Allows women to serve in combat
Brazil	X		X		X
Canada	X		X		X
China	X	X	X	X	
Costa Rica					
Israel	X	X	X	X	
Switzerland	X	X			
The United States	X		X		X
Venezuela	X		X		X

Facts about military service in eight countries:

1. _____*Only in*_____ Costa Rica _____*is there*_____ no military.
                                   (there / be)

2. Though officially neutral, _____ Switzerland _____ a military.
                                                              (have)

3. _____ three countries _____ required military service.
                                              (have)

4. _____ do Brazil, Canada, the United States, and Venezuela allow women to

serve in the military, _____ them to serve in combat.
                            (they / allow)

5. _____ to serve in combat in these four countries.
     (men / require)

6. _____ Israel and China _____ to do military service.
                                                  (women / require)

EXERCISE 6: Editing

There are seven mistakes in the use of adverbs in the letter. The first mistake is already corrected. Find and correct six more.

Dear Dad,

    I'm waiting for the 5:25 train, so ~~just I~~ *I just* thought I'd drop you a note. I've been at the global warming conference. Actually, I almost didn't get to the conference because almost we didn't get our taxes done on time. Vicky and I stayed up late last night, though, and I mailed the forms this morning.

    I hate income taxes! Only once in the last 10 years we have gotten a refund, and this time the form was so complicated that Vicky got even upset, and you know how calm she is. Maybe we should move to Antarctica or something. No taxes there.

    Besides that, we've been having problems with Donna. It's probably nothing more serious than teenage rebellion, but whenever we try to lay down the law, she gets defensive. Rarely if ever she takes criticism well. The other night she and her friend stayed out until 1 A.M., and when we asked what they'd been doing she said, "We were just talking and listening to music at the Teen Club. Why can't you leave me alone?" Then she stomped out of the room. Fortunately, Sam and Toby have been behaving like angels—but they're not teenagers!

    Meanwhile, Donna's school has started a new open-campus policy. Students can leave the campus whenever they don't have a class. Even they don't have to tell the school office where they're going or when they'll be back. No way do Vicky and I approve of that policy! School time, in our view, is for studying and learning, not for socializing. Little do those school officials realize how much trouble unsupervised teenagers can get into.

    Well, Dad, here the train comes. I'll sign off now. Write soon.

                Love,

                Ken

EXERCISE 7: Listening

A | *Listen to the next part of the radio call-in show. Where is the caller from?*

_____

B | *Listen again and circle the letter of the correct answer.*

1. The caller listens to the radio show _____.

   a. every day   **c.** twice a week

   b. once a week   **d.** once every two weeks

2. The caller likes the program _____.

   a. a lot   **c.** occasionally

   b. somewhat   **d.** very little

3. The caller is basically closer to the viewpoint of _____.

   a. the man from Jamaica   **b.** military leaders in her country   **c.** the woman from Canada   **d.** the U.N. secretary-general

4. The caller thinks military service should be _____.

   a. required   **b.** abolished   **c.** voluntary   **d.** only one of many service options

5. The caller thinks fighting in combat _____ a woman is unfeminine.

   a. doesn't mean   **b.** means   **c.** can mean   **d.** has always meant

6. The caller thinks combat isn't advisable for _____.

   a. any women   **b.** college educated women   **c.** women over 25   **d.** mothers

7. The caller thinks pro-military people in her country _____ support the idea of women in combat.

   a. do   **b.** don't   **c.** might   **d.** will eventually

8. The caller thinks national service is basically a _____ idea.

   a. foolish   **b.** good   **c.** complicated   **d.** very expensive

EXERCISE 8: Pronunciation

A | *Read and listen to the Pronunciation Note.*

> **Pronunciation Note**
>
> In sentences with focus adverbs, the word following the focus adverb usually has the strongest stress in the sentence.
>
> **EXAMPLES:** Even **I** like the cold weather. *(strongest stress on I)*
> I even **like** the cold weather. *(strongest stress on* like*)*

B | *Listen to the sentences. Underline the stressed words.*

> **EXAMPLES:** I love only <u>you</u>. (= You're the only one I love.)
> Only <u>I</u> love you. (= I'm the only one who loves you.)

1. Bill can even understand this math.

2. Even Bill can understand this math.

3. I don't just agree with Nancy.

4. I just don't agree with Nancy.

5. We don't even understand you.

6. Even we don't understand you.

7. Only women can visit this club.

8. Women can only visit this club.

C | *Listen again and repeat the sentences.*

EXERCISE 9: Personal Inventory

A | *Complete each of the sentences with the indicated adverbs, drawing from your own experience.*

1. Basically, I . . .

_____

2. Fortunately, I . . .

_____

3. Even I . . .

_____

(continued on next page)

4. I even . . .

_____

5. Rarely do I . . .

_____

6. I just don't . . .

_____

7. I don't just . . .

_____

8. Not only do I . . . but I also . . .

_____

B | *PAIRS: Discuss your answers. Report interesting examples to the class.*

EXERCISE 10: Pros / Cons

A | *PAIRS: Choose a controversial topic that might be discussed on a TV or radio call-in show. You may select a topic from the box or choose one of your own.*

capital punishment	the military draft
cloning	using hand-held cell phones while driving
electric vs. gas-powered cars	women in combat

B | *Brainstorm and write down points supporting both sides of the issue.*

EXERCISE 11: Debate

CLASS: Choose a topic from Exercise 10. Have a debate on that subject. Follow the steps to prepare for the debate:

- Divide into two groups that will argue the opposing viewpoints.
- Brainstorm and write down points supporting your group's side of the issue.
- Do research outside of class, using the Internet if possible.
- To maximize your side's performance, make certain that you can predict and understand the arguments that the opposing side might present.

EXERCISE 12: Writing

A | *Write five paragraphs on a controversial topic. You may use one of the topics in Exercise 10 (including the subject debated) or select another topic of your own. Follow these steps:*

- Do research on your topic outside of class, using the Internet if possible.
- Be objective: Find specifics that support your viewpoint, but also touch on points opposite to your view.
- Try to use at least two sentence adverbs, two focus adverbs, and two negative adverbs in your composition.

Organize your composition in this way:

- Paragraph 1: Introduction. State your viewpoint. Mention the viewpoints on the other side of the issue.
- Paragraph 2: First reason for your viewpoint.
- Paragraph 3: Second reason for your viewpoint.
- Paragraph 4: Third reason for your viewpoint.
- Paragraph 5: Conclusion.

B | *Check your work. Use the Editing Checklist.*

Editing Checklist

Did you use . . . ?
- ☐ sentence adverbs correctly
- ☐ focus adverbs correctly
- ☐ negative adverbs correctly

A | Circle the word or phrase that correctly completes each sentence.

1. Mom tries to get me to eat oatmeal, but I <u>don't just / just don't</u> like it.

2. Never <u>had we / we had</u> seen such a fine performance.

3. Bill is pro-military; <u>he even thinks / even he thinks</u> the draft should be renewed.

4. In our club <u>members can only / only members</u> can attend meetings.

5. I <u>just don't / don't just</u> love him; I want to marry him.

6. Pau is a terrible cook, but <u>even he can / he can even</u> boil eggs.

7. Rarely <u>does Eva / Eva does</u> arrive late at the office.

8. Here <u>the train comes / comes the train</u>.

B | Correct the mistakes, including errors of punctuation, in the underlined words or phrases.

1. Only in Australia <u>kangaroos are</u> found. _____

2. Something has to change <u>clearly</u>. _____

3. Not only should he hurry, <u>but should he</u> run. _____

4. Seldom <u>our team does lose</u>. _____

5. <u>Members just</u> can vote; non-members cannot. _____

6. Here <u>the money is</u> that I owe you. _____

7. <u>Actually</u> I did graduate from college. _____

8. There <u>the plane goes</u>. _____

C | Circle the letter of the one underlined word or phrase in each sentence that is not correct.

1. The author <u>clearly</u> shows that <u>rarely</u> <u>the law is applied</u> <u>fairly</u>.   **A B C D**
            A   B   C   D

2. I <u>actually</u> thought Ben wouldn't come <u>at all</u>, <u>but</u> <u>here comes he</u>.   **A B C D**
    A   B C   D

3. <u>Rarely</u> <u>will he accept</u> criticism, <u>and</u> at times <u>even he won't listen</u>.   **A B C D**
   A   B   C   D

4. <u>Never I have seen</u> as <u>clearly</u> as I do <u>now</u> how <u>very</u> absurd that is.   **A B C D**
        A   B   C   D

STEP 1 GRAMMAR IN CONTEXT

Before You Read

PAIRS: Discuss the questions.

1. What is your view of sports? Is it basically positive, negative, or somewhere in between?
2. What are some benefits of sports? What are some negative aspects of them?

Read

Read the editorial about sports.

EDITORIAL
ARE SPORTS STILL SPORTING?
by Buck Jacobs

As I write this editorial, the World Cup is in full swing in South Africa. The competition seems a big success, with the world's major soccer teams playing in attractive venues. Similarly, the 2008 Summer Olympics in Beijing and the 2010 Winter Olympics in Vancouver were artistic triumphs. But **while sports may look good on the surface**, problems are lurking underneath. Partisanship is increasing; **because he penalized a player** in the 2008 European Championships, a British referee received death threats. **Since there are ever-increasing**

Throwing the Javelin

possibilities for product endorsement by athletes, money is playing a larger role. Violence has certainly not diminished.

What is wrong? I've concluded that the whole sports scene is in need of repair and have identified three major excesses:

FIRST EXCESS: misplaced focus on fame. **When the Olympics began about 2,700 years ago in Greece**, the contests were related to war. The javelin throw, for example, paralleled the throwing of a spear in a battle. Running paralleled the physical exertion you might have to make **if an enemy was chasing you**. When the

(continued on next page)

EDITORIAL: ARE SPORTS STILL SPORTING?

modern Olympic games started in 1896, the philosophy had shifted to the promotion of peace. However, emphasis was still placed on demonstrating physical stamina and excellence in challenging contests.

How things have changed! **Although athletes still try to achieve their personal best**, the focus has shifted to the breaking of records and the achievement of fame. Can we really say that someone who finishes the 400-meter freestyle swim one-tenth of a second ahead of his or her nearest rival is a champion, **while that rival is an also-ran?**

SECOND EXCESS: money. Consider the cost of attending a major athletic competition. In the United States, the average cost of a ticket to a National Football League game in 2010 is about $72. **If you add the cost of taking a family of four to a game**, the total is over $388. A ticket to an NBA basketball game is about $49. Baseball is cheaper, **though it's not really a bargain at an average ticket cost of $27**. I wondered why tickets are so expensive **until I remembered the key factor**: players' salaries. Basketball star Kobe Bryant earns over $23 million a year. Baseball player Alex Rodriguez makes at least $33 million yearly. Is anyone worth that much money? The president of the United States earns $400,000 a year, and U.S. public schoolteachers make a yearly average of about $50,000. Who is more valuable to society? What we pay people says a lot about what we value.

THIRD EXCESS: prevalence of violence. We see it **wherever we look**, and it's certainly not decreasing. Fights occur frequently in professional sports, with ice hockey one of the worst offenders. In the 2003–2004 season, for instance, player Steve Moore had to be hospitalized **because another player hit him in the head with his stick.** Unfortunately, there seems to be increasing acceptance of violence as "just part of the game." But **once we assume violence is inevitable**, it will be almost impossible to stop. This sort of thing doesn't just happen in North America, either. We've all heard about the well-publicized violence surrounding soccer games in Europe.

Somehow, in becoming big business entertainment, sports have gone awry. What to do? Well, we can pay more attention to local athletics and events such as the Special Olympics. We can refuse to pay ridiculously high ticket prices. We can demand an end to violence. Above all we need to get back to this idea: It's not whether you win or lose; it's how you play the game.

After You Read

A | Vocabulary: *Complete the definitions with the correct word from the box.*

also-ran	inevitable	partisanship	stamina
awry	lurking	prevalence	venues

1. _____ are locations where events take place.

2. Something that is _____ is considered impossible to avoid.

3. Something that is waiting in hiding is said to be _____.

4. _____ is defined as strength of body or mind to complete a task.

5. The common, general, or wide existence of something is termed _____.

6. A loser in a competition is termed a(n) _____.

7. _____ is the condition of being devoted to or biased in support of a group or

   a cause.

8. Something that is away from the correct course is said to be _____.

B | Comprehension: *Refer to the reading and complete each sentence with a single word.*

1. When the Olympics began, athletic contests were related to _____.

2. The modern Olympic games were designed to promote _____.

3. In both the ancient and the revived Olympic games, the original emphasis was on the pursuit

   of _____ in physical contests.

4. According to the author of the editorial, the emphasis in today's Olympic games has shifted to

   the achievement of _____.

5. The author states that, while a ticket to a baseball game is less expensive than one to a football

   or basketball game, it's still hardly a _____.

6. The author says that the high cost of tickets today is most directly related to the need to pay

   the _____ of players.

7. According to the author, there is an increasing acceptance of _____ as being

   "just part of the game."

8. The author believes that we should support _____ athletic contests and events

   such as the Special Olympics.

ADVERB CLAUSES

Placement and Punctuation

Main Clause	Adverb Clause
We watched TV a lot	**when the Olympics were on.**
Tickets cost more	**because athletes earn so much.**

Adverb Clause	Main Clause
When the Olympics were on,	we watched TV a lot.
Because athletes earn so much,	tickets cost more.

Types

Adverb Clauses of Time	
Before I played basketball,	I was a soccer player.
The coach met with her players	**after the game was over.**
While the team was on the field,	the fans cheered continuously.

Adverb Clauses of Place	
I've seen children playing soccer	**everywhere I've been outside the United States.**
Anywhere you go,	sports stars are national heroes.
I work out at a gym	**wherever I travel.**

Adverb Clauses of Reason	
Since she plays well,	I want her on our team.
He was unable to play in the final game	**as he had hurt his ankle.**
Now that TV covers the games,	billions of people can see the Olympics.

Adverb Clauses of Condition	
Unless the tickets cost too much,	we'll go to the game next Saturday.
You'll be comfortable inside the dome	**even if it's cold and raining outside.**
Only if she wins the gold medal	will she get a professional contract.

Adverb Clauses of Contrast	
They won the game,	**though they didn't really deserve the victory.**
Although their team is talented,	they just didn't win.
Swimmers are rarely injured,	**whereas hockey players are often hurt.**

GRAMMAR NOTES

1 Remember that a **clause** is a group of words that contains at least one subject and a verb showing past, present, or future time. Clauses are either independent or dependent.

Independent clauses (also called main clauses) can stand alone as complete sentences.

Dependent clauses (also called subordinate clauses) cannot stand alone. They need another clause to be fully understood.

Sentences containing both an independent clause and a dependent clause are called **complex sentences**. In a complex sentence, the main idea is normally in the independent clause.

NOTE: In a complex sentence, the clauses can come in either order. If the dependent clause comes first, we place a comma after it.

- **You could win a medal**.
- **We'll go to the game**.

INDEPENDENT CLAUSE   DEPENDENT CLAUSE
- You could win a medal **if you practice enough**.

DEP. CLAUSE   INDEP. CLAUSE (MAIN IDEA)
- **If we can get tickets**, we'll go to the game.

- **Whenever I exercise**, I feel good.
- I feel good **whenever I exercise**.

2 **Adverb clauses** are dependent clauses that indicate **how**, **when**, **where**, **why**, or **under what conditions** things happen. Adverb clauses may also introduce a contrast.

Adverb clauses begin with **subordinating conjunctions** (also called subordinating adverbs), which can be either single words or phrases.

NOTE: Adverb clauses sometimes come inside independent clauses.

- I went home **when the game was over**. *(when)*
- She dropped out of the race **because she was injured**. *(why)*
- They won the game, **although the score was very close**. *(contrast)*

- It began to rain **while we were playing**.
- I have to practice a lot **now that I'm on the team**.

- Her ability **when she got to high school** was remarkable.

3 **Adverb clauses of time** indicate **when** something happens. They are introduced by *after, as, as soon as, before, by the time, once, since, until / till, when, whenever, while,* etc.

NOTE: *Once* means *starting from the moment something happens.*

NOTE: *Until* and *till* have the same meaning. *Till* is informal and used more in conversation.

BE CAREFUL! In complex sentences, do not use *will* and *be going to* in the dependent clause to show future time.

- The race will start **as soon as everyone is in place**.
- We always drink water **before we start a game**.

- She'll earn a good salary **once she starts playing regularly**.

- I'll wait here **until / till they arrive**.

- We'll leave **when they get here**.
  Not: We'll leave when they ~~will~~ get here.

(continued on next page)

4	**Adverb clauses of place** indicate **where** something happens. They are introduced by *anywhere*, *everywhere*, *where*, *wherever*, etc.	• Professional sports are played **where there are big stadiums**. • Major athletes are popular **wherever they go**.
5	**Adverb clauses of reason** indicate **why** something happens. They are introduced by *as*, *because*, *now that* (= because now), *since*, etc. **NOTE:** *Since* is used both in adverb clauses of reason and of time. **NOTE:** *As* is used both in adverb clauses of reason and of time.	• She won the medal **because she had practiced tirelessly**. • **Since he didn't register in time**, he can't play. • **Since Anna doesn't like sports**, she refused to go to the game. (*reason:* since = because) • Barry has played sports **since he entered high school**. (*time:* since = starting from that point) • **As he was badly hurt**, he had to drop out of the game. (*reason:* as = because) • He set a world record **as we were watching**. (*time:* as = while)
6	**Adverb clauses of condition** indicate **under what conditions** something happens. They are introduced by *even if*, *if*, *only if*, *unless*, *in case*, etc. *Even if* means that the condition does not matter; the result will be the same. *Only if* means that only one condition will produce the result. *Unless* means that something will happen or be true if another thing does not happen or is not true. *In case* means in order to be prepared for a possible future happening. **NOTE:** If the sentence begins with *only if*, the subject and verb of the main clause are inverted, and no comma is used. **BE CAREFUL!** Don't confuse *even if* or *even though* with *even*.	• You'll improve **if you practice daily**. • **Even if he practices constantly**, he won't make the team. • Bi-Yun will make the team **only if another athlete drops out**. • **Unless you train a great deal**, you won't be a champion. • We'd better take along some extra money **in case we run into difficulties**. • **Only if** another athlete drops out **will Bi-Yun** make the team. • **Even if** they win this game, they won't be the champions. • **Even** my mother understands the rules of baseball.

7 **Adverb clauses of contrast** make a contrast with the idea expressed in the independent clause. They are introduced by *although*, *even though*, *though*, *whereas*, *while*, etc.

- He lost the race, **although he was favored**.
- **Even though she is tall**, she doesn't score much.

We usually use *although*, *even though*, and *though* when we want to show an unexpected result.

- **Although / Even though / Though he is quite young**, he was selected for the team. (*comma after the clause*)

NOTE: We normally place a comma before or after a dependent clause of contrast.

- He was selected for the team, **though / although / even though he is quite young**.
- **Though / Although / Even though he is quite young**, he was selected for the team.

To make a direct contrast, we use *while* or *whereas*.

- **While / Whereas downhill skiing is very expensive**, cross-country skiing is cheap.

USAGE NOTE: *Whereas* is used in formal written English and careful speech.

NOTE: *While* is used to introduce both a clause of contrast and a clause of time.

- **While they lost the game**, they played their best. (*contrast*)
- We ate **while we were watching the game**. (*time*)

REFERENCE NOTE
For a list of **subordinating conjunctions**, see Appendix 20 on page A-9.

STEP 3 FOCUSED PRACTICE

EXERCISE 1: Discover the Grammar

In each of the sentences, underline the dependent clause once and the independent clause twice. Then write **contrast, place, time, reason,** *or* **condition** *above the dependent clauses.*

1. *time*
   As I write this editorial, the World Cup is in full swing in South Africa.

2. While sports may look good on the surface, problems are lurking underneath.

3. Because he penalized a player in the 2008 European Championships, a British referee received death threats.

4. When the Olympic games started about 2,700 years ago in Greece, the contests held were basically those related to war.

(continued on next page)

5. Running paralleled the physical exertion you might have to make if an enemy was chasing you.

6. Although athletes still try to achieve their personal best, the emphasis has shifted away from the individual pursuit of excellence.

7. I wondered why tickets are so expensive until I remembered the key factor: players' salaries.

8. Baseball is cheaper, though it's not really a bargain at an average ticket cost of $27.

9. We see violence wherever we look.

10. Once we assume violence is inevitable, it will be almost impossible to stop.

EXERCISE 2: Word Order

(Grammar Notes 3, 5–7)

Rearrange the words to make sentences, each containing an adverb clause. Add necessary punctuation.

1. ticket / can / to / Before / lift / buy / a / you / you / have / start

   Before you can start, you have to buy a lift ticket.

2. player's / love / zero / If / score / the / one / forty / is / is / score

   _____

3. unless / can't / You / you / ice / have / game / skates / and / this / play

   _____

4. free-throw / line / You / after / you've / go / the / to / fouled / been

   _____

5. use / head / hands / Though / may / you / you / your / your / use / can't

   _____

6. miles / You've / you've / 26.2 / course / finished / run / the / when

   _____

7. bat / until / Your / team / team / can't / outs / three / makes / the / other

   _____

8. touchdown / scores / If / team / your / earns / points / a / it / six

   _____

EXERCISE 3: Combining Sentences

(Grammar Notes 3, 5–6)

Combine each pair of sentences into one sentence containing an adverb clause and a main clause. Keep the clauses in the same order. Add necessary punctuation.

1. There are similarities between the ancient and modern Olympics. There are also differences.

   Though / Although / While / Even though there are similarities between the ancient and

   modern Olympics, there are also differences.

2. Greek city-states were often at war with one another. Olympic contestants stopped fighting during the games.

   _____

   _____

3. The ancient Olympic games were outlawed by the Roman Emperor Theodosius I. They had been held for over 1,000 years.

   _____

   _____

4. He outlawed them in 393. Romans thought the Greeks wore too few clothes.

   _____

   _____

5. French educator Pierre de Coubertin revived the Olympics. He thought they would promote international peace.

   _____

   _____

6. Tug-of-war was dropped from the Olympics in 1920. American and British athletes disagreed about how it should be played.

   _____

   _____

7. New Olympic sports often first appear as demonstration events. They are adopted as medal sports.

   _____

   _____

8. Any sport can potentially become a medal event. It can be scored and fulfills certain criteria.

   _____

   _____

EXERCISE 4: Writing Adverb Clauses

(Grammar Notes 3, 5–7)

Look at the pictures. Complete the sentence describing each picture with an adverb clause.
Use a different subordinating conjunction in each clause.

1. The Sharks will win the game _____
   (condition)
   _____
   _____

2. The other team can't win _____
   (condition)
   _____
   _____

3. _____
   (contrast)
   _____
   _____, their fans still love them.

4. The players are doing their best _____
   (contrast)
   _____
   _____

5. _____
   (reason)
   _____
   _____, the competition was postponed.

6. The competition won't be held _____
   (time)
   _____
   _____ improve.

EXERCISE 5: Editing

Read the student essay. There are eight mistakes in the use of adverb clauses, including incorrect subordinating conjunctions and incorrect verbs. The first mistake is already corrected. Find and correct seven more.

Why Sports?

by Jamal Jefferson

A lot of people are criticizing school sports these days. Some say there's too much
emphasis on football and basketball ~~if~~ *while* there's not enough emphasis on education.
Others say the idea of the scholar-athlete is a joke. Still others say sports provide a way
of encouraging violence. I think they're all wrong. If anything, school sports help prevent
violence, not encourage it. Why do I think sports are a positive force?

For one thing, sports are positive even though they give students opportunities to be
involved in something. Every day on TV we hear that violence is increasing. I think a lot
of people get involved in crime when they don't have enough to do to keep themselves
busy. After you'll play two or three hours of basketball, baseball, or any other kind of
sport, it's hard to commit a violent act even if you want to.

Second, sports teach people a lot of worthwhile things, especially at the high school
level. If they play on a team, students learn to get along and work with others. Wherever
their team wins, they learn how to be good winners; when their team will lose, they find
out that they have to struggle to improve. They discover that winning a few and losing a
few are part of the normal ups and downs of life. Also, there's no doubt that students
improve their physical condition by participating in sports.

Finally, sports are positive although they allow students who do not have enough
money to go to college to get sports scholarships and improve their chances for a
successful life. Unless a young basketball player from a small village in Nigeria can get
a scholarship to play for, say UCLA, he will have a chance to get an education and
probably make his life better. If a young woman with little money is accepted on the
University of Toronto swim team and gets a scholarship, she'll have the chance to earn
a college degree and go on to a high-paying job. Because school sports programs have
some deficiencies that need to be corrected, their benefits outweigh their disadvantages.
I should know because I'm one of those students who got a sports scholarship. School
sports must stay.

EXERCISE 6: Listening

A | *Listen to the interview. What country is Lillian Swanson from?*

_____

B | *Read the questions. Listen to the interview with a sports star. Then listen again and answer each question with a complete sentence containing an adverb clause.*

1. Why did Lillian Swanson become successful?

   Lillian Swanson became successful because her parents loved and supported her.

2. When did Lillian learn to swim?

   _____

3. Why does Lillian think she became a good swimmer?

   _____

4. Why did Lillian and her family spend a lot of time at the beach?

   _____

5. What did Lillian decide when she was 12?

   _____

6. Under what conditions did Lillian's parents agree to pay for lessons?

   _____

7. When did Lillian get discouraged?

   _____

8. Why can't Lillian imagine herself doing anything else?

   _____

9. What happened once Lillian started her lessons?

   _____

EXERCISE 7: Pronunciation

🎧 **A** | *Read and listen to the Pronunciation Note.*

> **Pronunciation Note**
>
> English speakers normally pause in a sentence in which a dependent adverb clause comes first in a complex sentence. They normally do not pause when a dependent clause comes second. However, a speaker normally pauses after or before an adverb clause that shows a contrast. The pause is indicated in writing with a comma.
>
> **EXAMPLES:**
>
> **As soon as she graduates,** she'll start her physical training. *(pause, comma)*
>
> She'll start her physical training **as soon as she graduates**. *(no pause, no comma)*
>
> **Though he has a lot of talent,** he doesn't work very hard at his sport. *(pause, comma)*
>
> He doesn't work very hard at his sport**, though he has a lot of talent**. *(pause, comma)*

🎧 **B** | *Listen and repeat the sentences. Place a comma wherever you hear a pause.*

1. As soon as the game was over, we left the stadium.

2. Elena swam laps while I did my calisthenics.

3. Even though the team scored 10 runs they still didn't win.

4. In case you haven't heard the manager was fired.

5. I always manage to go to a gym whenever I'm traveling.

6. He makes a lot of money now that he's a major league player.

7. The coach was not popular with his players although he took them to the championship.

8. Tickets to the game were very expensive though I'd have to say the expense was justified.

9. She always warms up by swimming extra laps before she begins a competition.

10. After Daoud scored the winning goal he was mobbed by his teammates.

11. The team won't make the playoffs unless they win their next eight games.

12. Once he started wearing contact lenses he became a much more accurate player.

C | *PAIRS: Practice the sentences, making sure to pause when there is a comma.*

EXERCISE 8: Personal Inventory

A | *Write sentences with adverb clauses about your possible future, using the subordinating conjunctions in parentheses. Place the dependent clause first in half of the sentences and second in the other half.*

EXAMPLE: **When I'm rich,** I'll sleep on a soft pillow.

1. (when) _____

_____

2. (if) _____

_____

3. (unless) _____

_____

4. (in case) _____

_____

5. (because) _____

_____

6. (after) _____

_____

7. (as soon as) _____

_____

8. (once) _____

_____

9. (before) _____

_____

10. (although) _____

_____

B | *PAIRS: Discuss your answers. Report interesting answers to the class.*

EXERCISE 9: Picture Discussion

A | *GROUPS: Discuss what is happening in the picture. In your view, how does the picture reflect sports in the world today? Have sports everywhere become too violent, or is this sort of behavior just "part of the game"?*

B | *Discuss your conclusions with the class.*

EXERCISE 10: Writing

A | *Choose one of the topics and write three or four paragraphs about it. If possible, support your ideas with examples from your personal experience. Use adverb clauses in your composition.*

- Sports are valuable to society because they provide entertainment.
- Sports have become too violent.
- Sports provide opportunities to people who have few other opportunities.
- Sports stars earn ridiculously large salaries.

EXAMPLE: Though many people say that sports are overemphasized in our culture, my opinion is that the advantages of sports outweigh their disadvantages. In particular, I strongly believe that sports provide opportunities to people who don't have many other opportunities. Consider the inner-city boy, for example, whose parents can't afford to send him to college, even though he's a good student. One of my best friends falls into this category. He . . .

B | *Check your work. Use the Editing Checklist.*

Editing Checklist

Did you use . . . ?
- ☐ correct placement and punctuation of adverb clauses
- ☐ adverb clauses of reason correctly
- ☐ adverb clauses of condition correctly
- ☐ adverb clauses of contrast correctly

Check your answers on page UR-3.
Do you need to review anything?

A | *Circle the word or phrase that correctly completes each sentence.*

1. You won't be a champion if / unless you practice regularly.

2. Since / Even though the team is in the playoffs, I doubt they'll win the title.

3. We're taking along our racquets in case / although there's time to play.

4. Whenever / As Hai was running toward the goal line, he sprained his ankle.

5. Once / As Bahdoon gets used to his new position, he'll be a great help.

6. Nelson and Elena don't go dancing once / now that they have children.

7. Famous athletes are in demand wherever / whereas they go.

8. We'll be leaving as soon as / since she arrives.

B | *Correct the mistakes in the underlined words or phrases.*

1. I visit my cousin wherever I'm in town.   _____

2. Until she arrives, we'll be leaving.   _____

3. Only if I study for days, I'm not likely to earn an "A."   _____

4. Although she's seldom at home, I don't often stop to see her.   _____

5. Whereas he exercises will he lose weight.   _____

6. Because they played with great skill, they lost the game.   _____

7. Since flying costs a lot, bus travel is inexpensive.   _____

8. That check is going to bounce when we make a deposit.   _____

C | *Circle the letter of the one underlined word or phrase in each sentence that is not correct.*

1. We'll start when they will get here, as long as they get here soon.   **A B C D**
      A   B   C   D

2. Even you explain the game to Mom, she won't understand what's going on.   **A B C D**
   A   B   C   D

3. As cars surely offer benefits, they unfortunately cause problems also.   **A B C D**
  A   B   C   D

4. We're angry because he's late, but I guess we'll wait until he'll arrive.   **A B C D**
     A   B C D

Adverb and Adverbial Phrases
COMPASSION

Before You Read

PAIRS: Discuss the questions.

1. What is your definition of compassion?
2. How important a value is compassion in society?

Read

Read the article about compassion.

Compassion

It was the evening of September 29, 1994. **Having spent a wonderful day exploring the ruins at Paestum in southern Italy**, Reg and Maggie Green were driving south in the area of Italy known as the boot, **their children Nicholas and Eleanor sleeping peacefully in the back seat**. Suddenly an old, decrepit car pulled up alongside them, and an Italian with a bandanna over his face screamed at them, **signaling them to stop. Not knowing what to do**, Reg carefully weighed the options. If they stopped, they risked a potentially deadly confrontation with criminals; if they sped away, they might escape. **Guessing that their newer-model car could probably elude the old car the criminals were driving**, Reg floored the gas pedal. Shots rang out, **shattering both windows on the driver's side of the car**. The Greens' car took off, **easily outdistancing the bandits' car**. **Checking the children**, Reg and Maggie

found them still **sleeping peacefully in the back seat**.

A bit farther down the road, Reg saw a police car parked on the shoulder and pulled over to alert the authorities. **Upon opening the door**, he saw blood oozing from the back of Nicholas's head. **After being rushed to a hospital**, Nicholas lay in a coma for two days. Then doctors declared him brain-dead.

This was not the end of the story, however. As Nicholas lay on his deathbed, Reg and Maggie decided that something good should come out of the situation. **Realizing that it would be far better to return good for evil than to seek revenge**, they offered Nicholas's organs for transplant. "Someone should have the future he lost," Reg said. **Profoundly moved by the gesture**, Italians poured out their emotions. Maurizio Costanzo, the host of a talk show, summed up the common feeling by saying, "You have given us a lesson in civility . . . shown us how to react in the face of pain and sorrow."

The great irony of this tragedy was that it was a mistake. Investigators later determined that Nicholas was killed by two petty criminals who thought the Greens were jewelers carrying precious stones. The criminals were placed on trial **after being turned over to the police**.

People all over Europe and North America reacted in sorrow. Headlines in Italian newspapers spoke of *La Nostra Vergogna* ("Our Shame"). Wherever the Greens went, they met Italians who begged their forgiveness. The Greens were given a medal, Italy's highest honor, by the prime minister.

Some good has indeed come out of Nicholas's death. Seven Italians received Nicholas's heart, liver, kidneys, islet cells (cells related to diabetes), and corneas. Perhaps more importantly, a blow was struck for organ donation. **Having heard Reg and Maggie speak on TV**, 40,000 French people pledged to donate their organs when they died. **On returning to the United States**, the Greens began to receive requests to tell their son's story and speak about organ donation. "It gradually dawned on us," said Reg, "that we'd been given a life's work."

Nicholas Green is gone, but others live on because of his parents' compassionate act. How many of us would do the same thing, **given the chance**?

After You Read

A **Vocabulary:** *Match the blue words and phrases on the left with their meanings on the right.*

_____ 1. Suddenly an old, **decrepit** car pulled up alongside them.

_____ 2. An Italian with a **bandanna** over his face screamed at them.

_____ 3. Reg carefully **weighed** the options.

_____ 4. Reg thought his newer-model vehicle could probably **elude** the criminals' car.

_____ 5. Reg **floored** the gas pedal.

_____ 6. He saw blood **oozing** from Nicholas's head.

_____ 7. Nicholas was killed by two **petty** criminals.

_____ 8. Seven Italians received Nicholas's heart, liver, kidneys, islet cells, and **corneas**.

_____ 9. **A blow was struck** for organ donation.

_____ 10. It gradually **dawned on** us that we'd been given a life's work.

a. pushed to the maximum extent

b. flowing slowly

c. became apparent to

d. progress was made

e. large handkerchief

f. considered

g. broken-down

h. coverings on the outer surface of your eyes

i. unimportant

j. escape from

B **Comprehension:** *Refer to the reading and complete each sentence with a single word.*

1. The Greens were traveling in the geographical area of Italy known as the _____.

2. The Greens' car was newer than the _____ car.

3. Shots shattered the windows on the _____ side of the Greens' car.

4. After the shooting, Nicholas lay in a _____ for two days.

5. The Greens offered Nicholas's organs for _____.

6. Italians were profoundly _____ by the Greens' donation of Nicholas's organs.

7. The ironic aspect of the Greens' tragedy was that it was a _____.

8. The criminals were placed on _____ after being turned over to the police.

ADVERB AND ADVERBIAL PHRASES

Reducing Adverb Clauses of Time to Adverb Phrases

Adverb Clause		Adverb Phrase	
While they were in Italy,	they had trouble.	While in Italy,	they had trouble.
While I was in Italy,		Ø*	
When I am traveling,	I keep a journal.	When traveling,	I keep a journal.
When Sue is traveling,		Ø	

*Ø = no change possible

Changing Adverb Clauses of Time to Adverb Phrases

Adverb Clause		Adverb Phrase	
Before we left,	we visited Rome.	Before leaving,	we visited Rome.
Before Ann left,		Ø	
After they (had) investigated,	the police identified the killers.	After investigating,	the police identified the killers.
		After having investigated,	
When they heard Reg speak,	many Italians were moved.	On / Upon hearing Reg speak,	many Italians were moved.

Changing Adverb Clauses of Time to Adverbial Phrases

Adverb Clause		Adverbial Phrase	
While they waited at the hospital,	they were deeply troubled.	Waiting at the hospital,	they were deeply troubled.
When they heard the news,	they decided what to do.	Hearing the news,	they decided what to do.

Changing Adverb Clauses of Reason to Adverbial Phrases

Adverb Clause		Adverbial Phrase	
As he saw the guns,	he chose to flee.	Seeing the guns,	he chose to flee.
Because they were unable to catch him,	the pursuers fired several shots.	Being unable to catch him,	the pursuers fired several shots.
Because I've been to Bari,	I hope to return.	Having been to Bari,	I hope to return.
Because I'd been to Bari,	I hoped to return.		I hoped to return.
Since they were accused by the police,	they had to appear in court.	Accused by the police,	they had to appear in court.

GRAMMAR NOTES

1 Remember that a **clause** is a group of words with a subject and a verb that shows time. A **phrase** does not have both a subject and a verb showing time. It commonly has a present or past participle.

CLAUSE
- **After he sped away**, he heard a shot.

PHRASE
- **After speeding away**, he heard a shot.

Some **adverb clauses** can be shortened to **adverb phrases** in ways similar to the ways adjective clauses can be shortened: by **reducing** the clauses or by **changing** them.

ADVERB CLAUSE
- We had a flat tire **while we were touring**.

ADVERB PHRASE (REDUCED)
- We had a flat tire **while touring**.

ADVERB CLAUSE
- **After we fixed the flat tire**, we were on our way again.

ADVERB PHRASE (CHANGED)
- **After fixing the flat tire**, we were on our way again.

Negative adverb phrases contain the word *not* or *never* before the participle.

- After **not eating** all day, we were very hungry.

2 **Adverb clauses** can be **reduced to adverb phrases** when the clause has a form of *be*. To reduce an adverb clause to a phrase, omit the subject pronoun and the form of *be*. If the original sentence has commas, keep the commas in the reduced sentence.

ADVERB CLAUSE
- **While they were driving**, they were attacked by bandits.

ADVERB PHRASE
- **While driving**, they were attacked by bandits.

BE CAREFUL! You can reduce an adverb clause to an adverb phrase only if the subjects in both clauses of the sentence refer to the same person or thing.

- **Reg and Maggie** drove while **the children** were sleeping.
NOT: Reg and Maggie drove ~~while sleeping~~.

NOTE: An adverb phrase can come first or second in the sentence. When it comes first, we usually place a comma after it.

- **While driving**, they were attacked by bandits.
- They were attacked by bandits **while driving**.

3 **Adverb clauses of time** beginning with *after*, *before*, *since*, and *while* can be **changed to adverb phrases** when the clause has no form of *be*. To change an adverb clause to a phrase, omit the subject pronoun and change the verb to its *-ing* form. Keep the subordinating conjunction and the original punctuation.

ADVERB CLAUSE
- **After they visited Paestum**, the Greens drove south.

ADVERB PHRASE
- **After visiting Paestum**, the Greens drove south.

BE CAREFUL! You can change an adverb clause to a phrase only if the subjects in the two clauses of the sentence refer to the same person or thing.

- After **the bandits** saw the Greens' car, **the Greens** sped away.
NOT: ~~After seeing the Greens' car~~, the Greens sped away.

4   A simple past or past perfect verb in an adverb clause changes to the *-ing* form or *having* + past participle in an adverb phrase.

- After they **(had) opened** the door, they saw the blood.
- After **opening** the door, they saw the blood.

OR

- **Having opened** the door, they saw the blood.

---

5   *Upon* or *on* + *-ing* in an adverb phrase usually has the same meaning as *when* in an adverb clause.

- **Upon / On realizing** what had happened, they pulled to the side of the road.

- **When they realized** what had happened, they pulled to the side of the road.

---

6   The **subordinating conjunction** is sometimes omitted in a phrase. A phrase without a subordinating conjunction is called an **adverbial phrase**.

- **While sitting on the porch**, I thought about my future.

- **Sitting on the porch**, I thought about my future.

BE CAREFUL! Do not omit the subordinating conjunction in a passive construction.

- I worked for two years **before being accepted** at the university.
  NOT: I worked for two years ~~being accepted~~ at the university.

---

7   **Adverb clauses of reason** can be **changed to adverbial phrases**. The subordinating conjunctions *because*, *since*, or *as* at the beginning of a clause must be omitted in an adverbial phrase of reason.

- **Because / Since / As the children were sleeping in the car**, they were not aware of what was happening.

- **Sleeping in the car**, the children were not aware of what was happening.
  NOT: ~~Because~~ sleeping in the car, the children were not aware of what was happening.

Because / Since / As + a form of *be* can be changed to *being* in an adverbial phrase.

- **Because / Since / As** they **were** not satisfied, they decided to do something about the problem.
- Not **being** satisfied, they decided to do something about the problem.

A present perfect or past perfect verb in an adverb clause can be changed to *having* + past participle in an adverbial phrase.

- Because they **had been** moved by the situation, people became organ donors.
- **Having been** moved by the situation, people became organ donors.

(continued on next page)

8 A **clause containing a passive verb** can be **changed** to an **adverbial phrase with just a past participle**. If the subordinating conjunction can be omitted without changing the meaning, delete the subject and any auxiliaries in the passive sentence.

BE CAREFUL! If the subordinating conjunction cannot be omitted without changing the meaning, as in some clauses of time, form an adverb phrase by deleting the subject and changing the form of *be* to *being*.

- **Since I was given two options**, I chose the harder of the two.
- **Given two options**, I chose the harder of the two.

- **Before I was told** the nature of the problem, I had no idea what to do.
- **Before being told** the nature of the problem, I had no idea what to do.
  Not: ~~Told the nature of the problem~~, I had no idea what to do.

REFERENCE NOTE
For **shortening adjective clauses to adjective phrases**, see Unit 13.

STEP 3 FOCUSED PRACTICE

EXERCISE 1: Discover the Grammar

A | *Underline the adverb phrase in each sentence. Circle the subordinating conjunction.*

1. Upon opening the door, he saw blood oozing from Nicholas's head.

2. Nicholas lay in a coma for two days after being rushed to a hospital.

3. On returning to the United States, Nicholas's parents received requests to tell their

    son's story.

4. The criminals were placed on trial after being turned over to the police.

B | *Read the sentences. Is the second sentence a correct rewriting of the first? Circle*
Y (Yes) *or* **N (No).**

1. Having spent a wonderful day exploring the ruins at Paestum, Reg and Maggie Green were driving south.
    Y   (N)   Spending a wonderful day exploring the ruins at Paestum, Reg and Maggie Green were driving south.

2. An Italian with a bandanna over his face screamed at them, signaling them to stop.
    Y   N   An Italian with a bandanna over his face screamed at them while signaling them to stop.

3. Not knowing what to do, Reg carefully weighed the options.
    Y   N   Because he didn't know what to do, Reg carefully weighed the options.

4. Shots rang out, shattering both windows on the driver's side of the car.

    Y   N   Having shattered both windows on the driver's side of the car, shots rang out.

5. The Greens' car took off, easily outdistancing the bandits' car.

    Y   N   Having outdistanced the bandits' car, the Green's car took off.

6. Upon opening the door, Reg saw blood oozing from the back of Nicholas's head.

    Y   N   When he opened the door, Reg saw blood oozing from the back of Nicholas's head.

7. After being rushed to a hospital, Nicholas lay in a coma for two days.

    Y   N   After he was rushed to a hospital, Nicholas lay in a coma for two days.

8. How many of us would do the same thing, given the chance?

    Y   N   How many of us would do the same thing if we were given the chance?

EXERCISE 2: Adverb Clauses to Phrases

(Grammar Notes 1–3)

Read the sentences. Circle the subjects in both clauses and connect the circles. If the subjects refer to the same person or thing, shorten the sentence by reducing or changing the adverb clause to a phrase. If the subjects are different, write **cannot be shortened.**

1. When a broken-down (car) pulled alongside their car, an (Italian) with a bandanna over his face screamed at them.

    cannot be shortened _____

2. Reg carefully considered the options before he sped away.

    _____

3. Because the criminals were a deadly threat, Reg floored the gas pedal.

    _____

4. When Reg saw a police car parked on the shoulder, he pulled over to alert the authorities.

    _____

5. As Nicholas lay on his deathbed, Reg and Maggie decided that something good should come out of the situation.

    _____

6. Because the criminals thought the Greens had precious stones, they fired shots that killed Nicholas.

    _____

A | *Read the article about an apparently grieving animal.*

A Caring Elephant That Died of Grief

By Sutapa Mukerjee, The Associated Press

LUCKNOW, INDIA. Distressed by a companion's death, Damini refused to move, to eat, to drink. For 24 days, zookeepers and veterinarians tried everything they could think of to save an elephant who seemed determined to die.

Despite all their efforts, Damini died yesterday in her enclosure. After she had suffered for so long, loose gray skin hung over her protruding bones, and bedsores covered much of her body.

Zoo officials said Damini was 72. She came to the zoo last year after she was taken from owners who were illegally transporting her. She was alone for five months until the arrival in September of a pregnant younger elephant named Champakali.

Champakali came from Dudhwa National Park, where she had worked carrying around tourists. When she became pregnant, park officials decided to send her to the zoo in Lucknow for a kind of maternity leave.

The two elephants "became inseparable in no time," said the zookeeper. Damini made herself available at all hours for Champakali, who seemed to love the attention.

"Elephants are very social animals. They can form very close bonds with others in their social group," said Pat Thomas, curator of mammals at the Bronx Zoo in New York City. "It's been pretty well documented that they do exhibit emotions that we would consider grieving" when a calf or other elephant dies.

However, he said, an age-related medical problem should not be discounted as well in the case of an elephant as old as Damini.

On April 11, giving birth to a stillborn calf, Champakali died. Damini seemed to shed tears, then showed little interest in food or anything else, according to zoo officials.

For days, Damini stood still in her enclosure, barely nibbling at the two tons of sugarcane, bananas, and grass heaped in front of her.

Her legs soon swelled up and eventually gave way. After that, Damini lay still on her side, head and ears drooping, trunk curled. Tears rolled from her eyes, and the 4-ton elephant rapidly lost weight.

A week ago, Damini completely stopped eating or drinking her usual daily quota of 40 gallons of water, despite the 116-degree heat.

Alarmed, veterinarians pumped more than 25 gallons of glucose, saline, and vitamins through a vein in her ear.

Yesterday, Damini died.

"It will take me some time to get over the death of my two loved ones," her keeper said.

B | *Refer to the article and follow the instructions.*

1. Rewrite the adverbial phrase in this sentence as an adverb clause.

   Distressed by a companion's death, Damini refused to move, to eat, to drink.

   Because Damini was distressed by a companion's death, _____

2. Read the original and revised sentences. Is the revised sentence correct?

   Original: After she had suffered for so long, loose gray skin hung over her protruding bones, and bedsores covered much of her body.

   Revised: After suffering for so long, loose gray skin hung over her protruding bones, and bedsores covered much of her body.

   _____ yes   _____ no

3. Rewrite this sentence, changing the adverb clause to an adverb phrase.

   She came to the zoo last year after she was taken from owners.

   _____

4. Read the original and revised sentences. Is the revised sentence correct?

   Original: When she became pregnant, park officials decided to send her to the zoo in Lucknow.

   Revised: Becoming pregnant, park officials decided to send her to the zoo in Lucknow.

   _____ yes   _____ no

5. Read the original and combined sentences. Is the combined sentence correct?

   Original: Elephants are very social animals. They can form very close bonds with others in their social group.

   Combined sentence: Being very social animals, elephants can form very close bonds with others in their social group.

   _____ yes   _____ no

6. Rewrite the adverbial phrase as an adverb phrase by adding a subordinating conjunction.

   On April 11, Champakali died giving birth to a stillborn calf.

   _____

7. Rewrite the sentence as two independent clauses.

   Damini stood still in her enclosure, barely nibbling at the two tons of food in front of her.

   _____

EXERCISE 4: Adverb Phrases / Main Clauses

(Grammar Notes 3–8)

Look at the pictures, which are connected in a story. Write a sentence with an adverb or adverbial phrase and a main clause to describe each situation. Use the prompts.

1.

(present participle)

Coming out of the train station, the

tourists saw a boy selling guidebooks.

2.

(present participle)

_____

_____

3.

(*not* + present participle)

_____

_____

4.

(past participle)

_____

_____

5.

(present participle)

_____

_____

6.

(*having* + past participle)

_____

_____

7.

(*after* + present participle)

_____

_____

8.

(*having* + present participle)

_____

_____

EXERCISE 5: Editing

Read the magazine article. There are seven mistakes involving the use of adverb and adverbial phrases. The first mistake is already corrected. Find and correct six more.

A Helping Hand
by Jim Lamoureaux

If you're at all like me, you tire of requests to help others. ~~Barraging~~ *Barraged* by seemingly constant appeals for money to support homeless shelters, the Special Olympics, or the like, I tend to tune out, my brain numbed. I don't think I'm selfish. But subjecting to so many requests, I only remember the flashy ones. By arguing that I don't have enough money to help others, I am able to ignore the requests. Or at least that was the way I saw the situation before sent by my magazine to South America to do a human interest story on homeless children. Having heard many TV requests asking viewers to sponsor a child overseas, I always said to myself, "I'll bet the money is pocketed by some local politician." My opinion changed when I saw the reality of the life of a poor child.

While landing in Santa Simona, I took a taxi to my hotel in the center of town, where I met Elena, a girl of 10 or 11. Sat on a dirty blanket on the sidewalk in front of the hotel, she caught my eye. Elena was trying to earn a living by selling mangoes. Smiling at me, she asked, "*Mangos, señor?* —Mangoes, sir?" I bought some mangoes and some other fruit, and we talked together. Elena's life had been difficult. Her parents were both dead, and she lived with an elderly aunt. Having polio at the age of five, she now walked with a limp. She and her aunt often went hungry.

Investigated the question the next day, I talked to several different authorities. Having become convinced that money from sponsors does in fact get to those who need it, I knew my attitude had to change. Learning that I could sponsor Elena for less than a dollar a day, I began to feel ashamed; after all, I spend more than that on my dogs. But what remains most vivid in my mind is my vision of Elena. She didn't beg or feel sorry for herself. Selling her mangoes, she earned a living, and her spirit shone through in the process. So I say to all of you reading this: The next time you hear an ad about sponsoring a child, pay attention.

EXERCISE 6: Listening

A | *Listen to the news broadcast. Check (✓) the two subjects that are <u>not</u> mentioned.*

- ☐ political struggles in the nation of Franconia
- ☐ an oil spill in the Mediterranean
- ☐ a new vaccine for AIDS
- ☐ a new nation comes into existence
- ☐ World Cup news
- ☐ a rescue in a swimming pool

B | *Read the questions. Listen again to the news broadcast. Then answer each question in a complete sentence.*

1. When asked whether he would attend next week's peace conference, did rebel leader Amalde commit himself?

   No, he declined to commit himself.

2. According to Mr. Amalde, how could Mr. Tintor demonstrate good faith?

3. Did the president's aide speak on or off the record?

4. What did researchers from the Global Health Foundation acknowledge?

5. How is the new nation to be known?

6. What will it need in order to become a viable state?

7. Why had Michaels almost given up hope of being rescued?

8. How did Hutchinson save him?

EXERCISE 7: Pronunciation

🎧 **A** | *Read and listen to the Pronunciation Note.*

Pronunciation Note

Notice how the pronunciation of vowels in English changes when the stress shifts in words that are members of the same family:

EXAMPLES:

She has always been interested in **politics**. (stress on the first syllable; the vowel in the second syllable has the schwa sound, /ə/)

She comes from a **political** family. (stress on the second syllable; the vowel in this syllable assumes the pronunciation of a full vowel)

🎧 **B** | *Listen and repeat the sentences. In the boldfaced words, circle the syllables that have stress.*

1. The Greens were traveling in **Italy**.

2. They made a great impression on many **Italians**.

3. The Greens risked a deadly **confrontation** with the bandits.

4. The bandits **confronted** the Greens.

5. The **criminals** fired shots at the Greens' car.

6. These bandits engaged in **criminality**.

7. The great **irony** of this tragedy was that it was a mistake.

8. It was **ironic** that the bandits thought the Greens were jewelers.

9. The Greens **realized** they'd been given a life's work.

10. The **reality** of the situation was that Nicholas lost his life.

C | *PAIRS: Practice the sentences, taking turns so that each partner pronounces each sentence.*

EXERCISE 8: Personal Inventory

A | *Complete the sentences according to your personal experience.*

1. Having finished . . . , I . . .

   _____

2. Given the chance to . . . , I . . .

   _____

3. Not wanting to . . . , I . . .

   _____

4. Being unable to . . . , I . . .

   _____

5. While driving . . . , I . . .

   _____

6. After visiting . . . , I . . .

   _____

B | *PAIRS: Discuss your answers. Report interesting examples to the class.*

EXERCISE 9: Group Discussion

A | *PAIRS: Review the article "A Caring Elephant That Died of Grief" on page 348. In small groups, discuss the questions.*

1. Compare animals and humans in regard to showing emotion. Do you think animals are capable of grief or any other kind of emotion?
2. Give a personal example of an animal showing grief or another emotion.

   EXAMPLE: **A:** I don't think animals show emotion.
   B: I disagree.
   A: Why?
   B: My aunt died last year. Her dog . . .

B | *Share your answers with the class.*

EXERCISE 10: Writing

A | *Write three or four paragraphs about an act you have witnessed that you believe qualifies as compassionate. Describe the situation fully. What made the act compassionate? Did the compassionate person have anything to gain from showing compassion? Use adverb and/or adverbial phrases in your composition.*

EXAMPLE: Perhaps the best example of compassion I have witnessed occurred about a year ago. Having attended an office party, I finally managed to leave about 10:00 P.M. Driving home on a major expressway, I suddenly felt the car slow down and heard a grinding noise. Realizing that I probably had a flat tire, I quickly pulled over to the side of the road. I looked for the jack to change the flat but couldn't find it. I thought about calling my brother but couldn't find my cell phone, either. Just then a group of teenagers slowed down and stopped . . .

B | *Check your work. Use the Editing Checklist.*

Editing Checklist

Did you use . . . ?
- ☐ adverb phrases of time correctly
- ☐ adverbial phrases of time correctly
- ☐ adverbial phrases of reason correctly

A | *Circle the word or phrase that correctly completes each sentence.*

1. Not knowing / Because not knowing what to do, we called the service department.

2. Having caught cheating / Caught cheating, she failed the course.

3. Getting the tickets / Having gotten the tickets, we were able to leave.

4. Taksim turned off the lights before leaving / before left home.

5. On realizing / When realizing what had happened, we called the police.

6. During relaxing / Relaxing at home, I reminisced about the trip.

7. Having visited / Visiting Asia, I wanted to return some day.

8. We didn't know where to go before given / being given directions.

B | *Correct the mistakes in the underlined words or phrases.*

1. Heard a noise downstairs, Melinda called 911.　　　　　　　　　_____

2. Juan listens to music while does his homework.　　　　　　　　_____

3. Having eating too fast, Bill got a bad case of indigestion.　　　　_____

4. Upon finished the project, the crew celebrated.　　　　　　　　_____

5. Being to France before, we skipped it on our last trip.　　　　　_____

6. Sam recovered after taking to the hospital.　　　　　　　　　　_____

7. Having feared the weather, we took umbrellas.　　　　　　　　　_____

8. Having given the choice, I decided to walk to work.　　　　　　　_____

C | *Circle the letter of the one underlined word or phrase that is not correct.*

1. Believed I clearly had time, I narrowly missed the plane I was taking.　　**A B C D**
　　　A　　　　B　　　　　　　　C　　　　　　　　　　　D

2. I firmly refused to give money, to feel that the pleas were only frauds.　　**A B C D**
　　　A　　　　　　B　　　　　　C　　　　　　　　　　D

3. Being new to the job, I didn't know what to do before told.　　　　　　**A B C D**
　　A　　　　　　　　　　　　　　　　B　　C　　D

4. Upon realize we were right, they complied, not wanting to anger us.　　**A B C D**
　　A　　B　　　　　　　　　　　　　　　　　C　　　D

Unit 20 Review: Adverb and Adverbial Phrases　　**357**

21 Connectors
MEMORY

Before You Read

PAIRS: Discuss the questions.

1. What is your earliest memory?
2. What are methods that help you to remember things?

Read

Read the article about memory.

TRY TO
REMEMBER
by Helen Giuliani

Picture this: You're with a friend, **and** suddenly up walks somebody you've known for a long time. You want to introduce this person to your friend. **However**, just as you say, "Nancy, I'd like you to meet . . . ," your mind goes blank, and you don't remember the person's name. It's embarrassing and maybe a little worrisome. I wouldn't be too concerned, **though**, **for** it's also very common. As we get older, we tend to become more forgetful.

How does memory work, and what can we do to improve it? I was worried about memory loss on my part; **therefore**, I decided to do some research into the problem. Here's what I learned:

First: There are two types of memory, long-term and short-term. Long-term memory refers to things that we experienced some time ago and that form the core of our knowledge of ourselves. Short-term memory can be called "working" memory—the type we use in processing such things as phone numbers, names of new people we meet, and email addresses. As we grow older, our long-term memory holds up remarkably well. **Thus**, we are able to remember the vacation we took at the age of 10 to the Everglades and the alligators we saw there. **Meanwhile**, things have been happening to our short-term memory, which, **in contrast**, doesn't hold up as well as our long-term memory does. **Because** our short-term memory sometimes fails us, we may have difficulty remembering a name right after we meet someone or a phone number we've heard only twice.

TRY TO REMEMBER ·

Memory problems are generally short-term memory problems.

Second: Short-term memory operations occur in the frontal lobes of the brain. As we age, these lobes tend to lose mass, as much as 5 to 10 percent per decade. **However**, we can slow memory decline. Maintaining a steady supply of glucose can mitigate the problem of shrinking lobes. **Consequently**, elderly people would do well to eat several small meals each day rather than two or three big ones. There is evidence, **moreover**, that staying mentally active can help prevent memory deterioration.

Third: There are many materials on the market designed to help us remember things better. Do they work? Well, yes and no. All memory aids depend on the creation of a peg, or mental picture, on which to hang something we want to recollect. Suppose, **for example**, you have difficulty remembering names. Let's say you're at a party and are introduced to a woman named Sarah Baer. She has long, thick hair, rather like a bear's fur. Baer = Bear. **Furthermore**, the first syllable of "Sarah" rhymes with "bear." Sar and Baer. It might work. The point is to create a mental picture you can relate to the person, place, or thing you want to recall. The more vivid the association is, the greater is the chance that you'll remember it.

Most importantly, memory improvement takes work. The real problem in remembering something we learned is often the fact that we weren't paying enough attention when we learned it. Think about the last time you were introduced to someone whose name you immediately forgot. Were you really paying attention to the person's name, **or** were you focusing on the impression you might be making? Memory courses can work, of course, **but** they depend on techniques we can create and perform for ourselves. The real trick lies in our willingness to tap and use what's within us.

memory improvement takes work

After You Read

A | **Vocabulary:** *Match the blue words on the left with their meanings on the right.*

_____ **1.** Long-term memories form the **core** of our knowledge of ourselves.

_____ **2.** Short-term memory operations occur in the frontal **lobes** of the brain.

_____ **3.** Maintaining a steady supply of **glucose** can mitigate the problem of shrinking lobes.

_____ **4.** Maintaining a steady supply of glucose can **mitigate** the problem of shrinking lobes.

_____ **5.** All memory aids depend on the creation of a **peg** on which to hang something.

_____ **6.** We need a peg on which to hang something we wish to **recollect**.

_____ **7.** The more **vivid** the association is, the greater is the chance that you'll remember it.

_____ **8.** The real trick lies in our willingness to **tap** and use what's within us.

a. lessen the seriousness of a harmful action

b. remember

c. something that can serve as a key organizing principle or example

d. most important or central part of something

e. sharp, clear, colorful

f. a natural form of sugar

g. use or draw from

h. rounded divisions of an organ, for example, the brain

B | Comprehension: *Circle* **T (True)** *or* **F (False)**. *Correct the false statements.*

1. Forgetting things such as another person's name is quite uncommon.   T   F

2. Long-term memory refers to things we experienced some time ago.   T   F

3. Short-term memory can be termed "working" memory.   T   F

4. Our short-term memory holds up better than our long-term memory.   T   F

5. Memory problems are generally short-term memory problems.   T   F

6. Elderly people would do better to eat several small meals daily instead   T   F
   of two or three big ones.

7. There is no evidence that staying mentally active can slow memory   T   F
   deterioration.

8. A key reason we forget things is that we often weren't paying enough   T   F
   attention when we learned something.

STEP 2 GRAMMAR PRESENTATION

CONNECTORS

Connectors: Placement and Punctuation	
Type of Connector	**Examples**
COORDINATING CONJUNCTION	I was worried, **so** I did some research.
SUBORDINATING CONJUNCTION	**Because** I was worried, I did some research.
	I did some research **because** I was worried.
TRANSITION	I was worried. **Therefore,** I did some research.
	I was worried. I, **therefore,** did some research.
	I was worried. I did some research, **therefore.**

Connectors: Functions

Function	Coordinating Conjunctions	Subordinating Conjunctions	Transitions
ADDITION	and, nor, or		besides, furthermore, indeed, in addition, moreover
CONDITION	or	if, even if, only if, unless	otherwise
CONTRAST	but, or, yet	although, though, even though, whereas, while	however, nevertheless, nonetheless, on the contrary, on the other hand
CAUSE / REASON	for	as, because, since	
EFFECT / RESULT	so		consequently, otherwise, therefore, thus
TIME		after, before, when, while	afterwards, meanwhile, next

Transitions: Connecting Sentences

Functions	Examples	
ADDITION	She couldn't remember names.	**Furthermore**, she forgot addresses.
	Human brains lose mass.	**Indeed**, they may lose 10 percent a year.
CONDITION	Older people should eat several small meals a day.	**Otherwise**, their memory might deteriorate.
CONTRAST	I often have trouble with names.	**However**, I always remember faces.
	We all forget things.	**Nevertheless**, we shouldn't worry.
EFFECT / RESULT	I wasn't concentrating when we met.	**Consequently**, I couldn't recall her name.
	He wanted to improve his memory.	**Therefore**, he took a memory course.
TIME	He studied for his course.	**Meanwhile**, his wife read a book.
	She completed the book.	**Next**, she bought a memory video.

Transitions: Connecting Blocks of Text

Functions	Examples
LISTING IDEAS IN ORDER OF TIME / IMPORTANCE	**First of all**, we need to distinguish between two types of memory.
GIVING EXAMPLES	**For example**, you need to stay mentally active.
SUMMARIZING	**To summarize**: Memory improvement requires work.
ADDING A CONCLUSION	**In conclusion**, we can prevent the deterioration of memory.

GRAMMAR NOTES

1   **Connectors** (often called discourse connectors) are words and phrases that connect ideas both within sentences and between sentences or larger blocks of text.

Three types of connectors are
a. **coordinating conjunctions**

b. **subordinating conjunctions**

c. **transitions**

- I try hard, **but** I can never remember new people's names.
- I can't remember her name, **although** I can remember her face.
- I spent a lot on a memory improvement course. **However**, it was a waste of money.

2   **Coordinating conjunctions** join two independent clauses. Coordinating conjunctions come between clauses and are normally preceded by a comma.

Subordinating conjunctions connect ideas within sentences. They come at the beginning of a subordinate (= dependent) clause. If the subordinate clause comes first in a sentence, it is followed by a comma. If the subordinate clause follows the independent clause, it is not usually preceded by a comma unless the clause sets up a contrast.

- I often forget things, **so** I write everything down.
- I heard what you said, **but** what did you mean?

- **Because** I often forget things, I write everything down.
- I write everything down **because** I often forget things.

3   **Transitions** connect ideas between sentences or larger sections of text. Transitions that connect sentences can come at the beginning of a sentence, within it, or at the end. Common transitions include *besides*, *consequently*, *however*, *in addition*, *nevertheless*, *otherwise*, and *therefore*.

At the beginning of a sentence, a transition is preceded by a period or semicolon and followed by a comma. In the middle of a sentence, it is preceded and followed by a comma. At the end of a sentence, it is preceded by a comma.

- He said he would support the idea. **However**, I wouldn't count on him.
- He said he would support the idea. I wouldn't, **however**, count on him.
- He said he would support the idea. I wouldn't count on him, **however**.

4 There are five principal types of **transitions that connect sentences**:

a. Some transitions show **addition**. These include *additionally*, *besides*, *furthermore*, *in addition*, *likewise*, *moreover*, and *plus*.

- I remember her telephone number. **In addition**, I remember what street she lives on.
- I live too far away to visit you. **Besides**, I can never remember your address.

b. One transition of **condition**, *otherwise*, indicates that a result opposite to what is expected will happen if a certain action isn't taken.

- I need to write down your email address. **Otherwise**, I'll never remember it.

c. Some transitions show **contrast**. These include *however*, *in contrast*, *in spite of this*, *instead*, *nevertheless*, *nonetheless*, *still*, and *though*.

- Her speech was good; **nevertheless**, I can't support her ideas.
- Jim thinks I'm against his ideas. **On the contrary**, I'm one of his biggest supporters.

NOTE: *Though* is a contrast transition when it occurs at the end of an independent clause, when its meaning is equivalent to that of *however*. In other positions it is a subordinating conjunction.

- I carefully wrote down her name on a piece of paper. I lost the piece of paper, **though**. (*transition*)
- **Though** I've told him my name several times, he never remembers it. (*subordinating conjunction*)

d. Some transitions show **effect / result**. These include *accordingly*, *as a result*, *because of this*, *consequently*, *on account of this*, *otherwise*, *therefore*, and *thus*.

- I was not paying close attention when she was introduced. **Consequently**, her name escapes me.
- This new memory technique is helpful. **On account of this**, I recommend it to you.

e. Some transitions show **relationships** of actions, events, and ideas **in time**. These include *after that*, *afterwards*, *in the meantime*, *meanwhile*, *next*, and *then*.

- Bob spent three years in the military. **Meanwhile**, his brother was earning a college degree.
- I went to a memory workshop. **Afterwards**, I couldn't remember a single thing.

(continued on next page)

5 Some **transitions connect blocks of text**. They usually come at the beginning of a sentence and are commonly followed by a comma.

Such transitions have these uses:

a. to **list ideas in order of time or importance**. These include *finally, first of all, most importantly, next, second, third*, etc.

- **First of all**, let's consider the question of short-term memory.
- **Most importantly**, let's consider the question of memory improvement courses.

b. to **give examples**. These include *for example* and *for instance*.

- I can remember lots of things about people. **For example**, I always remember what they're wearing.

c. to **summarize**. These include *all in all, in summary, overall, to summarize*.

- **In summary**, these are the key points about memory loss.

d. to **add a conclusion**. These include *in conclusion* and *to conclude*.

- **To conclude**, let me just say that we can all improve our memory if we work at it.

REFERENCE NOTES

For more on **subordinating conjunctions**, see Unit 19.
For more complete lists of **transitions**, see Appendices 21 and 22 on pages A-9 and A-10.
For more practice on **connectors**, see **From Grammar to Writing** for Part VIII.

STEP 3 FOCUSED PRACTICE

EXERCISE 1: Discover the Grammar

A | *Identify the boldfaced words and phrases as coordinating conjunctions* (**C**), *subordinating conjunctions* (**S**), *or transitions* (**T**).

1. I wouldn't be too concerned, though, **for** it's also very common.   _C_

2. I was worried about memory loss on my part; **therefore**, I decided to do some research into the problem.   ____

3. **Meanwhile**, things have been happening to our short-term memory.   ____

4. **Because** our short-term memory sometimes fails us, we may have difficulty remembering a name right after we meet someone.   ____

5. Suppose, **for example**, you have difficulty remembering names.   ____

6. Were you really paying attention, **or** were you focusing on the impression you might be making?   ____

B | *Underline the transition in each sentence. Then identify it as a transition of addition (**A**), contrast (**C**), effect / result (**R**), time (**T**), or order of importance or presentation (**O**).*

1. <u>However</u>, just as you start to introduce your friend, your mind goes blank, and you don't remember the person's name.   *C*

2. I was worried about memory loss on my part; therefore, I decided to do some research into the problem.   _____

3. First: There are two types of memory, long-term and short-term.   _____

4. Thus, we are able to remember the vacation we took at the age of 10 to the Everglades and the alligators we saw there.   _____

5. Meanwhile, things have been happening to our short-term memory.   _____

6. There is evidence, moreover, that staying mentally active can help prevent memory deterioration.   _____

7. Furthermore, the first syllable of "Sarah" rhymes with "bear."   _____

8. Most importantly, memory improvement takes work.   _____

EXERCISE 2: Combining Sentences with Connectors

(Grammar Notes 2–5)

Combine each of the pairs of sentences into one sentence. Rewrite items 1–3 using a coordinating conjunction, a subordinating conjunction, and a transition. Rewrite item 4 with only a coordinating conjunction and a transition.

1. Jim is a wonderful man. I can't see myself married to him. (contrast)

   Jim is a wonderful man, but I can't see myself married to him.

   Although Jim is a wonderful man, I can't see myself married to him.

   Jim is a wonderful man; however, I can't see myself married to him.

2. He was having problems remembering his appointments. He bought a daily planner. (effect / result)

   _____

   _____

   _____

3. It's important for Nancy to take her medications. She forgot today. (contrast)

   _____

   _____

   _____

(continued on next page)

4. Jack remembers everyone's name. He never forgets a face. (addition)

_____

_____

EXERCISE 3: Completing Sentences with Connectors

(Grammar Notes 2–5)

Read a segment of a radio broadcast. Fill in the blanks with the connectors from the box. Use each connector once.

first	in addition	meanwhile	otherwise	therefore
however	in fact	~~next~~		second

_____Next_____ we focus on the aftermath of the earthquake. Investigators have
1.

determined that it will cost approximately $8 billion to rebuild damaged highways. According

to the governor, two actions have to be taken: _____, the federal government
2.

will have to approve disaster funds to pay for reconstruction; _____, insurance
3.

investigators will need to determine how much their companies will have to pay in the rebuilding

effort. With luck, the governor says, some key highways could be rebuilt within six months.

He cautioned, _____, that the six-month figure is only an estimate. The process
4.

depends on timely allocation of funds, and certain insurance companies have been slow to approve

such funds in the past. The rebuilding effort could, _____, drag on for at least
5.

a year. _____, bad weather could prevent the speedy completion of the project.
6.

_____, it is taking some people as long as four hours to commute to work, and
7.

others haven't been able to get to work at all. Interviewed by our news team, one commuter who

works in an office downtown said, "This has been ridiculous. It took me three hours to drive to work

last Friday. I knew I'd have to find some other way of getting there; _____, I'd never
8.

make it. Well, yesterday the train got me there in 50 minutes, and the trip was really pleasant. I even

had the chance to read the morning paper. _____, I'm going to switch permanently to
9.

the train."

EXERCISE 4: Writing Sentences with Conjunctions / Transitions *(Grammar Notes 2–4)*

Look at the pictures. Write two sentences describing what happened to Hank in each picture. Use the prompts. Use commas to join clauses connected by coordinating conjunctions (and by the phrase in item 5). Use semicolons to join clauses connected by transitions.

1.

(and / in addition)

2.

(but / however)

3.

(so / consequently)

4.

(and / besides that)

5.

(while this was happening / meanwhile)

6.

(or / otherwise)

EXERCISE 5: Editing

There are seven mistakes involving connectors in this student composition. The first mistake is already corrected. Find and correct six more. You may add or eliminate words, but do not change word order or punctuation.

My Car Is Moving to the Suburbs

by Ed Snyder

October 12

Yesterday I drove my car to the downtown campus of the college. I usually have

trouble finding a parking place, ~~however~~ *but* this time it was almost impossible. There were

simply no parking places anywhere near the campus, so I had to park in the downtown

mall, which is about a mile away. When I finished class, I walked back to the mall.

Therefore, I couldn't remember where I'd parked my car! Believe it or not, it took me

45 minutes to find it, and I was about ready to panic when I finally did. That was the

last straw. I've decided that I'm going to send my car to a new home in the suburbs.

I used to think that a car was the most wonderful thing in the world. I loved the

freedom of being able to come and go to my part-time job or to the college whenever I

wanted. A year ago I was in a carpool with four other people, nevertheless I hated

having to wait around if my carpool members weren't ready to leave, so I started

driving alone.

Although, I've changed my mind since then. Now it's clear to me that there are just

too many disadvantages to having a car in town. For example, sitting stalled in your car

in a traffic jam is stressful; besides, it's a phenomenal waste of time. In addition, it

would cost me $200 a month to park my car in the city (which is why I don't do that);

therefore, there's always the chance it will be vandalized.

Nonetheless, I've decided to leave it at my cousin Brent's house in the suburbs.

Otherwise, I'll end up going broke paying for parking and a course in memory

improvement. My car will have a good home, and I'll use it just for longer trips. When

I'm in the city, though, I'll take the bus or the tram, otherwise I'll walk. Who knows?

They say you can meet some interesting people on the bus. Maybe I'll find the love of

my life. My only problem will be remembering which bus to take.

EXERCISE 6: Listening

A | *Listen to the excerpt from a memory training workshop. Check (✓) the two things that are true.*

☐ The workshop visitor says he's from Hawaii.

☐ The visitor has a Hawaiian name.

☐ The visitor is wearing a tuxedo.

☐ The visitor is wearing brown shoes.

B | *Read the questions. Then listen again and answer the questions in complete sentences.*

1. What is the first point the workshop leader makes?

   It's important to get people's names in your short-term memory.

2. According to her, why is it important to remember clients' names?

   _____

3. What is the second point the leader makes?

   _____

4. What did the visitor tell the people in the workshop to do?

   _____

5. What are the two reasons one of the participants knows the visit was planned and not real?

   a. _____

   b. _____

(continued on next page)

6. Why were all the participants able to remember the last word the visitor said?

_____

7. According to the workshop leader, what is the most important thing the participants in the workshop have to learn to do?

_____

EXERCISE 7: Pronunciation

A | _Read and listen to the Pronunciation Note._

> **Pronunciation Note**
>
> Notice the difference in pronunciation of clauses connected by coordinating conjunctions and those connected by transitions:
>
> **EXAMPLES:** We visited Mexico on our trip, **and** we went to Costa Rica as well. (a small pause before the coordinating conjunction _and_; no pause after it)
>
> We visited Mexico on our trip; **in addition**, we went to Costa Rica. (a major pause before the transition _in addition_, and a small pause after the transition)
>
> A comma indicates a small pause; a semicolon indicates a major pause. Remember that a semicolon is equivalent to a period.

B | _Listen and repeat the sentences. Then insert semicolons and commas in the places where you hear major pauses and small pauses, respectively._

1. Frank has an excellent memory; however, he doesn't use it to good advantage.

2. Frank has an excellent memory but he doesn't use it to good advantage.

3. Marta was having trouble remembering things so she signed up for a memory course.

4. Marta was having trouble remembering things consequently she signed up for a memory course.

5. You need to start writing things down otherwise you'll miss out on key appointments.

6. You need to start writing things down or you'll miss out on key appointments.

7. I have trouble remembering people's names yet I can always remember their faces.

8. I have trouble remembering people's names on the other hand I can always remember their faces.

9. You live awfully far away to visit besides you never come to see me.

10. You live awfully far away to visit and you never come to see me.

C | _PAIRS: Practice the sentences._

EXERCISE 8: Game

Form two teams. Everyone writes a statement involving personal or general knowledge and containing a connector. One team makes its statements while the other team listens and takes notes. Teams take turns making statements. When all the statements have been made, teams attempt to reproduce the other team's statements. Score one point for each correctly remembered statement, and one point for a correct connector.

> EXAMPLE: **Team A:** Washington, D.C., is the capital of the United States; however, it's not the largest city.
> **Team B:** I have been to France three times, and I've been to Britain twice.

EXERCISE 9: Picture Discussion

PAIRS: Study the painting for two minutes. Then close your book. Write down as many details as you can remember. Then open your book again and check your memory. Which details were you able to remember best? Why?

> EXAMPLE: I can remember _____. I also remember _____.
> However, I can't remember _____.

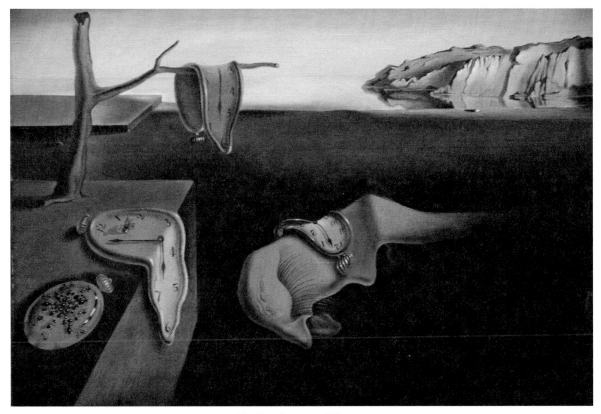

The Persistence of Memory
Salvador Dalí (Spanish, 1904–1989)

EXERCISE 10: Writing

A | *Write three or four paragraphs about a significant memory you have. Explain clearly why this memory is important to you, and speculate as to why you remember it well. Use specific details to support your ideas and statements. Include appropriate connectors in your composition.*

> **EXAMPLE:** One of my most significant, and most painful, memories is of my accordion recital when I was 13 years old. I had been taking accordion lessons for three years and was told by my teacher that I had made excellent progress. She scheduled me for a recital in which I was to play two easy songs and one difficult one. I looked forward to the recital and practiced hard. However, things didn't go at all as planned . . .

B | *Check your work. Use the Editing Checklist.*

Editing Checklist
Did you use . . . ?   ☐ coordinating conjunctions correctly   ☐ subordinating conjunctions correctly   ☐ transitions correctly

A | *Circle the word or phrase that correctly completes each sentence.*

1. I never forget a face; <u>and / however</u>, I have trouble remembering names.

2. I never forget a face, <u>besides / though</u> I have trouble remembering names.

3. <u>Because / Besides</u> Hari forgot to pay his utility bill, the city turned off his water.

4. Hari forgot to pay his utility bill; <u>and / consequently</u>, the city turned off his water.

5. The house is too expensive for us; <u>otherwise / besides</u>, I don't really like it.

6. The house is too expensive for us, <u>and / though</u> I don't really like it.

7. You'd better get up right now, <u>or / because</u> you'll miss the bus.

8. You'd better get up right now; <u>however / otherwise</u>, you'll miss the bus.

B | *Correct the mistakes in the underlined words or phrases.*

1. I was exhausted, <u>but</u> I went to bed at 8:00 P.M.   _____

2. It's too early to get up; <u>and</u> I want to sleep in.   _____

3. We need to get tickets, <u>otherwise</u> we won't get seats.   _____

4. Nora didn't leave on time; <u>so</u>, she missed her flight.   _____

5. <u>However</u> Bao has a degree, he has a very poor job.   _____

6. <u>Next</u> the train arrived, I got a taxi to the hotel.   _____

7. You're too young to have a car. <u>Therefore</u>, cars are expensive.   _____

8. The café was cheap; <u>furthermore</u>, we decided to eat there.   _____

C | *Circle the letter of the one underlined word or phrase that is not correct.*

1. Pets <u>admittedly</u> cause problems; <u>yet</u>, they <u>often</u> bring love <u>also</u>.   **A B C D**
      A   B   C   D

2. <u>Indeed</u>, Lee is <u>highly</u> qualified. <u>Example</u>, she has an <u>advanced</u> degree.   **A B C D**
   A   B   C   D

3. I got up <u>late</u>, <u>and</u> I missed the bus, <u>so</u> <u>consequently</u> I got to work late.   **A B C D**
         A B   C   D

4. <u>First</u>, study; <u>or</u> <u>second</u>, attend class; <u>otherwise</u>, you'll fail.   **A B C D**
   A   B C   D

PART VIII

From Grammar to Writing
USING TRANSITIONS

A key aspect of effective writing is the use of **transitions**: words and expressions that tie sentences and paragraphs together and give the reader an overall sense of where a piece of writing is going and where it has been.

There are two main types of transitions: (1) those that connect sentences and independent clauses; and (2) those that connect larger blocks of text.

EXAMPLES: Events in Geraldine's life had been going extremely well for years. **However**, just when she had come to feel secure, her fortunes changed dramatically.
(The transition *however* connects two sentences and introduces a contrast.)

There are several reasons why Andrew was not accepted at the university. **First**, his high school grades, while reasonably good, were not high enough. . . .
(The transition *first* is the type that connects larger blocks of text. It shows the reader that this is the initial reason the writer is giving to support the main idea. The reader will expect a similar transition—e.g., *second* or *another reason*—to introduce the next reason.)

Refer to Unit 21 for more information on transitions. Also see Appendices 21 and 22 on pages A-9 and A-10.

1 | *Complete the paragraph with the transitions from the box.*

besides that   consequently   first   however   most importantly   second

Recently the lives of Stella and Hank Wang have improved in several ways.

_____, they both secured new jobs that make them better off financially. Stella

got a position as a proofreader and editor at a publishing company pioneering new workplace

methods, and Hank was hired as a full-time consultant for an engineering firm.

_____, their new jobs have made their lives much less stressful. The difference

between their new jobs and their old ones can be summed up in one word: flextime. Until they

secured these new positions, Stella and Hank had a very difficult time raising their two small

children. They were at the mercy of a nine-to-five schedule; _____, they had to

pay a lot for day care. In order to get to work on time, they had to have the children at the day

care center by 7:30 every morning. Both of their new companies, _____, offer a flextime schedule. As long as Stella and Hank both put in their 40 hours a week, they are free to work when it is convenient for them. _____, they can take turns staying home with the children, and day care is just a memory. _____, Stella and Hank feel that they are now doing a good job of parenting. The children are much happier because they are getting the attention they need.

2 | *Add appropriate transitions to the paragraph.*

There are a number of reasons why I prefer going out to movies to watching DVDs on TV. _____, I often fall asleep when watching the TV screen, no matter how interesting the DVD is. The other night, _____, I was watching *Gone with the Wind* on my flat screen TV. It was compelling for a while, but pretty soon my eyelids started getting heavy, and before I knew it I was in dreamland. _____, watching movies is basically a social experience. There's a lot to be said for experiencing the group reaction to a film seen in a theater. When I watch movies on a TV screen, _____, I'm often alone. I love my cat, but she doesn't make many perceptive comments about movies. _____, the TV screen, no matter how large it is, diminishes the impact you get when watching a movie on the big screen. I have a 58-inch flat screen TV, and I love the programs I see on it. It's not the same as going out to a cinema, _____. _____, my recommendation is to find a friend who also likes movies and go out to the flicks.

3 | *Before you write . . .*

1. Most of us have clear opinions on a variety of topics. Think of an issue that concerns you and/or that you feel strongly about.
2. Describe your opinion / issue to a partner. Listen to your partner's description.
3. Ask and answer questions about your and your partner's issue. What are your reasons for thinking as you do? What are some reasons why people might disagree with you?

4 | *Write a draft of a composition in which you present your opinion. Follow the model. Remember to include information that your partner asked about. Use both types of transitions in your paragraph.*

Reasons why I think as I do:

_____

_____

_____

_____

Reasons why people might disagree with me:

_____

_____

_____

_____

5 | *Exchange compositions with a different partner. Complete the chart.*

1. The writer used both types of transitions. **Yes** ☐ **No** ☐

2. What I liked in the composition:

_____

_____

_____

3. Questions I'd like the writer to answer about the composition:

Who _____?

What _____?

When _____?

Where _____?

Why _____?

How _____?

(Your own question) _____?

6 | *Work with your partner. Discuss each other's chart from Exercise 5. Then rewrite your own composition and make any necessary changes.*

CONDITIONALS AND THE SUBJUNCTIVE

22 Conditionals; Other Ways to Express Unreality

INTUITION

STEP 1 GRAMMAR IN CONTEXT

Before You Read

PAIRS: Discuss the questions.

1. What do you understand by "intuition"? Do you believe in intuition?
2. Have you had any experiences in which your or someone else's intuition proved correct?

Read

Read the story about trusting intuition.

Intuition

It was a sweltering day. Donna and Thain were driving down Maple Street, looking for a yard sale, when they spotted the old man hailing them.

"Nine-thirty in the morning, and it's already beastly hot. I **wish** I **had** an iced tea right now."

"Wow! Look at that old fellow, Donna. I**'d** sure **get** out of this heat **if** I **were** him … Pull over, will you? He**'s going to faint if** he **doesn't get** out of the sun."

"Thain, I **wish** you **would stop** taking pity on every weirdo you see. He**'ll** probably **kill** us and **steal** the car **if** we **pick** him **up**."

"I don't think so. He looks harmless to me."

"But, sweetie, we've got to get to the sale. There **won't be** anything worth buying **if** we **don't get** there soon. **If only** that bureau **would** still **be** there!"

"Well, it's just an inkling, but my male intuition is telling me we'd better stop."

"**If** I **had** a nickel for all the times we've done things because of your male intuition, I**'d be** rich. Aren't females supposed to have the intuition, anyway? OK, but I **hope** we **don't end up** in the headlines. I can see it all now: YOUNG MARRIED COUPLE MUTILATED BY SERIAL KILLER."

Intuition

They pulled up to the curb in front of the old man. "Need some help, sir?" Thain asked.

The old man smiled. "Yes, thanks. Could you take me to a pharmacy? I'm diabetic, and I've run out of medicine. I'm on a cross-country trip, but I keep forgetting to buy enough insulin. **If** I **don't take** my medicine regularly, I **go** into shock. **If only** I **weren't** so forgetful . . ."

They found a pharmacy and got the insulin. The old man said, "Now, **if** you **can** just **take** me to the bus station, I'**ll be** on my way."

Thain said, "Sure. We can do that."

At the bus station, they helped the old man out of the car. "Can you tell me your names and your address? When I get back home, I'll send you a token of my appreciation." They gave him their names and address, said good-bye, and proceeded to the yard sale.

As Donna had predicted, all of the good merchandise had been sold. "We'**d** probably **have** that bureau **if** we'**d gotten** here earlier, but I'm glad we helped the old guy. I'**ll be** surprised **if** we ever **hear** from him, though. You don't really believe he's taking a trip around the country, do you, Thain?"

In a few days they had forgotten about the incident. Three months later, on returning from a vacation, Donna was going through a pile of mail. She opened a long envelope with no return address.

"What in the world? Thain, come here and look at this!" There was a letter, neatly typed, which said,

> Dear Thain and Donna,
> I finished my trip around the country and had a marvelous time. I'm now back at home and expect I won't be traveling anymore. I met some wonderful people in my travels, the two of you among them.
>
> Thank you for your kindness to a forgetful old man. **If** you **hadn't come** along when you did, I **might have died**. At the very least, I **would have become** quite ill **if** you **hadn't been** there to help. I **wish** there **had been** time for us to get to know one another. **If** I **had been** fortunate enough to have children of my own, I **couldn't have had** any nicer ones than you two. At any rate, I am enclosing a token of my gratitude.
>
> My warmest regards,
> Quentin Wilkerson

Something fluttered out of a second sheet of folded paper. It was a check for $100,000.

After You Read

A | Vocabulary: *Circle the letter of best meaning for the blue words from the reading.*

1. It was a **sweltering** day.

    a. quite cool   **b.** rather warm   **c.** very hot   **d.** cold and windy

2. They spotted the old man **hailing** them.

    a. waving at   **b.** shouting at   **c.** looking at   **d.** coming at

3. It's 9:30 A.M., and it's already **beastly** hot.

    a. unfortunately   **b.** extremely   **c.** unpredictably   **d.** violently

4. I wish you would stop taking pity on every **weirdo** you see.

    a. random person   **b.** old person   **c.** strange person   **d.** interesting person

5. If only that **bureau** would still be there!

    a. dresser   **b.** sofa   **c.** bookcase   **d.** armchair

6. Well, it's just an **inkling**, but my male intuition is telling me we'd better stop.

    a. conclusion   **b.** slight idea   **c.** strong belief   **d.** statement

7. I can see it all now: YOUNG MARRIED COUPLE MUTILATED BY SERIAL KILLER.

    a. deliberately attacked   **b.** fatally shot   **c.** severely injured   **d.** robbed

8. I'll send you a **token** of my appreciation.

    a. acknowledgment   **b.** official statement   **c.** testimony   **d.** small remembrance

9. Something **fluttered** out of a second sheet of folded paper.

    a. dropped lightly   **b.** zoomed   **c.** appeared suddenly   **d.** fell heavily

B | Comprehension: *Refer to the reading and complete each sentence with a single word.*

1. At the beginning of the story, Donna and Thain are looking for a _____ sale.

2. The old man may _____ if he doesn't get out of the sun soon.

3. Donna is afraid that the old man might _____ them if they pick him up.

4. Donna and Thain are a young _____ couple.

5. The old man's medical problem is that he is _____.

6. He needs to go to a pharmacy to get _____.

7. When Donna and Thain got to the sale, all the good _____ had been sold.

8. Judging from the gift he sent, we can assume the old man is _____.

CONDITIONALS; OTHER WAYS TO EXPRESS UNREALITY

Present and Future Real Conditional

Present Conditionals	
If Clause	Result Clause
If it **is** hot,	I **drink** iced tea.
If it **isn't** hot,	I **don't drink** iced tea.

Future Conditionals	
If Clause	Result Clause
If it **rains**,	we **will close** the windows.
If it **doesn't rain**,	we **won't close** the windows.

Present Unreal Conditionals

Actual Situations	Conditionals	
	If Clause	Result Clause
It **is** rarely hot in Antarctica.	If it **were** hot in Antarctica,	
It **is** usually hot in Egypt.	If it **weren't** hot in Egypt,	it **would be** unusual.
It rarely **rains** in the Sahara.	If it **rained** in the Sahara,	
It usually **rains** in the jungle.	If it **didn't rain** in the jungle,	

Past Unreal Conditionals

Actual Situations	Conditionals	
	If Clause	Result Clause
They **stopped**, so they **were** late.	If they **hadn't stopped**,	they **wouldn't have been** late.
They **didn't stop**, so they **weren't** late.	If they **had stopped**,	they **would have been** late.
They **helped** the man, so he **sent** a gift.	If they **hadn't helped** the man,	he **wouldn't have sent** a gift.
They **didn't help** the man, so he **didn't send** a gift.	If they **had helped** the man,	he **would have sent** a gift.

"Mixed" Conditionals

Actual Situations	Conditionals	
	If Clause	Result Clause
He **didn't have** children, so he **is** alone.	PAST If he **had had** children,	PRESENT he **wouldn't be** alone.
His memory **is not** good, so he **didn't buy** his medicine.	PRESENT If his memory **were** good,	PAST he **would have bought** his medicine.

Other Ways to Express Unreality

Actual Situations	Wish / If only Statement
She **will miss** the sale.	She **wishes** (that) she **wouldn't miss** the sale. **If only** she **wouldn't miss** the sale.
They **can't buy** the bureau.	They **wish** (that) they **could buy** the bureau. **If only** they **could buy** the bureau.
They **arrived** late.	They **wish** (that) they **hadn't arrived** late. **If only** they **hadn't arrived** late.

GRAMMAR NOTES

1

Conditional sentences describe situations that occur (or do not occur) because of certain conditions. They consist of two clauses, a **dependent condition clause** (also called the *if* **clause**) and an **independent result clause**. There are two types of conditional sentences: real and unreal.

Real (or factual) **conditionals** are sentences that describe situations that

a. occur regularly

b. are likely or possible in the future

Unreal conditionals are sentences that describe situations that are untrue, unlikely, or impossible in the present or the past.

NOTE: In conditional sentences, the clauses can come in either order. The meaning is the same. We place a comma after the *if* clause if it comes first. We don't generally place a comma after the result clause if it comes first. Either or both clauses can be negative.

RESULT   CONDITION
- Water **boils** if it **reaches** 100° C.

CONDITION   RESULT
- If we **study**, we **will pass**.

CONDITION   RESULT
- If I **were** rich, I**'d buy** a car.

RESULT   CONDITION
- I **would have helped** if you **had asked**.

- **If I don't finish my work early**, I won't be able to attend.
  OR
- I won't be able to attend **if I don't finish my work early**.

2 We use **present real conditional** sentences to talk about general truths, scientific facts, or habits and repeated events. We use the simple present in both clauses. We can also use the present progressive in the *if* clause.

- Plants **die** if they **don't get** enough water.
- People with diabetes **can control** their disease if they **take** insulin regularly.
- If I**'m flying**, I always feel nervous.

In **future-time situations**, we use the simple present or the present progressive in the *if* clause and the future with *will* or *be going to*, *may*, *might*, *can*, *could*, or *should* in the result clause.

- If Barry **passes** the final exam, he **might pass** the course.
- Unless he **studies** hard, however, he **won't pass** the final exam.

BE CAREFUL! Use the simple present in the *if* clause, even though the time referred to is future.

- I'll contact you as soon as I **hear** from her.
  Not: I'll contact you as soon as I'll hear from her.

3 Use the **present unreal conditional** to talk about unreal, untrue, imagined, or impossible conditions and their results. Use the simple past form of the verb in the *if* clause. If the verb is *be*, use *were* for all persons. Use *could*, *might*, or *would* + the base form of the verb in the result clause.

- If I **loved** you, I**'d ask** you to marry me.
- We **wouldn't stay up** so late if we **were** parents.
- I **might watch** videos if I **had** the day off.
- If I **were** you, I **wouldn't accept** the offer.

BE CAREFUL! The simple past in the *if* clause is **past in form only**. It is not past in meaning.

BE CAREFUL! Don't use *would* in the *if* clause in present unreal conditional sentences.

- I'd buy a new car if **I had** the money.
  Not: I'd buy a new car if I would have the money.

4 Use the **past unreal conditional** to talk about past unreal, untrue, imagined, or impossible conditions and their unreal results. Use the past perfect in the *if* clause. Use *could*, *might*, or *would* + *have* + past participle in the result clause.

- If I **had listened** to my inner voice, I **wouldn't have made** that mistake.
- Mary **would have accepted** your proposal if you**'d asked** in time.

We often use the past unreal conditional to express regret about a situation that actually happened in the past.

- I **would have lent** you money if I **had known** you were in financial difficulty.

BE CAREFUL! Don't use *would have* in the *if* clause in past unreal conditional sentences.

Not: I **would have lent** you money if I would have known you were in financial difficulty.

(continued on next page)

5 The times of the *if* clause and the result clause are sometimes different. Present unreal and past unreal conditional forms can be "**mixed**" in the same sentence.

PAST ACTION   PRESENT RESULT

• If I **hadn't gone** to college, I**'d** still **be working** at the hardware store.
(I went to college. I'm not working at the hardware store.)

          PRESENT ACTION   PAST RESULT

• If Sam **were coming**, he **would have arrived** by now.
(Sam isn't coming. He hasn't arrived.)

---

6 We often use **unreal conditionals** to express regret or sadness. In a similar way, we use *wish* + noun clause to express sadness or a desire for a different situation.

• I'd earn more **if I had a better job**.
• I **wish** (that) **I had a better job**.

a. Use *wish* + *could* / *would* + base form to express a wish about the future.

• I **wish** (that) you **would change** your mind about buying that house.

b. Use *wish* + the simple past to express a wish about the present.

• My wife **wishes** (that) I **helped** her with the housework more.

c. Use *wish* + the past perfect to express a wish about the past.

• My son **wishes** (that) he **hadn't taken** that job.

BE CAREFUL! Don't confuse *wish* and *hope*. Use *wish* to express regrets about things that are unlikely or impossible to change. Use *hope* to express a desire about events that are possible or probable.

• I **wish** (that) she **would accept** my proposal. *(I don't think she will.)*
• I **hope** (that) she **accepts / will accept** my proposal. *(It's possible or probable that she will.)*

---

7 *If only* has a meaning similar to that of *wish*. *If only* is followed by a noun clause without *that*.

• I **wish** (that) I were good at sports.
• **If only** I were good at sports.

Use the simple past after *if only* to express a wish about something that is contrary to fact at present.

• **If only we weren't** so busy.

Use the past perfect after *if only* to express a wish that something had happened differently in the past.

• **If only I hadn't said** that.

BE CAREFUL! Don't confuse *if only* with *only if*.

• **If only** Jerry studied more.
(= I wish he would study more.)
• **Only if** Jerry studied more would he have a chance of passing.
(= This would be the only way for him to pass.)

EXERCISE 1: Discover the Grammar

A | *Identify the sentences as real (**R**) or unreal (**U**) conditionals.*

1. I'd sure get out of the heat if I were him. _U_

2. He's going to faint if he doesn't get out of the sun. _____

3. He'll probably kill us and steal the car if we stop and pick him up. _____

4. There won't be anything worth buying if we don't get there soon. _____

5. If I had a nickel for all the times we've done things because of your male intuition, I'd be rich. _____

6. If I don't take my medicine regularly, I go into shock. _____

7. We'd probably have the bureau if we'd gotten here earlier. _____

8. I'll be surprised if we ever hear from him, though. _____

B | *Identify the time of the conditional sentences as **past, present, future,** or **mixed.***

1. I wish I had an iced tea right now. _present_

2. I'd sure get out of this heat if I were him. _____

3. I wish you'd stop taking pity on every weirdo you see. _____

4. If only that bureau would still be there. _____

5. If only I weren't so forgetful. _____

6. We'd probably have that bureau if we'd gotten here earlier. _____

7. If you hadn't come along when you did, I might have died. _____

8. I would have become quite ill if you hadn't been there to help. _____

EXERCISE 2: Present Real Conditionals

(Grammar Notes 1–2)

Arrange the words in the correct order to create present real conditional sentences. Use correct punctuation.

1. sometimes / below / Farmers / temperature / drops / crops / zero / springtime / the / their / if / lose

   Farmers sometimes lose their crops if the springtime temperature drops below zero.

2. their / If / go / into / don't / shock / take / diabetics / sometimes / insulin / they

   _____

(continued on next page)

3. out / sources / if / energy / run / will / We / develop / alternative / of / don't / fuel / we

_____

4. continues / warming / If / icecaps / the / global / could / polar / melt

_____

5. dies / Venus / it / A / doesn't / water / enough / flytrap / if / get

_____

6. by / population / world / trends / will / If / billion / the / reach / 2060 / continue / present / nine

_____

EXERCISE 3: Present / Future Conditionals

(Grammar Notes 2–3)

Use the phrases from the box to complete the story with present and future conditional forms.

how would you feel	I'd want	I'll do	what would you do
I'd call	~~if I ask~~	it weren't	will you give
I'd keep	if I were	I will	you found
I'd take	if you really think	I wouldn't be	you were

MARISA: Hello?

FABIO: Hi, Marisa. This is Fabio. Got a couple of minutes for your little brother?

MARISA: Always. What's up?

FABIO: _____ _If I ask_ _____ you a question, _____ me an honest answer? Tell me
                        1.   **2.**

   what you really think, not what you think I want to hear?

MARISA: Of course _____. Shoot.
                                      3.

FABIO: _____ if _____ some money in a motel room?
                        4.   **5.**

MARISA: _____ it to the front desk. Why?
                        6.

FABIO: Ana and I found $200 in our room at the motel we were staying at. She says we should

   keep it, but a little voice told me I should call and ask you. If _____ so much
                                                                                       7.

   money, _____ concerned. _____ it. But $200 is quite a bit.
                   8.   **9.**

MARISA: You mean you think this all depends on the amount of money?

FABIO: Well, yes. Two hundred dollars is a significant amount, isn't it?

Marisa: I think it is. My take on this is that the previous occupants forgot it. _____ if

                                       10.

         _____ the one who left it?

             11.

Fabio: I guess _____ someone to return it.

                      12.

Marisa: Yeah. _____ you, _____ the front office and ask if anyone has

                  13.   14.

        inquired about it.

Fabio: OK, big sister. _____ it _____ it's the right thing.

                            15.   16.

Marisa: I do. But it's your choice, of course.

EXERCISE 4: *Wish / If Only* Sentences

(Grammar Notes 6–7)

A | *Look at the pictures. Write a sentence with* **wish** *for each.*

1.

They wish the weather were better.

2.

_____

3.

YES, OF COURSE.

_____

4.

NO, I CAN'T!

_____

(continued on next page)

5.

6.

_____   _____

B | _Now rewrite each sentence with_ **if only**. _Change subject pronouns and possessive adjectives where appropriate._

1. _If only the weather were better._ _____

2. _____

3. _____

4. _____

5. _____

6. _____

EXERCISE 5: Mixed / Past Unreal Conditionals

(Grammar Notes 4–5)

Complete the story with mixed or past unreal conditional sentences.

Mai and Dinh were at the new racetrack one afternoon to meet their friends Kenny and Allison

and then go to dinner. Time passed, and Kenny and Allison didn't show up, so Mai and Dinh began

to grow impatient.

Dinh said, "Let's go. They _____*would have arrived*_____ by now if they

                          1. (arrive)

_____." Now Mai and Dinh had never bet on a horse before and
    2. (be / coming)

_____ so this time if Kenny and Allison _____
    3. (not / do)   **4. (be)**

there. There's a first time for everything, however, and Mai said, "OK, but we might as well bet

on a horse as long as we're here." They studied the racing form. Dinh wanted to bet on Magic

Dancer, a horse that had won many times. Mai's intuition, however, was to go with Static, the

horse that had won the fewest races. It's a good thing they followed Mai's intuition because things

_____ quite differently if _____. They went to the
    5. (turn out)   **6. (they / not)**

stands to watch the race. At first it looked like Dinh's original idea had been right: Magic Dancer,

the favored horse, was running in the lead. In the final seconds, though, Static moved up suddenly

and finally passed Magic Dancer just before the finish line. Mai and Dinh couldn't believe their eyes.

They'd won $10,000.

The next day they told Kenny and Allison about their adventure. "Sorry we didn't make it," Kenny

said, "but we had a family emergency and couldn't call. I certainly _____
                                            7. (not pick)

Static if _____. Just think how much money _____
    8. (I / be / betting)   **9. (you / win)**

if _____ $50 or $100 instead of $20! _____ rich
    10. (you / bet)   **11. (you / be)**

now." Mai said, "It's too bad you had an emergency, but at least something good happened. We

_____ $10,000 richer right now if _____. So we
    12. (not / be)   **13. (you / make it)**

have you guys to thank."

EXERCISE 6: Editing

There are six mistakes in the use of conditionals and related forms in the diary entry. The first mistake is already corrected. Find and correct five more.

> ### June 4
>
> This has been one of those days when I wish I ~~would have~~ *had* stayed in bed.
> It started at 7:30 this morning when Trudy called me up and asked me for "a
> little favor." She's always asking me to do things for her and never wants to
> take any responsibility for herself. She acts as if the world owes her a living.
> I wish she doesn't think like that. Today she wanted me to take her to the
> mall because she had to get her mother a birthday present. At first I said I
> couldn't because I had to be downtown at 11 A.M. for a job interview. Trudy
> said she'd do the same for me if I would ask her. Then she said it wouldn't
> take long to drive to the mall, and I'd have plenty of time to get downtown
> from there. I gave in and agreed to take her, but something told me I
> shouldn't. If I had listened to my inner voice, I might have had a job right
> now. When we were on the freeway, there was a major accident, and traffic
> was tied up for over an hour. By the time we got to the mall, it was 11:30, so I
> missed the appointment. I think I probably would get the job if I had
> managed to make it to the interview because my qualifications are strong. If
> only I wouldn't have listened to Trudy! I just wish she doesn't ask me to do
> things like this. If she asks me again, I hope I can resist.

STEP 4 COMMUNICATION PRACTICE

EXERCISE 7: Listening

A | *Listen to the conversation. Check (✓) the three subjects that are not mentioned.*

☐ math class

☐ French class

☐ turning in a completed workbook

☐ turning in a completed term paper

☐ breaking up with a boyfriend

☐ finding a new boyfriend

B | *Listen again to the conversation. Answer the questions in complete sentences.*

1. What does April wish?

   April wishes she and Bob weren't going together.

2. What does Sally wish April hadn't done?

3. What did April think Bob would do if she refused?

4. What would Sally have done?

5. What will the teacher do if she finds out?

6. What would Sally do if she were April?

7. What does Sally think April should tell Bob?

8. What should April do if Bob gets mad and says he wants to break up?

EXERCISE 8: Pronunciation

A | *Read and listen to the Pronunciation Note.*

> **Pronunciation Note**
>
> In conversational or rapid speech, we often contract both *would* and *had* to /d/. Therefore, perceiving the pronunciation of the verb following these auxiliaries is important for understanding different sentences.
>
> **EXAMPLES:** I wish **you'd try** my dessert. (= would try)
> I wish **you'd tried** my dessert. (= had tried)
>
> The key consideration is whether the verb after the auxiliary is a base form or a past participle.

1. I wish you (**'d stop**) / 'd stopped riding motorcycles.

2. I wish you 'd stop / 'd stopped riding motorcycles.

3. Mary wishes I 'd accept / 'd accepted the job.

4. Mary wishes I 'd accept / 'd accepted the job.

5. I sure wish she 'd call / 'd called me.

6. I sure wish she 'd call / 'd called me.

7. My dad wishes I 'd visit / 'd visited more often.

8. My dad wishes I 'd visit / 'd visited more often.

9. I wish it 'd rain / 'd rained more.

10. I wish it 'd rain / 'd rained more.

C | *PAIRS: Practice the sentences in random order, making sure to contract **would** and **had**. Your partner says which sentences he or she hears.*

EXERCISE 9: Conditional Game

Form two teams. Each team uses the prompts to construct eight conditional questions, four in the present and four in the past. Then each team creates two questions of its own, for a total of 10 questions. Take turns asking questions. The other team guesses what person or thing is being referred to. For answers, see page G-AK4.

EXAMPLE: What / doing / if / spelunking
A: What would you be doing if you were spelunking?
B: We'd be exploring a cave.

Team A's Prompts

1. Where / be / if / in the capital of Honduras

2. How old / have to / be / if / the president of the United States

3. Where / traveling / if / the monetary unit / the won

4. Where / be / if / visiting Angkor Wat

5. Who / been / if / the emperor of France in 1804

6. Who / been / if / the first prime minister of India

7. What country / been from / if / Marco Polo

8. What mountain / climbed / if / with Edmund Hillary and Tenzing Norgay

9. _____

10. _____

    1. How old / be / if / an octogenarian

    2. Where / be traveling / if / in Machu Picchu

    3. What / be / if / the largest mammal

    4. What country / be in / if / standing and looking at Angel Falls

    5. Who / been / if / the inventor of the telephone

    6. What kind of creature / been / if / a stegosaurus

    7. What / been your occupation / if / Genghis Khan

    8. Who / been / if / Siddartha Gautama

    9. _____

    10. _____

EXERCISE 10: Personal Inventory

A | *Complete the sentences according to your own experience.*

    1. If I were _____.
                                        (present)

    2. I wish _____.
                                        (present)

    3. I wish _____.
                                        (past)

    4. If only I hadn't _____.
                                        (past)

    5. I wish _____.
                                        (future)

    6. I hope _____.
                                        (future)

    7. I would have _____.
                                        (past)

    8. I wouldn't have _____.
                                        (past)

B | *PAIRS: Discuss your answers. Report interesting examples to the class.*

EXERCISE 11: Group Discussion

A | *GROUPS: Look again at the opening reading. How do you think the story ended? Would it have been ethical for Thain and Donna to cash the check Mr. Wilkerson sent them? Would it have been proper to keep the money? What would you have done if you had been in their situation?*

    EXAMPLE: **A:** If I'd been in their situation, I wouldn't have cashed the check.
                       B: Why not?

B | *Tell the class about what your group has decided. Discuss the issue further as a class.*

EXERCISE 12: Writing

A | *Write four or five paragraphs about a time when you ignored your intuition and inner voice and instead made a seemingly logical decision that turned out badly. Describe your original intuitive feelings, explain why you ignored them, and speculate on what would or might have happened if you had acted intuitively. Use conditional sentences and clauses with* **wish** *where appropriate.*

> **EXAMPLE:**   A year ago I had an experience that taught me the advisability of going with my intuition. Looking back on the situation now, I wish I had paid attention to what my inner voice was telling me. Unfortunately, I didn't do that, and I had to suffer the consequences. I had saved up enough money for the down payment on a new car and was ready to close the deal. When a cousin heard of my plans, however, he offered to sell me his two-year-old car for half the price of the down payment. Something told me this was the wrong thing to do, but . . .

B | *Check your work. Use the Editing Checklist.*

Editing Checklist

Did you use . . . ?
- ☐ conditional sentences correctly
- ☐ clauses with *wish* correctly
- ☐ sentences with *if only* correctly

A | Circle the word or phrase that correctly completes each sentence.

1. We won't be able to go on the picnic if it <u>will rain / rains</u> tomorrow.

2. I hope it <u>doesn't / wouldn't</u> rain tomorrow.

3. I'd like living here more if it <u>rains / rained</u> less.

4. If only it <u>wouldn't / won't</u> rain tomorrow!

5. I wouldn't be worried about tomorrow if it <u>weren't / isn't</u> raining now.

6. If it <u>didn't rain / hadn't rained</u>, we could have had the picnic last week.

7. If it weren't raining, I <u>'d / 'll</u> be dry.

8. The sky would be darker if it <u>would / were going to</u> rain.

B | Correct the mistakes in the underlined words or phrases in the story.

1. Bao <u>hopes</u> he hadn't forgotten to change the oil in his car.   _____

2. If he had changed the oil, the engine <u>won't</u> have seized.   _____

3. If the engine <u>will not have</u> seized, the car wouldn't have stopped.   _____

4. He wouldn't <u>have to</u> pay a towing bill.   _____

5. He <u>won't</u> have had to replace the engine.   _____

6. He could have <u>make</u> it to the job interview.   _____

7. He probably <u>will not</u> be unemployed now.   _____

8. Bao wishes he <u>listened</u> to his inner voice.   _____

C | Circle the letter of the one underlined word or phrase in each sentence that is not correct.

1. <u>If only</u> we <u>would have</u> <u>been able to</u> finish the job in the time we <u>had</u>.   **A B C D**
     A   B   C   D

2. If I <u>was</u> you, I <u>wouldn't</u> <u>accept</u> the offer until I <u>knew</u> more.   **A B C D**
        A   B   C   D

3. Toshi <u>would have</u> <u>arrived</u> by now if he <u>would be</u> planning to <u>come</u>.   **A B C D**
             A   B   C   D

4. <u>If</u> Omar <u>had</u> <u>had</u> children, he <u>has</u> someone to care for him.   **A B C D**
    A   B   C   D

More Conditions; The Subjunctive
ADVICE

Before You Read

PAIRS: Discuss the questions.

1. Do you ever read advice columns? Do you think they contain useful information?
2. What is a problem that you might potentially ask a columnist about?

Read

Read the letters to the advice columnist and her responses.

ASK ROSA

Dear Rosa,

Hank and I were best friends in high school, so when he **suggested we room** together in college I thought it was a great idea. Wrong! **Had I known** what a slob Hank really is, I never would have agreed. We have a small suite that has become a pigsty because Hank thinks it's beneath him to wash a dish and is convinced the floor is the place to keep clothes. Whenever I talk to Hank about it, he just says, "Hey, Jason, you need to lighten up. You're too solemn." I'm no neatnik, but I do prefer a semblance of order. I still like Hank and want to stay friends, but I'm feeling more like a doormat every day. What would you **recommend I do?**

Jason

Dear Jason,

No one should have to feel like a doormat. Unfortunately, there's no easy solution to your problem. I can suggest three potential remedies: First, Hank may be unaware there's actually a problem. **If so**, ask him if he really likes having dirty dishes and bugs all over the place. If he doesn't, he might lend his muscles and help with the cleaning. There's a chance this approach will work, but **if not**, remedy two is teaching him how to clean up—he just may not be used to it. You might **suggest he do** the dishes one day and you the next. **Should that not work**, remedy three is to remind him you both have a right to a reasonably clean and orderly living space, and you feel your rights are being violated. Sometimes an appeal to a person's sense of fairness can do the trick. Whatever you do, **it's important that Hank not feel** criticized. **Otherwise**, he'll probably become intransigent, so be moderate in your suggestions. Good luck.

Rosa

ASK ROSA

Dear Rosa,

Jim and I have been married for over four years now, and our marriage would be ideal **were it not** for the overbearing qualities of some of his extended family. I love Jim dearly, but there are times when I feel like I'm married to his family members as well. They often drop in without letting me know they're coming, and at this point I'm spending more time with them than with Jim. Besides that, his sister Hannah constantly bombards me with requests that I do favors for her. For example, she **insists I take** her grocery shopping every week, even though she has her own car and is perfectly capable of doing this on her own. Even worse, his cousin Helen often **requests I lend** her money. At this point, Helen owes me about $750, but if I mention it she just says, "Carla, you know I'm good for it. I just need to get some bills paid off, and then I can pay you back." Rosa, I feel like I'm being taken advantage of. I know how important Jim's extended family is to him, but I'm at the end of my rope. What would you **suggest that I do**?

Carla

Dear Carla,

You're experiencing one of the most common problems faced by young marrieds, so don't feel you're alone. The problem sounds quite fixable. My guess is that your husband probably doesn't know what's going on and doesn't realize the depth of your frustration. Here's my advice: have a heart-to-heart talk with Jim. First tell him you appreciate his extended family but also feel you and he need more time alone together, that **without** it, your relationship can't develop as it should. **Suggest they** only **come over** at designated times. Also tell him you want to be helpful but feel his sister and cousin are asking too much of you. I'll bet he'll be willing to speak to them privately. When you're telling Jim about this, of course, **it's essential that you not criticize** his family members. That will probably cause resentment. Just give an honest statement of your feelings. **With** a little bit of extra communication with Jim, you can right the ship and make your marriage stronger. Good luck, and hang in there!

Rosa

After You Read

A | **Vocabulary:** *Match the blue words and phrases on the left with their meanings on the right.*

_____ 1. Had I known what a **slob** Hank is, I never would have agreed.

_____ 2. We have a small suite that has become a **pigsty**.

_____ 3. Jason, you need to **lighten up**.

_____ 4. I'm no **neatnik**, but I do prefer a semblance of order.

_____ 5. I'm no neatnik, but I do prefer a **semblance** of order.

_____ 6. I'm feeling more like a **doormat** every day.

_____ 7. Otherwise, he'll probably become **intransigent**.

_____ 8. Our marriage would be ideal were it not for the **overbearing** qualities of some of his extended family.

_____ 9. I'm **at the end of my rope**.

_____ 10. With a little bit of extra communication, you can **right the ship**.

a. outward appearance

b. stubbornly resistant

c. almost desperate

d. tending to order other people around

e. fix the situation

f. very dirty room or house

g. person excessively concerned about cleanliness and order

h. lazy, dirty, or messy person

i. one who allows others to dominate him or her

j. stop taking things so seriously

B | **Comprehension:** *Refer to the reading and complete each sentence with a single word.*

1. It was Hank's suggestion that he and Jason _____ together in college.

2. Hank is not a _____ person.

3. Jason is not a compulsively neat person, but he likes a certain amount of _____.

4. Rosa says Hank may just not be _____ to cleaning up.

5. Rosa suggests that appealing to Hank's sense of _____ may help the situation.

6. Carla is bothered by the fact that some of her husband's extended family _____ in without letting her know they're coming.

7. Rosa says intrusiveness on the part of in-laws is a common problem faced by young _____.

8. Rosa says Carla should suggest to Jim that his family members come over only at _____ times.

9. Rosa says it's essential that Carla not _____ Jim's family.

MORE CONDITIONS; THE SUBJUNCTIVE

Implied Conditions

Nonstandard Condition	(= Implied Condition)	Result Clause
With a bit of luck,	(If we have a bit of luck,)	we can fix the problem.
Without your help,	(If you hadn't helped,)	I wouldn't have succeeded.
But for his investments,	(If he didn't have investments,)	he'd have no income.
She might be lucky; **if so**,	(If she is lucky,)	she'll meet some new friends.
He might get the chance; **if not**,	(If he doesn't get the chance,)	he won't take the job.
She is lonely; **otherwise**,	(If she weren't lonely,)	she wouldn't need company.

Inverted Conditions

Inverted Condition	(= Standard Condition)	Result Clause
Were he in love,	(If he **were** in love,)	he would get married.
Were he **not** in love,	(If he **weren't** in love,)	he wouldn't get married.
Had I **seen** her,	(If I **had seen** her,)	I would have called you.
Should we **do** it,	(If we **should do** it,)	we will celebrate.

The Subjunctive in Noun Clauses

Verbs of Advice, Necessity, and Urgency + Subjunctive	
Main Clause	**Noun Clause**
Frank's teacher **suggested**	(that) he **take** an additional class.
The boss **demanded**	(that) Rosa **arrive** at work by 9:00.
The fireman **insisted**	(that) she **leave** the burning building immediately.

Adjectives of Advice, Necessity, and Urgency + Subjunctive	
Main Clause	**Noun Clause**
It is **advisable**	(that) he **arrive** one-half hour before the appointment.
It is **mandatory**	(that) no one **enter** the building without a permit.
It is **urgent**	(that) she **call** home at once.

GRAMMAR NOTES

1 **Conditions in conditional sentences** are sometimes implied rather than stated directly in an *if* clause.

Conditions may be implied by using *but for*, *if not*, *if so*, *otherwise*, *with*, *without*, etc.

- Your brother may be lonely. **If so**, he should join a singles group.
  (*= If he is lonely . . .*)

In a sentence with an implied condition, there is no change in the result clause.

- Mary needs to be part of the decision. Otherwise, **she'll never be happy**.
  (*= If she isn't part of the decision, she'll never be happy.*)

As with other conditional sentences, the condition may precede or follow the result clause.

- **With a little extra communication**, you can fix the problem.
- You can fix the problem **with a little extra communication**.

2 **Unreal conditions** with *had* (past perfect), *should*, and *were* are sometimes expressed by deleting *if* and **inverting** the subject and the verb.

- **If I had known** he was lazy, I wouldn't have roomed with him.
- **Had I known** he was lazy, I wouldn't have roomed with him.

If there is an inverted condition, there is no change in the result clause.

- If I were to accept the job, **I would insist on benefits**.
- Were I to accept the job, **I would insist on benefits**.

As with other conditional sentences, the inverted condition clause can precede or follow the result clause.

- **If I were to move,** I'd have to get a new roommate.
- I'd have to get a new roommate **if I were to move**.

NOTE: Inverted conditional sentences with *should* imply that an action or event is unlikely to happen. The meaning of *should* in this type of sentence is much different from its usual meaning.

- **Should something go wrong**, we need to have a backup plan. (*= It is unlikely that something will go wrong, but we need to be prepared.*)

BE CAREFUL! Negative inversion is formed by adding *not* after the inverted verb and the subject. Don't contract *not* and the verb.

- **Had I not received** the phone call, I wouldn't have been able to help.
  Not: ~~Hadn't I~~ received the phone call, I wouldn't have been able to help.

USAGE NOTE: Sentences with inverted condition clauses have the same meaning as conditionals with *if* but are more formal.

3

The **subjunctive** is somewhat uncommon in English. However, one common example is the use of *were* in unreal conditions.

BE CAREFUL! This use of *were* occurs only in present unreal conditions. It is not used for past situations.

- If I **were** you, I'd visit my parents more often.
- We could go on a picnic if it **weren't** raining.

- If I **were** there, I would help her.
  Nᴏᴛ: ~~If I were there~~, I would have helped her.

4

Another form of the **subjunctive** uses the **base form** of a verb in noun clauses.

BE CAREFUL! The main verb in a noun clause can be past, present, or future. However, the subjunctive verb is the base form.

Form the negative of a subjunctive verb by placing *not* before the base form.

To form a passive subjunctive, use *be* + the past participle.

NOTE: In noun clauses with subjunctive constructions, we can usually omit the word *that*.

MAIN CLAUSE	NOUN CLAUSE

- We recommend (that) he **see** a lawyer.

- We recommended (that) he **sell** his house.
  Nᴏᴛ: We recommended (that) he ~~sold~~ his house.

- My aunt and uncle insisted (that) we **not come** to visit them today.

- The doctor recommends (that) Uncle John **be hospitalized**.

5

The **subjunctive** with the base form of the verb is used in noun clauses following **verbs of advice**, **necessity**, and **urgency**, such as *demand*, *insist*, *propose*, *recommend*, and *suggest*.

BE CAREFUL! We do not use infinitives after these verbs.

Note that *insist (on)*, *propose*, *recommend*, and *suggest* can also be followed by a gerund phrase. The meaning of this structure is similar to the meaning of a sentence with a subjunctive in a noun clause.

Note that the verbs *ask*, *order*, *require*, *urge*, etc., may also occur in the pattern verb + object + infinitive. When they are used in subjunctive constructions, the word *that* is usually not omitted.

- I **propose** (that) we **ask** Mom and Dad about their wishes.
- My parents **insisted** (that) I **come** to visit them often.

- He **suggested** (that) we **talk**.
  Nᴏᴛ: He suggested (that) we ~~to talk~~.

- We **insist on / propose / recommend / suggest getting** another bid for the job.

- I **asked** that my brothers and sisters **be** present.
  ᴏʀ
- I **asked** my brothers and sisters **to be** present.

(continued on next page)

6 The **subjunctive** is also used after **adjectives of advice**, **necessity**, and **urgency**, such as *advisable, crucial, desirable, essential, important, mandatory, necessary,* and *urgent.* Subjunctive verbs after adjectives of urgency, necessity, and advice occur in the pattern *It + be* + adjective + *that* clause. We do not usually omit the word *that* in this type of clause.

NOTE: The pattern shown above can be replaced with *It + be* + adjective + *for* + noun or object pronoun + infinitive, which is more informal.

- It is **essential** that elderly people **be treated** with dignity.
- It's **important** that she **understand** her options.
- It was **necessary** that my brother **see** a lawyer.

- It's **important for her to understand** her options.
- It was **necessary for my brother to see** a lawyer.

REFERENCE NOTE
For a list of **verbs and phrases followed by the subjunctive**, see Appendix 24 on page A-10.

STEP 3 FOCUSED PRACTICE

EXERCISE 1: Discover the Grammar

A | *Read the sentences. Do the underlined words and phrases show implied conditionals (**IM**), inverted conditionals (**IV**), or subjunctive verb (**S**) constructions?*

1. Hank <u>suggested we room</u> together in college.   *S*

2. <u>Had I known</u> what a slob Hank really is, I never would have agreed. _____

3. What would you <u>recommend I do</u>?   _____

4. This may work, but <u>if not</u>, try teaching him how to clean up.   _____

5. <u>Should that not work</u>, remedy three is to appeal to his sense of fairness. _____

6. Our marriage would be ideal <u>were it not</u> for the overbearing qualities of some of his extended family.   _____

7. Be moderate in your suggestions; <u>otherwise</u>, he may become intransigent. _____

8. It's <u>essential that you not criticize</u> his family.   _____

9. <u>With</u> a little bit of extra communication, you can right the ship.   _____

B | *Read the pairs of sentences. Is the second sentence a correct rewriting of the first? Circle* **Y (Yes)** *or* **N (No).**

1. I would have recommended she sell it a long time ago.

   Ⓨ   N   I would have recommended her selling it a long time ago.

2. She's always said it's important for her to keep her independence.

   Y   N   She's always said it's important that she keep her independence.

3. I propose you make a new offer on the house.

   Y   N   I propose you to make a new offer on the house.

4. I'd recommend you look into joining a singles group.

   Y   N   I'd recommend you to join a singles group.

5. It's essential that you understand what your job responsibilities would be.

   Y   N   It's essential for you to understand what your job responsibilities would be.

6. Our marriage would be ideal were it not for the overbearing qualities of some of his extended family.

   Y   N   If it weren't for the overbearing qualities of some of his extended family, our marriage would be ideal.

EXERCISE 2: Implied Conditionals   *(Grammar Note 1)*

Read the conversation between a man and his doctor. There are six conditional sentences. The first sentence is underlined. Underline five more sentences. Rewrite the sentences by replacing the **if** *clauses with these nonstandard conditions:* **if so, if not, otherwise, with, without.** *One will be used twice.*

Doctor: Bob, you've got to improve your diet. <u>If you don't, you're going to get sick.</u> Too much fast

food is not good for you.

Bob: There isn't time to go to a decent restaurant. I'm working 12 hours a day.

Doctor: Maybe your boss will let you have an extra half hour for lunch. If he will, that would solve

your problem.

Bob: And if he won't, what can I do? He's a task master.

Doctor: Then I'd suggest you pack yourself a lunch every day. But now here's another thing: You

need to stop smoking.

(continued on next page)

Bob: Impossible. If I don't have cigarettes, I can't make it through the day.

Doctor: There must be a way. You can do it if you find a buddy who has the same problem. You have friends at work, don't you?

Bob: I sure do. I'd hate my job if I didn't have my friends. Maybe there's someone else who's trying to stop smoking.

Doctor: Hopefully there is. Anyway, promise me you'll try to quit.

Bob: OK. I can promise to try.

1. _Otherwise, you're going to get sick._

2. _____

3. _____

4. _____

5. _____

6. _____

EXERCISE 3: Inverted / Implied Conditionals

(Grammar Notes 1–2)

A | *Fill in the blanks in the story with the items from the box.*

had she known	if so	~~were she to stay~~
if not	otherwise	with

Doris Allen had just moved to St. Louis from Russellville, the small city where she had grown up and attended college. For some time, Doris had felt it was necessary for her to leave Russellville.
_____Were she to stay_____ there, she felt, she would just fall into a rut she would never escape
         1.
from, so she decided to go to the big city and start a new life. At the age of 23, however, she needed to work. _____ how difficult it would be to find employment, she might
                              2.
have stayed in her hometown. She loved the big city, though, and she had been looking hard for a job. The only problem was that Doris needed to find a job fairly soon; _____,
                                                                                                              3.

she wouldn't be able to afford her apartment. A good deal of her savings were already gone. There

was another problem: Having spent the last five years in college, Doris had worked only in the

summers and was unaccustomed to job hunting. One day she was wandering around downtown,

feeling that _____ a bit of luck she might find something. She saw a

4.

pleasant-looking florist's shop. Maybe they were hiring; _____, she might

5.

get a job. _____, she wouldn't lose anything by going in and asking.

6.

Without even thinking further, she walked in. "I'm Doris Allen, and I was wondering whether you

were doing any hiring. I was a botany major in college, and I have a lot of experience with flowers

and gardening."

The manager said, "Actually, we're expanding and do need someone to work part-time. The

position could become full-time eventually. I was just going to put up a sign in the window. Tell me

more about your experience."

Doris got the job.

B | *Rewrite each word or phrase from Part A with an* **if** *clause that restates the condition.*

1. _If she were to stay_____

2. _____

3. _____

4. _____

5. _____

6. _____

EXERCISE 4: Verbs of Urgency and Subjunctives

(Grammar Notes 4–5)

Describe the action of each picture by completing each sentence on the next page. Use subjunctive verb forms and appropriate subjects.

1.

2.

3.

4.

5.

6.

1. The police officer is suggesting _the woman call a towing company_____.

2. The workers are demanding _____.

3. The wife is insisting _____.

4. The woman is proposing _____.

5. The real estate agent is recommending _____.

6. The travel agent is suggesting _____.

EXERCISE 5: Adjectives of Urgency and Subjunctives

(Grammar Note 6)

A | *What do young people need for a good start to adult life? Complete each sentence with the adjective in parentheses and a verb from the box.*

communicate	find	~~have~~	make	stay	take

1. It is ____*desirable that they have*____ good self-esteem.
   (desirable)

2. It is _____ responsibility for their own actions.
   (necessary)

3. It is _____ satisfying employment.
   (important)

4. It is _____ most of their own decisions.
   (essential)

5. If they are married, it is _____ with each other.
   (crucial)

6. It is _____ in touch with family and close friends.
   (advisable)

B | *Now rewrite each sentence in Part A using* **for** *+ noun or object pronoun + infinitive.*

1. _It is desirable for them to have good self-esteem._____

2. _____

3. _____

4. _____

5. _____

6. _____

EXERCISE 6: Editing

Read the letter. It has seven mistakes in verb constructions. The first mistake is already corrected. Find and correct six more.

December 10

Dear Hei-Rim,

It's time I wrote and filled you in on what's been happening since I left

Russellville. I finally got a job! Remember when you suggested I just ~~went~~ go walking

around, getting a sense of what St. Louis was like? A few weeks ago I was getting

rather worried since I had spent most of the money I had saved to get me through

the job-hunting period. It's not all that easy for someone fresh out of college to find a

job, you know. I had gotten to the point where it was absolutely essential that I found

something or come back to Russellville. So I decided to follow your advice. I had

known how easy this would be, I would have tried it the first week I was here. I

started walking around in the downtown area, and before I knew it, I saw a beautiful

little florist's shop. I walked right in, unafraid, and asked if they needed anyone. Can

you believe that they did?

I was really happy in my job until my boss hired a new assistant manager who

has been making my life miserable. Among other things, he demands me to make coffee

for him. He also insists that I'm doing other things that aren't in my job description.

I took this job to work with plants, not to serve him coffee. I think I need to tell him

where I stand. It's important that he stops treating me as his personal assistant. I

have a few days off for the holidays. Do you have some time off? If so, how about

coming down here for a visit? Wouldn't that be fun? I have a spare bedroom in my

apartment. If you can come, I suggest you to drive, as it isn't far. Please write or

email and let me know.

Love,

Doris

EXERCISE 7: Listening

A | *Listen to the conversation. Why is the daughter working so much?*

_____

B | *Read the questions. Listen again to the telephone conversation and answer the questions in complete sentences.*

1. What did the daughter ask her mother to do?

   The daughter asked her mother to babysit.

2. What did the daughter almost do when the mother said no?

   _____

3. Had the mother known who was calling, what would she have done?

   _____

4. What did the mother have to do the last time this happened?

   _____

5. According to her mother, what is it important that the daughter do?

   _____

6. What does the mother's friend suggest she do?

   _____

EXERCISE 8: Pronunciation

A | *Read and listen to the Pronunciation Note.*

Pronunciation Note

English has "silent" consonants that are not pronounced in many words but are pronounced in other words in the same family.

EXAMPLES: You're too **solemn**. ("n" is not pronounced)
There are times when **solemnity** is a good thing. ("n" is pronounced)

B | *Listen to the sentences. Cross out silent consonants that are not pronounced. Circle the same consonants in words where they are pronounced.*

1. **a.** Your marriage is already strong.

   b. You can make it stronger.

2. **a.** Too much exercise can give you muscular aches.

   b. Maybe he'll lend his muscles and help with the cleaning.

3. **a.** I love autumn more than any other season.

   b. The autumnal equinox occurs around September 21 in the Northern Hemisphere.

4. **a.** Ask them to come over at designated times.

   b. We've designed our new house and are going to have it built.

5. **a.** There are plenty of people who want to ban the bomb.

   b. We're bombarded with attention.

6. **a.** There are crumbs all over the floor.

   b. Their relationship has crumbled.

C | *PAIRS: Practice the sentences.*

EXERCISE 9: Personal Inventory

A | *Complete each of the sentences, drawing from your own experience or opinions. Use subjunctive verb forms where appropriate.*

1. My parents suggested _____

2. My parents insisted _____

3. It's essential that I _____

4. It's important for me _____

5. It's essential that a person _____

6. Had I known _____

7. Were I _____

8. Should I _____

B | *PAIRS: Discuss your answers. Report interesting examples to the class.*

EXERCISE 10: Group Discussion

A | *Read the statements. Write* **A (Agree)**, **D (Disagree)**, *or* **IB (In Between)**, *according to your personal beliefs.*

_____ **1.** It's desirable that young people work for a year or two before going to college.

_____ **2.** It is advisable that young people not be allowed to drive until they are at least 18.

_____ **3.** It is essential that national governments pay for the health care of the citizens.

_____ **4.** It is reasonable that national governments provide low-cost loans to students who want to attend college.

_____ **5.** It is important that young people participate in some form of national service.

B | *SMALL GROUPS: Discuss your answers. Share your group's opinions with the rest of the class.*

    EXAMPLE: **A:** I think it is desirable that young people work for a year or two before going to college.
                 B: Why?
                 A: They need a break from at least 12 years of school.

EXERCISE 11: Picture Discussion

GROUPS: Discuss one of the pictures. The daughter or son of a friend is going to make a visit to one of these countries and has asked for your input. Give advice, using subjunctive verb constructions with **suggest, recommend,** *and* **it is essential that** *plus any others that are appropriate. Include a negative sentence.*

    EXAMPLES: If the person is visiting the United Kingdom, I suggest he / she stay in bed and breakfasts.
                   I recommend he / she pack a raincoat and a sweater.
                   It's essential that he / she visit Stonehenge.
                   It's crucial that he / she not forget to take his / her passport.

China

France

Egypt

Brazil

EXERCISE 12: Writing

A | *Write four or five paragraphs about a time when you took some good advice or a time when you took some bad advice. Explain the situation fully and show why the advice was good or bad. In your composition use subjunctive verb constructions (such as* **suggest, recommend, necessary that,** *etc.) and at least one implied conditional.*

EXAMPLE: One of the worst pieces of advice I've ever taken was to go out for the football team in high school. My friend Mark had suggested I try to make the team and had assured me I would make it if I did. I've never been very good at football, and I knew that in the back of my mind, but for the sake of popularity and togetherness I took Mark's suggestion. Had I known how badly the situation would turn out, I never would have done it. Here's what happened . . .

B | *Check your work. Use the Editing Checklist.*

Editing Checklist

Did you use . . . ?
- ☐ subjunctives with verbs of advice correctly
- ☐ subjunctives with adverbs of necessity correctly
- ☐ implied conditionals correctly
- ☐ inverted conditionals correctly

UNIT **23** **Review**

Check your answers on page UR-3.
Do you need to review anything?

A | Circle the word or phrase that correctly completes each sentence.

1. You need to get some job retraining. <u>With / Without</u> it, you risk being laid off.

2. Juan may or may not go to college. <u>If so / If not</u>, he'll be working for his father.

3. I think something is wrong with the car. <u>If so / If not</u>, we'd better have it fixed.

4. You have to take notes; <u>if not / otherwise</u>, you'll forget.

5. Our house is on the market. <u>If so / With</u> a bit of luck, the sale will go through.

6. I may not pass the class; <u>if not / if so</u>, I'll have to take it over.

7. Ana has a daughter; <u>without / if not</u> her daughter, she'd be all alone.

8. The traffic is heavy, but <u>with / if</u> a bit of luck, we'll be on time.

B | Correct the mistakes in the underlined words or phrases.

1. Give me a call; <u>but for that</u>, I may forget the meeting. _____

2. <u>Hadn't I</u> reminded Jiro of the party, he would have forgotten. _____

3. Hana suggested that I <u>called</u> the airline, but I didn't. _____

4. I might be late. <u>That should happen</u>, go without me. _____

5. <u>But</u> her pension, she would never be able to survive financially. _____

6. It's crucial that Linh <u>understands</u> the gravity of his situation. _____

7. Jae-Yong may be coming; <u>if not</u>, you can ride back with him. _____

8. It is surprising that Jane <u>like</u> to scuba dive. _____

C | Circle the letter of the one underlined word or phrase in each sentence that is not correct.

1. <u>I had known</u> how you <u>would act</u>, I <u>wouldn't have suggested</u> you <u>come</u>. **A B C D**
       A   B   C   D

2. I <u>suggest</u> Aki <u>to attend</u> class. <u>She'll be</u> more likely to pass if she <u>does</u>. **A B C D**
       A   B   C   D

3. Dev <u>would ask</u> Frida <u>to marry</u> him <u>he were</u> in love, but he <u>isn't</u>. **A B C D**
           A   B   C   D

4. I'm glad you <u>suggested</u> I <u>followed</u> my intuition. I <u>did</u>, and it <u>worked</u>. **A B C D**
           A   B   C   D

From Grammar to Writing

AVOIDING RUN-ON SENTENCES AND COMMA SPLICES

To strengthen your writing and make it effective, you should avoid two common types of errors: the **run-on sentence** and the **comma splice**. A run-on sentence is a group of words containing at least two independent clauses without any punctuation separating them. A comma splice is the joining of two independent clauses with only a comma.

> **EXAMPLES:** The old man felt ill he needed to get out of the sun quickly.
> *(run-on sentence—No punctuation separates the two independent clauses.)*
>
> The old man felt ill, he needed to get out of the sun quickly.
> *(comma splice—A comma separates the two clauses, but a comma is not adequate punctuation.)*

Correct run-on sentences and comma splices in the following ways:

1. Insert a period between the independent clauses.
   The old man felt ill. **H**e needed to get out of the sun quickly.

2. Insert a semicolon between the independent clauses: (Don't capitalize the word after the semicolon unless it is a proper noun or *I*.)
   The old man felt ill**;** he needed to get out of the sun quickly.

3. Join the two independent clauses with a comma and a coordinating conjunction:
   The old man felt ill, **so** he needed to get out of the sun quickly.

4. Make one of the independent clauses dependent by adding a subordinating conjunction, and separate the two clauses with a comma if the dependent clause comes first:
   Because the old man felt ill, he needed to get out of the sun quickly.

5. Convert one of the two clauses into an adverbial phrase if the subjects of the two clauses are the same:
   Feeling ill, the old man had to get out of the sun quickly.

1 | *Correct the run-on sentences and comma splices by using the method given in parentheses.*

1. Nancy says she wants to do something worthwhile if so, she should consider volunteer work. *(period)*

2. I need to get a bank loan, otherwise, I'll have to file for bankruptcy. *(semicolon)*

3. Donna didn't want to stop for the old man Thain persuaded her it was a necessity. *(comma and coordinating conjunction)*

4. I was learning to be assertive I learned many things about myself. *(subordinating conjunction and comma)*

5. Nancy felt dominated by her mother-in-law, she needed to take assertive action. *(Make the first clause an adverbial phrase.)*

2 | *Read the passage. Correct the nine mistakes consisting of run-on sentences and comma splices. Capitalize where necessary.*

Call it either intuition or good vibrations. Whatever you want to call it, it works. Last summer I was on a committee to hire a new head nurse at the nursing home where I work, we interviewed two candidates as finalists, a man named Bob and a woman named Sarah on paper, Bob was better qualified he had a master's degree while Sarah had only a bachelor's degree, however, Sarah was the one who really impressed us she answered all of the questions straightforwardly and simply, Bob, on the other hand, evaded some of our questions while simultaneously trying to make us think he knew everything and could do everything all of us on the committee just liked Sarah better in fact, she got the job because she was the person we all felt we wanted to work with. Our intuition wasn't wrong, she's turned out to be a wonderful nurse.

3 | *Before you write . . .*

1. We are sometimes encouraged to act according to our intuition. Think of a time when you or a friend acted according to intuitive feelings, and those feelings turned out to be correct.
2. Describe your experience to a partner. Listen to your partner's description.
3. Ask and answer questions about your and your partner's topic. Why do you think following intuition worked successfully? Does this mean we should always act intuitively?

4 | *Write a draft of a composition about your (or a friend's) intuitive experience. Follow the model. Remember to include information that your partner asked about. Read your draft aloud and correct any run-on sentences or comma splices.*

Details about my (or my friend's) intuitive experience:

_____

_____

_____

_____

(continued on next page)

My explanation of why I think it worked to act on the basis of intuition:

_____

_____

_____

_____

Reasons why I think we should / should not always follow our intuition:

_____

_____

_____

_____

5 | *Exchange compositions with a different partner. Complete the chart.*

1. The writer's composition is free of run-on sentences and comma splices.   **Yes** ☐   **No** ☐

2. What I liked in the composition:

_____

_____

_____

3. Questions I'd like the writer to answer about the composition:

Who _____ ?

What _____ ?

When _____ ?

Where _____ ?

Why _____ ?

How _____ ?

(Your own question) _____ ?

6 | *Work with your partner. Discuss each other's chart from Exercise 5. Then rewrite your own composition and make any necessary changes.*

1 Irregular Verbs

Base Form	Simple Past	Past Participle	Base Form	Simple Past	Past Participle
arise	arose	arisen	forgo	forwent	forgone
awake	awoke	awoken	forsake	forsook	forsaken
be	was/were	been	freeze	froze	frozen
bear	bore	born/borne	get	got	gotten/got
beat	beat	beaten/beat	give	gave	given
become	became	become	go	went	gone
begin	began	begun	grind	ground	ground
bend	bent	bent	grow	grew	grown
bet	bet	bet	hang	hung*/hanged**	hung*/hanged**
bite	bit	bitten	have	had	had
bleed	bled	bled	hear	heard	heard
blow	blew	blown	hide	hid	hidden
break	broke	broken	hit	hit	hit
bring	brought	brought	hold	held	held
broadcast	broadcast/broadcasted	broadcast/broadcasted	hurt	hurt	hurt
build	built	built	keep	kept	kept
burn	burned/burnt	burned/burnt	kneel	knelt/kneeled	knelt/kneeled
burst	burst	burst	knit	knit/knitted	knit/knitted
buy	bought	bought	know	knew	known
cast	cast	cast	lay	laid	laid
catch	caught	caught	lead	led	led
choose	chose	chosen	leap	leaped/leapt	leaped/leapt
cling	clung	clung	learn	learned/learnt	learned/learnt
come	came	come	leave	left	left
cost	cost	cost	lend	lent	lent
creep	crept	crept	let	let	let
cut	cut	cut	lie *(down)*	lay	lain
deal	dealt	dealt	light	lit/lighted	lit/lighted
dig	dug	dug	lose	lost	lost
dive	dived/dove	dived	make	made	made
do	did	done	mean	meant	meant
draw	drew	drawn	meet	met	met
dream	dreamed/dreamt	dreamed/dreamt	pay	paid	paid
drink	drank	drunk	plead	pleaded/pled	pleaded/pled
drive	drove	driven	prove	proved	proved/proven
eat	ate	eaten	put	put	put
fall	fell	fallen	quit	quit	quit
feed	fed	fed	read	read	read
feel	felt	felt	rid	rid	rid
fight	fought	fought	ride	rode	ridden
find	found	found	ring	rang	rung
fit	fitted/fit	fitted/fit	rise	rose	risen
flee	fled	fled	run	ran	run
fling	flung	flung	saw	sawed	sawed/sawn
fly	flew	flown	say	said	said
forbid	forbade/forbid	forbidden			
forget	forgot	forgotten			
forgive	forgave	forgiven			

  * hung = hung an object
 ** hanged = executed by hanging

(continued on next page)

Base Form	Simple Past	Past Participle	Base Form	Simple Past	Past Participle
see	saw	seen	stand	stood	stood
seek	sought	sought	steal	stole	stolen
sell	sold	sold	stick	stuck	stuck
send	sent	sent	sting	stung	stung
set	set	set	stink	stank/stunk	stunk
sew	sewed	sewn/sewed	strike	struck	struck/stricken
shake	shook	shaken	swear	swore	sworn
shave	shaved	shaved/shaven	sweep	swept	swept
shear	sheared	sheared/shorn	swim	swam	swum
shine	shone*/shined**	shone*/shined**	swing	swung	swung
shoot	shot	shot	take	took	taken
show	showed	shown	teach	taught	taught
shrink	shrank/shrunk	shrunk/shrunken	tear	tore	torn
shut	shut	shut	tell	told	told
sing	sang	sung	think	thought	thought
sink	sank/sunk	sunk	throw	threw	thrown
sit	sat	sat	understand	understood	understood
slay	slew/slayed	slain/slayed	upset	upset	upset
sleep	slept	slept	wake	woke	woken
slide	slid	slid	wear	wore	worn
sneak	sneaked/snuck	sneaked/snuck	weave	wove/weaved	woven/weaved
speak	spoke	spoken	weep	wept	wept
speed	sped/speeded	sped/speeded	win	won	won
spend	spent	spent	wind	wound	wound
spill	spilled/spilt	spilled/spilt	withdraw	withdrew	withdrawn
spin	spun	spun	wring	wrung	wrung
spit	spat/spit	spat	write	wrote	written
split	split	split			
spread	spread	spread			
spring	sprang	sprung			

* shone = intransitive: *The sun shone brightly.*
** shined = transitive: *He shined his shoes.*

2 Non-Action Verbs

Examples: She **seems** happy in her new job.
I **have** a terrible headache.
The food **smells** good.
Mary **owes** me money.

Appearances	Emotions	Mental States		Senses and Perception	Possession	Wants and Preferences
appear	abhor	agree	hesitate	ache	belong	desire
be	admire	amaze	hope	feel	have	need
concern	adore	amuse	imagine	hear	own	prefer
indicate	appreciate	annoy	imply	hurt	pertain	want
look	care	assume	impress	notice	possess	wish
mean (= signify)	desire	astonish	infer	observe		
parallel	detest	believe	know	perceive		**Other**
represent	dislike	bore	mean	see		cost
resemble	doubt	care	mind	sense		include
seem	empathize	consider	presume	smart		lack
signify (= mean)	envy	deem	realize	smell		matter
	fear	deny	recognize	sound		owe
	hate	disagree	recollect	taste		refuse
	hope	disbelieve	remember			suffice
	like	entertain (= amuse)	revere			weigh
	love	estimate	see (= understand)			
	regret	expect	suit			
	respect	fancy	suppose			
	sympathize	favor	suspect			
	trust	feel (= believe)	think (= believe)			
		figure (= assume)	tire			
		find (= believe)	understand			
		guess	wonder			

A-2

3 Non-Action Verbs Sometimes Used in the Progressive

EXAMPLES: The students **are being** silly today.
We**'re having** dinner right now. Can I call you back?
Mary **is smelling** the roses.
The cook **is tasting** the soup.

ache	bore	expect	hear	include	perceive	sense
admire	consider	favor	hesitate	indicate	presume	smell
agree	deny	feel	hope	lack	realize	sympathize
amuse	disagree	figure	hurt	look	refuse	taste
annoy	doubt	find	imagine	notice	represent	think
assume	empathize	guess	imply	observe	see	wonder
be	entertain	have	impress			

4 Irregular Noun Plurals

SINGULAR FORM	PLURAL FORM	SINGULAR FORM	PLURAL FORM	SINGULAR FORM	PLURAL FORM
alumna	alumnae	elf	elves	paramecium	paramecia
alumnus	alumni	fish	fish/fishes*	people***	peoples
amoeba	amoebas/amoebae	foot	feet	person	people
analysis	analyses	genus	genera	phenomenon	phenomena
antenna	antennae/antennas	goose	geese	—	police
appendix	appendixes/appendices	half	halves	policeman	policemen
axis	axes	index	indexes/indices	policewoman	policewomen
basis	bases	knife	knives	protozoan	protozoa/protozoans
businessman	businessmen	leaf	leaves	radius	radii
businesswoman	businesswomen	life	lives	series	series
cactus	cacti/cactuses	loaf	loaves	sheaf	sheaves
calf	calves	louse	lice	sheep	sheep
—	cattle	man	men	shelf	shelves
child	children	millennium	millennia/millenniums	species	species
crisis	crises	money	moneys/monies**	thesis	theses
criterion	criteria	moose	moose	tooth	teeth
datum	data	mouse	mice	vertebra	vertebrae/vertebras
deer	deer	octopus	octopuses/octopi	wife	wives
dwarf	dwarfs/dwarves	ox	oxen	woman	women

   * fishes = different species of fish
  ** monies/moneys = separate amounts or sources of money
*** a people = an ethnic group

ABSTRACTIONS

advice	integrity
anarchy	love
behavior	luck
chance	momentum
decay	oppression
democracy	peace
energy	pollution
entertainment	responsibility
evil	slavery
freedom	socialism
fun	spontaneity
good	stupidity
happiness	time
hate	totalitarianism
hatred	truth
honesty	violence
inertia	

ACTIVITIES

badminton	hockey
baseball	judo
basketball	karate
biking	reading
billiards	sailing
bowling	singing
boxing	skating
canoeing	soccer
cards	surfing
conversation	taekwon do
cycling	talking
dancing	tennis
football	volleyball
golf	wrestling
hiking	

DISEASES

AIDS
appendicitis
bronchitis
cancer
chickenpox
cholera
diabetes
diphtheria
flu (influenza)
heart disease
malaria
measles
mumps
pneumonia
polio
smallpox
strep throat
tuberculosis (TB)

FOODS

barley
beef
bread
broccoli
cake
candy
chicken
corn
fish
meat
oats
pie
rice
wheat

GASES

carbon dioxide
helium
hydrogen
neon
nitrogen
oxygen

LIQUIDS

coffee
gasoline
juice
milk
oil
soda
tea
water

NATURAL PHENOMENA

air
cold
electricity
fog
hail
heat
ice
lightning
mist
rain
sleet
slush
smog
smoke
snow
steam
thunder
warmth
wind

OCCUPATIONS

banking
computer
  technology
construction
dentistry
engineering
farming
fishing
law
manufacturing
medicine
nursing
retail
sales
teaching
writing
work

PARTICLES

dust
gravel
pepper
salt
sand
spice
sugar

SOLID ELEMENTS

aluminum
calcium
carbon
copper
gold
iron
lead
magnesium
platinum
plutonium
radium
silver
sodium
tin
titanium
uranium

SUBJECTS

accounting
art
astronomy
biology
business
chemistry
civics
computer science
economics
geography
history
linguistics
literature
mathematics
music
physics
psychology
science
sociology
speech
writing

OTHER

clothing
equipment
film
furniture
news

6 Ways of Making Non-Count Nouns Countable

ABSTRACTIONS
a piece of advice
a matter of choice
a unit of energy
a type/form of entertainment
a piece/bit of luck

ACTIVITIES
a game of badminton/baseball/basketball/
  cards/football/golf/soccer/tennis, etc.
a badminton game/a baseball game, etc.

FOODS
a grain of barley
a cut/piece/slice of beef
a loaf of bread
a piece of cake
a piece/wedge of pie
a grain of rice
a portion/serving of . . .

LIQUIDS
a cup of coffee, tea, cocoa
a gallon/liter of gasoline
a can of oil
a glass of milk, water, juice
a can/glass of soda

NATURAL PHENOMENA
a bolt/current of electricity
a bolt/flash of lightning
a drop of rain
a clap of thunder

PARTICLES
a speck of dust
a grain of pepper, salt, sand, sugar

SUBJECTS
a branch of accounting/art/
astronomy/biology/chemistry/
economics/geography/linguistics/
literature/mathematics/music/
physics/psychology/sociology, etc.

OTHER
an article of clothing
a piece of equipment
a piece/article of furniture
a piece of news/a news item/an item
  of news
a period of time

7 Nouns Often Used with the Definite Article

the air
the atmosphere
the authorities
the Bhagavad Gita
the Bible
the cosmos
the Creator

the earth
the economy
the Empire State
  Building
the environment
the European Union
the flu

the gross national
  product (GNP)
the Internet
the Koran
the measles
the Milky Way
  (galaxy)

the moon
the movies
the mumps
the ocean
the police
the *Queen Mary*

the radio
the sky
the solar system
the stock market
the stratosphere
the sun

the Taj Mahal
the *Titanic*
the United Nations
the universe
the Vatican
the world

8 Countries Whose Names Contain the Definite Article

the Bahamas
the Cayman Islands
the Central African Republic
the Channel Islands
the Comoros
the Czech Republic

the Dominican Republic
the Falkland Islands
the Gambia
the Isle of Man
the Ivory Coast
the Leeward Islands

the Maldives (the Maldive Islands)
the Marshall Islands
the Netherlands
the Netherlands Antilles
the Philippines
the Solomon Islands

the Turks and Caicos Islands
the United Arab Emirates
the United Kingdom (of Great
  Britain and Northern Ireland)
the United States (of America)
the Virgin Islands

9 Selected Geographical Features Whose Names Contain the Definite Article

GULFS, OCEANS, SEAS, AND STRAITS

the Adriatic Sea
the Aegean Sea
the Arabian Sea
the Arctic Ocean
the Atlantic (Ocean)
the Baltic (Sea)
the Black Sea
the Caribbean (Sea)
the Caspian (Sea)
the Coral Sea
the Gulf of Aden
the Gulf of Mexico
the Gulf of Oman

the Indian Ocean
the Mediterranean (Sea)
the North Sea
the Pacific (Ocean)
the Persian Gulf
the Philippine Sea
the Red Sea
the Sea of Japan
the South China Sea
the Strait of Gibraltar
the Strait of Magellan
the Yellow Sea

MOUNTAIN RANGES

the Alps
the Andes
the Appalachians
the Atlas Mountains
the Caucasus

the Himalayas
the Pyrenees
the Rockies (the Rocky
   Mountains)
the Urals

RIVERS
(all of the following can contain the word *River*)

the Amazon
the Colorado
the Columbia
the Danube
the Don
the Euphrates
the Ganges
the Huang
the Hudson
the Indus
the Jordan
the Lena
the Mackenzie
the Mekong
the Mississippi
the Missouri
the Niger

the Nile
the Ob
the Ohio
the Orinoco
the Po
the Rhine
the Rhone
the Rio Grande
the St. Lawrence
the Seine
the Tagus
the Thames
the Tiber
the Tigris
the Volga
the Yangtze

OTHER FEATURES

the Arctic Circle
the Antarctic Circle
the equator
the Far East
the Gobi (Desert)
the Kalahari (Desert)
the Middle East
the Near East
the North Pole
the Occident
the Orient
the Panama Canal
the Sahara (Desert)
the South Pole
the Suez Canal
the Tropic of Cancer
the Tropic of Capricorn

10 Verbs Used in the Passive Followed by a *That* Clause

EXAMPLE: It **is alleged that** he committed the crime.

allege	believe	fear	hold	predict	theorize
assume	claim	feel	postulate	say	think

11 Stative Passive Verbs + Prepositions

EXAMPLE: The island of Hispaniola **is divided into** two separate nations.

be bordered by	be divided into/by	be known as	be measured by
be composed of	be filled with	be listed in/as	be placed near/in
be comprised of	be found in/on, etc.	be located in/on, etc.	be positioned near/in
be connected to/with/by	be intended	be made (out) of	be related to
be covered by/with	be joined to	be made up of	be surrounded by

12 Verbs Followed by the Gerund

EXAMPLE: Jane **enjoys playing** tennis and **gardening**.

abhor	confess	endure	give up (= stop)	postpone	resume
acknowledge	consider	enjoy	imagine	practice	risk
admit	defend	escape	keep (= continue)	prevent	shirk
advise	delay	evade	keep on	put off	shun
allow	deny	explain	mention	recall	suggest
anticipate	detest	fancy	mind (= object to)	recollect	support
appreciate	discontinue	fear	miss	recommend	tolerate
avoid	discuss	feel like	necessitate	report	understand
be worth	dislike	feign	omit	resent	urge
can't help	dispute	finish	permit	resist	warrant
celebrate	dread	forgive	picture		

13 Verbs Followed by the Infinitive

EXAMPLE: The Baxters **decided to sell** their house.

agree	care	determine	hurry	plan	say	venture
appear	chance	elect	incline	prepare	seek	volunteer
arrange	choose	endeavor	learn	pretend	seem	wait
ask	claim	expect	manage	profess	shudder	want
attempt	come	fail	mean (=	promise	strive	wish
beg	consent	get	intend)	prove	struggle	would like
can/cannot	dare	grow (up)	need	refuse	swear	yearn
afford	decide	guarantee	neglect	remain	tend	
can/cannot	demand	hesitate	offer	request	threaten	
wait	deserve	hope	pay	resolve	turn out	

14 Verbs Followed by the Gerund or Infinitive without a Significant Change in Meaning

EXAMPLES: Martha **hates to go** to bed early.
Martha **hates going** to bed early.

begin	can't stand	hate	love	propose
can't bear	continue	like	prefer	start

15 Verbs Followed by the Gerund or the Infinitive with a Significant Change in Meaning

forget
I've almost **forgotten meeting** him. (= At present, I can hardly remember.)
I almost **forgot to meet** him. (= I almost didn't remember to meet him.)

go on
Jack **went on writing** novels. (= Jack continued to write novels.)
Carrie **went on to write** novels. (= Carrie ended some other activity and began to write novels.)

quit
Ella **quit working** at Sloan's. (= She isn't working there anymore.)
Frank **quit to work** at Sloan's. (= He quit another job in order to work at Sloan's.)

regret
I **regret telling** you I'm taking the job. (= I'm sorry that I said I would take it.)
I **regret to tell** you I'm taking the job. (= I'm telling you now that I'm taking the job, and I'm sorry I'm taking it.)

remember
Velma **remembered writing** to Bill. (= Velma remembered the previous activity of writing to Bill.)
Melissa **remembered to write** to Bill. (= Melissa didn't forget to write to Bill. She wrote to him.)

stop
Hank **stopped eating**. (= He stopped the activity of eating.)
Bruce **stopped to eat**. (= He stopped doing something else in order to eat.)

try
Martin **tried skiing**. (= Martin sampled the activity of skiing.)
Helen **tried to ski**. (= Helen attempted to ski but didn't succeed.)

16 Adjective + Preposition Combinations

These phrases are followed by nouns, pronouns, or gerunds.

EXAMPLES: I'm not **familiar with** that writer.
I'm **amazed at** her.
We're **excited about** going.

accustomed to	capable of	famous for	incapable of	poor at	suited to
afraid of	careful of	fascinated with/by	intent on	ready for	surprised at/about/
amazed at/by	concerned with/	fed up with	interested in	responsible for	by
angry at/with	about	fond of	intrigued by/at	sad about	terrible at
ashamed of	content with	furious with/at	mad at (=angry at/	safe from	tired from
astonished at/by	curious about	glad about	with)	satisfied with	tired of
aware of	different from	good at	nervous about	shocked at/by	used to
awful at	excellent at	good with	obsessed with/about	sick of	weary of
bad at	excited about	guilty of	opposed to	slow at	worried about
bored with/by	familiar with	happy about	pleased about/with	sorry for/about	

17 Verbs Followed by Noun / Pronoun + Infinitive

EXAMPLE: I **asked** Sally **to lend** me her car.

advise	choose*	forbid	invite	pay*	remind	tell	warn
allow	convince	force	need*	permit	require	urge	would like*
ask*	encourage	get*	order	persuade	teach	want*	
cause	expect*	hire					

*These verbs can also be followed by the infinitive without an object.

EXAMPLES: I **want** Jerry **to go**.
I **want to go**.

18 Adjectives Followed by the Infinitive

EXAMPLE: I was **glad to hear** about that.

advisable*	careful	disappointed	essential*	happy	lucky	proud	sorry
afraid	crucial*	distressed	excited	hard	mandatory*	ready	surprised
alarmed	curious	disturbed	fascinated	hesitant	necessary*	relieved	touched
amazed	delighted	eager	fortunate	important*	nice	reluctant	unlikely
angry	depressed	easy	frightened	impossible	obligatory*	right	unnecessary*
anxious	desirable*	ecstatic	furious	interested	pleased	sad	upset
ashamed	determined*	embarrassed	glad	intrigued	possible	scared	willing
astonished	difficult	encouraged	good	likely	prepared	shocked	wrong

* These adjectives can also be followed with a noun clause containing a subjunctive verb form.

EXAMPLES: It's **essential to communicate**.
It's **essential that she communicate with her parents**.

19 Sentence Adverbs

EXAMPLES: **Clearly**, this is the best course of action.
This is **clearly** the best course of action.
This is the best course of action, **clearly**.

actually	certainly	evidently	happily	mainly	perhaps	significantly	thankfully
amazingly	clearly	fortunately	honestly	maybe	possibly	surely	understandably
apparently	definitely	frankly	hopefully	mercifully	probably	surprisingly	unfortunately
basically	essentially	generally	importantly	overall			

20 Words That Begin Dependent Clauses

SUBORDINATING CONJUNCTIONS (TO INTRODUCE ADVERB CLAUSES)		RELATIVE PRONOUNS (TO INTRODUCE ADJECTIVE CLAUSES)	OTHERS (TO INTRODUCE NOUN CLAUSES)
after	no matter if	that	how
although	no matter whether	when	how far
anywhere	now that	where	how long
as	on account of the fact that	which	how many
as if	once	who	how much
as long as	only if	whom	however (= the way in which)
as many as	plus the fact that	whose	if
as much as	provided (that)		that
as soon as	providing (that)		the fact that
as though	since		what
because	so that		what color
because of the fact that	so . . . that (= in order to)		whatever
before	such . . . that		what time
despite the fact that	though		when
due to the fact that	till		where
even if	unless		whether (or not)
even though	until		whichever (one)
even when	when		whoever
everywhere	whenever		whomever
if	where		why
if only	whereas		
inasmuch as	wherever		
in case	whether (or not)		
in spite of the fact that	while		

21 Transitions: Sentence Connectors

TO SHOW ADDITION	TO SHOW A CONTRAST	TO SHOW AN EFFECT / RESULT	TO SHOW TIME AND SEQUENCE
additionally	actually	accordingly	after this/that
along with this/that	anyhow	as a result	afterwards
also	anyway	because of this/that	an hour later (several hours later, etc.)
alternatively	as a matter of fact	consequently	
as a matter of fact	at any rate	for this/that reason	at last
besides	despite this/that	hence	at this moment
furthermore	even so	in consequence	before this/that
in addition	however	on account of this/that	from now on
indeed	in any case	otherwise	henceforth
in fact	in contrast	then	hitherto
in other words	in either case	therefore	in the meantime
in the same way	in fact	this/that being so	just then
likewise	in spite of this/that	thus	meanwhile
moreover	instead (of this/that)	to this end	next
plus	nevertheless		on another occasion
	nonetheless		previously
	on the contrary		then
	on the other hand		under the circumstances
	rather		until then
	still		up to now
	though		

22 Transitions: Blocks of Text

all in all	in short	second(ly)	to conclude
another reason/point, etc.	in sum	the most important reason/factor, etc.	to resume
finally	in summary	third(ly) (fourth[ly], etc.)	to return to the point
first(ly)	last(ly)		to summarize
in conclusion	most importantly		

23 Reporting Verbs

EXAMPLE: "This is the best course of action," Jack **added**.

add	claim	maintain	point out	respond	tell
allege	comment	murmur	query	say	wonder
allow	confess	note	report	shout	yell
ask	exclaim	observe			

24 Verbs and Expressions Followed by the Subjunctive (Base Form)

EXAMPLES: We **demand (that)** he **do** it.
It is **essential (that)** he **do** it.
The professor **suggested (that)** we **buy** his book.

AFTER SINGLE VERBS
ask*
demand
insist
move (= formally propose something in a meeting)
order*
prefer*
propose
recommend
request*
require*
suggest
urge*

AFTER *IT* + ADJECTIVE + NOUN CLAUSE
it is advisable that
it is crucial that
it is desirable that
it is essential that
it is important that
it is mandatory that
it is necessary that
it is obligatory that
it is reasonable that
it is required that
it is unnecessary that
it is unreasonable that

* These verbs also take the form verb + object pronoun + infinitive.

EXAMPLES: We **asked that** she **be** present.
We **asked her to be** present.

These are the pronunciation symbols used in this text. Listen to the pronunciation of the key words.

VOWELS				**CONSONANTS**			
Symbol	**Key Word**	**Symbol**	**Key Word**	**Symbol**	**Key Word**	**Symbol**	**Key Word**
i	beat, feed	ə	banana, among	p	pack, happy	ʃ	ship, machine, station, special, discussion
ɪ	bit, did	ɚ	shirt, murder	b	back, rubber		
eɪ	date, paid	aɪ	bite, cry, buy, eye	t	tie	ʒ	measure, vision
ɛ	bet, bed	aʊ	about, how	d	die	h	hot, who
æ	bat, bad	ɔɪ	voice, boy	k	came, key, quick	m	men
ɑ	box, odd, father	ɪr	beer	g	game, guest	n	sun, know, pneumonia
ɔ	bought, dog	ɛr	bare	tʃ	church, nature, watch	ŋ	sung, ringing
oʊ	boat, road	ɑr	bar	dʒ	judge, general, major	w	wet, white
ʊ	book, good	ɔr	door	f	fan, photograph	l	light, long
u	boot, food, student	ʊr	tour	v	van	r	right, wrong
ʌ	but, mud, mother			θ	thing, breath	y	yes, use, music
				ð	then, breathe	t̬	butter, bottle
				s	sip, city, psychology		
				z	zip, please, goes		

GLOSSARY OF GRAMMAR TERMS

action verb A verb that describes an action.
- James **telecommutes** three days a week.

active sentence A sentence in which the subject acts upon the object.
- **William Shakespeare** wrote **Hamlet**.

adjective A part of speech modifying a noun or pronoun.
- The **blue** sofa is **beautiful**, but it's also **expensive**.

adjective clause A clause that identifies or gives additional information about a noun.
- The man **who directed the film** won an Oscar.

adjective phrase A phrase that identifies or gives additional information about a noun.
- In that movie, the actress **playing the heroine** is Penélope Cruz.

adverb A part of speech modifying a verb, an adjective, another adverb, or an entire sentence.
- Ben drives his **incredibly** valuable car **very carefully**.

adverb clause A dependent clause that indicates how, when, where, why, or under what conditions things happen; or which establishes a contrast. An adverb clause begins with a subordinating conjunction and modifies an independent clause.
- We're going to leave for the airport **as soon as Jack gets home**.

adverb / adverbial phrase A phrase that indicates how, when, where, why, or under what conditions things happen. An adverb phrase modifies an independent clause.
- We learned a great deal of Spanish **while traveling in Mexico**.

An adverbial phrase performs the same functions as an adverb phrase but does not contain a subordinating conjunction.
- **Having had the professor for a previous class**, I knew what to expect.

auxiliary (helping) verb A verb that occurs with and "helps" a main verb.
- **Did** Mary contact you? No. She **should have** called at least.

base form The form of a verb listed in a dictionary. It has no endings (-s, -ed, etc.).
- It is mandatory that Sally **be** there and **participate** in the discussion.

causative A verb construction showing that someone arranges for or causes something to happen. **Get** and **have** are the two most common causative verbs.
- We **got** Martha to help us when we **had** the house remodeled.

clause A group of words with a subject and a verb that shows time. An **independent clause** can stand by itself. A **dependent clause** needs to be attached to an independent clause to be understood fully.

INDEPENDENT   DEPENDENT
- We'll go out for dinner when Mom gets back from the bank.

comma splice An error resulting from joining two independent clauses with only a comma.
- I understand the point he made, however, I don't agree with it. (comma splice)
- I understand the point he made; however, I don't agree with it. (correction)

common noun A noun that does not name a particular thing or individual.
- We bought a **turkey**, cranberry **sauce**, mashed **potatoes**, and **rolls** for the special **dinner**.

complement A noun or adjective (phrase) that describes or explains a subject or direct object.
- Hal is **a man with unusual tastes**. He painted his house **orange**.

compound modifier A modifier of a noun that is composed of more than one word. A compound modifier is usually hyphenated when it precedes a noun.
- My **five-year-old** daughter can already read.

conditional sentence A sentence containing a dependent clause showing a condition and an independent clause showing a result. The condition may or may not be fulfilled.

CONDITION   RESULT
- If I had enough time, I would visit Morocco.

coordinating conjunction A word connecting independent clauses or items in a series. The seven coordinating conjunctions are **and**, **but**, **for**, **nor**, **or**, **so**, and **yet**.

- *Mom had forgotten to buy groceries, **so** we had a supper of cold pizza, salad, **and** water.*

count noun A noun that can be counted in its basic sense. Count nouns have plural forms.

- *The **students** in my **class** all have at least one **sibling**.*

definite article The article **the**; it indicates that the person or thing being talked about is unique or is known or identified to the speaker and listener.

- *China is **the** most populous nation in **the** world.*

definite past The simple past form; it shows an action, state, or event at a particular time or period in the past.

- *I **lived** in Spain in the '90s and **visited** there again last year.*

dependent clause A dependent clause is a group of words that cannot stand alone as a sentence: It requires a main (independent) clause for its meaning.

MAIN CLAUSE   DEPENDENT CLAUSE
- *They saw the bandit, who was wearing a bandanna.*

direct object A noun or pronoun that receives the action of a verb.

- *Martin discovered an autographed **copy** of the novel.*

direct (quoted) speech The exact words (or thoughts) of a speaker, which are enclosed in quotation marks.

- *"**Barry**," Phyllis said, "**I want you to tell me the truth.**"*

embedded question A question that is inside another sentence.

- *He didn't know **what he should buy for his mother**.*

focus adverb An adverb that focuses attention on a word or phrase. Focus adverbs come before the word or phrase they focus on.

- ***Even** I don't support that idea. It's too radical.*

fragment A group of words that is not a complete sentence. It is often considered an error.

- *Because he doesn't know what to do about the situation. (fragment)*
- *He's asking for our help because he doesn't know what to do about the situation. (correction)*

future in the past A verb construction showing a state, action, or event now past but future from some point of time in the past.

- *We **were going to help** Tim move but couldn't. Sam said he **would help** instead.*

generic Referred to in general; including all the members of the class to which something belongs.

- ***The computer** has become essential in today's world.*
- ***Whales** are endangered.*
- ***An orangutan** is a primate living in Borneo and Sumatra.*

gerund A verbal noun made by adding **-ing** to a verb.

- *Dad loves **cooking**, and we love **eating** what he cooks.*

identifying (essential) clauses and phrases Clauses and phrases that distinguish one person or thing from others. They are not enclosed in commas.

- *The student **who is sitting at the end of the second row** is my niece.*
- *The film **starring Johnny Depp** is the one I want to see.*

if clause The clause in a conditional sentence that states the condition.

- ***If it rains**, they will cancel the picnic.*

implied condition A condition that is suggested or implied but not stated fully. Implied conditional sentences use expressions such as *if so, if not, otherwise, with,* and *without*.

- *You may be able to get the item for half price. **If so**, please buy one for me as well. (= if you are able to get the item for half price)*

indefinite article The articles **a** and **an**; they occur with count nouns and indicate that what is referred to is not a particular or identified person or thing.

- *In the last year I have bought **an** old **house** and **a** new **car**.*

indefinite past The present perfect; it shows a past action, event, or state not occurring at any particular or identified time.

- *We **have seen** that movie several times.*

indirect object A noun or pronoun that shows the person or thing that receives something as a result of the action of the verb.

- *Martin gave **Priscilla** an autographed copy of his new novel. He also gave **her** a DVD.*

indirect (reported) speech   A report of the words of a speaker. Indirect speech does not include all of a speaker's exact words and is not enclosed in quotation marks.

- *Phyllis told Barry **that she wanted him to tell her the truth**.*

infinitive   ***To*** + the base form of a verb.

- *Frank Jones is said **to be** the author of that article.*

inverted condition   The condition of a conditional sentence, stated without the word *if*. Inverted conditions occur with the verbs *had, were,* and *should,* which come first in the sentence and are followed by the subject.

- ***Had I** known that would happen, I never would have agreed.*

main (independent) clause   A clause that can stand alone as a sentence.

| MAIN CLAUSE | DEPENDENT CLAUSE |

- *They saw the bandit, who was wearing a bandanna.*

mixed conditional   A conditional sentence that shows the hypothetical present result of a past unreal situation or the hypothetical past result of a present unreal situation.

- *If I had taken that job, I would be living in Bucharest now.*
- *Sam would have arrived by now if he were planning to come.*

modal (auxiliary)   A type of helping verb. ***Can, could, had better, may, might, must, ought to, shall, should, will,*** and ***would*** are modals. They each have one form and no endings.

- *You certainly **can** do that; the question is whether you **should** do it.*

modal-like expression   An expression with a meaning similar to that of a modal. Modal-like expressions have endings and show time.

- *Russell **has to** find a new job.*

non-action (stative) verb   A verb that in its basic sense does not show action.

- *It **seems** to me that Joe **has** a problem.*

non-count noun   A noun that in its basic sense cannot be counted.

- ***Smoke** from the **fire** filled the **air**.*

nonidentifying (nonessential) clauses and phrases   Clauses and phrases that add extra information but do not distinguish one person or thing from others. They are enclosed in commas.

- *Henry, **who is a member of the hockey team,** is also a star basketball player.*

noun clause   A dependent clause that performs the same function as a noun. Noun clauses function as subjects, objects, objects of prepositions, and complements.

- ***What I want to do** is spend a week relaxing on the beach.*

noun modifier   A noun that modifies another noun.

- *What did you buy, **milk** chocolate or **chocolate** milk?*

parallelism (parallel structure)   The placing of items in a series in the same grammatical form.

- *Marie loves **hiking, riding** horses, and **collecting** artifacts.*

participial adjective   An adjective formed from present and past participial forms of verbs.

- *The **bored** students were not paying attention to the **boring** speaker.*

passive causative   A verb structure formed with ***have*** or ***get*** + **object** + **past participle**. It is used to talk about services that you arrange for someone to do for you.

- *I usually **have my dresses made** by Chantal.*

passive sentence   A sentence that shows the subject being acted upon by the object.

- ***Hamlet** was written by **William Shakespeare**.*

perfect forms   Verb constructions formed with the auxiliary verbs ***had, has,*** and ***have*** and a past participle. They include the **past perfect, present perfect,** and **future perfect**.

- *I **had** never **been** to Brazil before 1990. Since then **I've been** there eight times. By this time next year, **I'll have been** there ten times.*

phrase   A group of related words without a subject or a verb showing time.

- ***Relaxing in the hammock**, I pondered my future.*

proper noun   The name of a particular individual or thing. Proper nouns are capitalized.

- ***Stella** and I both think that **Rio de Janeiro** and **Paris** are the world's two most beautiful cities.*

quantifier   A word or phrase showing the amount or number of something.

- *Ken earned **a lot of** money selling books. I bought **a few of** them myself.*

relative pronoun   A pronoun used to form adjective clauses. ***That**, **when**, **where**, **which**, **who**, **whom**,* and ***whose*** are relative pronouns.

- *The fairy tale **that** always scared me when I was a child was "Rumpelstiltskin."*

reporting verb   A verb such as ***said**, **told**,* or ***asked**,* which introduces both direct and indirect speech. It can also come after the quotation in direct speech.

- *The mayor **said**, "I've read the report."* OR *"I've read the report," the mayor **said**.*

result clause   The clause in a conditional sentence that indicates what happens if the condition occurs.

- *If it rains, **they'll cancel the picnic**.*

run-on sentence   An error resulting from the joining of two independent clauses with no punctuation.

- *I think therefore, I am. (run-on sentence)*
- *I think; therefore, I am. (correction)*

sentence adverb   An adverb that modifies an entire sentence. It can occur at the beginning, in the middle, or at the end of a sentence.

- ***Fortunately,** Sarah was not hurt badly in the accident.*

stative passive   A passive form used to describe situations or states.

- *North and South America **are connected by** the Isthmus of Panama.*

subjunctive   A verb form using the base form of a verb and normally following a verb or expression showing advice, necessity, or urgency. The verb *be* has the special subjunctive form *were*, which is used for all persons.

- *We always **insist** that our daughter **do** her homework before watching TV.*
- *If I **were** you, I would pay off my mortgage as soon as possible.*

subordinating conjunction   A connecting word used to begin an adverb clause.

- *We were relieved **when** Jack finally called at 1 A.M.*

tag question   A statement + tag. The **tag** is a short question that follows the statement. Tag questions are used to check information or comment on a situation.

- *She's an actor, **isn't she?***

topic sentence   A general sentence that indicates the content of a paragraph.

- *There are several things to keep in mind when you visit a Japanese home.*

transition   A word or phrase showing a connection between sentences or between larger blocks of text.

- *Climate change is a serious problem. **However,** it is not as serious as the problem of poverty.*

unreal conditional sentence   A sentence that talks about untrue, imagined, or impossible conditions and their results.

- *If I were you, I would study a lot harder.*

zero article   The absence of a definite or indefinite article. The zero article occurs before unidentified plurals or non-count nouns.

- ***Whales** are endangered.*
- ***Water** is necessary for survival.*

UNIT REVIEW ANSWER KEY

Note: In this answer key, where the contracted verb form is given, it is the preferred form, though the full form is also acceptable. Where the full verb form is given, it is the preferred form, though the contracted form is also acceptable.

UNIT 1

A 1. are doing   5. seem
   2. loves   6. attends
   3. takes   7. is playing
   4. 'm getting   8. like

B 1. have lived   4. have owned
   2. has directed   5. have been remodeling
   3. has been working   6. has been running

C 1. B   2. C   3. D   4. B   5. A   6. D

UNIT 2

A 1. got   5. was
   2. have done   6. went
   3. have been   7. wanted
   4. have visited   8. have never known

B 1. met   4. was
   2. attended   5. had known
   3. had invited   6. proposed

C 1. D   2. B   3. A   4. D   5. C   6. D

UNIT 3

A 1. have to   4. lets
   2. 'll be   5. 'll stop by
   3. 'll call   6. get

B 1. taking   6. 're spending OR
   2. leaves OR is leaving   'll spend OR
   3. get   're going to spend
   4. 'll have been flying 7. 'll send
      OR will have flown   8. 're
   5. 'll be

C 1. C   2. B   3. C   4. A   5. C   6. D

UNIT 4

A 1. weren't supposed to 6. must have
   2. didn't have to   7. 's got to
   3. shouldn't have   8. aren't allowed to
   4. could   9. could have
   5. 'd better not   10. Hadn't we better

B 1. must OR have got to
   2. should
   3. can't OR must not
   4. must (simply) OR has to (simply)
   5. should you

C 1. A   2. A   3. C   4. B   5. C

UNIT 5

A 1. must   6. ought not to
   2. might   7. had to
   3. might   8. 's got to be
   4. couldn't   9. must have been
   5. should   10. must

B *Possible answers*
   1. Jeremy may have had to work late.
   2. Mari must have missed her flight.
   3. They can't have heard the news.
   4. We should know the answer soon.
   5. You could have gotten a scholarship.

C 1. C   2. C   3. C   4. A   5. B

UNIT 6

A 1. C   3. NC   5. NC   7. NC
   2. NC   4. C   6. C

B 1. a. any   b. a drop of
   2. a. some   b. some pieces of
   3. a. any   b. a grain of
   4. a. some   b. a game of

C 1. C   2. D   3. C   4. B   5. A

UNIT 7

A 1. G   3. D   5. G   7. N
   2. N   4. G   6. D   8. N

B 1. The   3. the   5. The   7. —
   2. a   4. an   6. —

C 1. B   2. C   3. A   4. B   5. D

UNIT 8

A 1. Most   6. The number of
   2. amount of   7. many
   3. any   8. little
   4. a lot of   9. plenty of
   5. a couple of   10. no

B *Possible answers*
   1. many   3. a lot of   5. a lot of
   2. much   4. a few   6. Every

C 1. B   2. C   3. D   4. A

UNIT 9

A
1. sweltering humid summer
2. chilly late winter
3. new pink silk
4. handsome young European
5. beautiful new brick
6. dirty little old

B
1. an eleven-year-old son
2. a 900-page novel
3. a short-haired bandit
4. six 55-minute periods
5. a voter-initiated proposal
6. strange-looking people
7. Chinese ivory statue
8. a gray short-haired cat

C 1. A 2. C 3. D 4. C 5. C

UNIT 10

A
1. what the punch line of the joke was
2. why he always tells that joke
3. what time the meeting starts
4. what *hyperbole* means
5. whether Samira liked the party
6. what Mary does for a living
7. how long she's been a writer
8. whether or not

B
1. what Mary meant
2. whether or not Bob
3. Whatever you want
4. That Alison loves Kahlil
5. what we should give Russell
6. the fact that Ben helped us
7. that she was

C 1. D 2. B 3. A 4. C

UNIT 11

A
1. it was
2. had finished
3. if she was
4. to be sure
5. not to
6. if he would
7. she would come by
8. could

B
1. if he would
2. told
3. she didn't feel well
   OR, "I don't . . ."
4. needed
5. if he had ever
6. have seen
7. not to
8. "We didn't."

C 1. D 2. A 3. C 4. A 5. C

UNIT 12

A
1. who
2. where
3. whom
4. whose
5. which
6. when
7. sees
8. who

B
1. who lives next door
2. The book that Sara bought OR The book Sara bought
3. whose dog is barking
4. whom we met
5. where I was born
6. when we spoke
7. ,who is a student,
8. whose parents work here

C 1. A 2. A 3. D 4. D

UNIT 13

A
1. which
2. whose
3. whom
4. which
5. whom
6. interested
7. which was
8. starring

B
1. which
2. which
3. whom
4. which
5. whom
6. who
7. who
8. which

C 1. C 2. C 3. C 4. D

UNIT 14

A
1. is being constructed
2. had his car serviced
3. were caught
4. died
5. been
6. being
7. been
8. the job done by noon

B
1. is reported
2. is being reported
3. has been reported
4. was reported
5. was being reported
6. had been reported
7. will be reported
8. will have been reported

C 1. B 2. A 3. B 4. D

UNIT 15

A
1. is bordered by
2. as
3. is claimed
4. is believed to be
5. by
6. is located in
7. is thought to
8. are alleged

B
1. by
2. is said
3. is surrounded
4. are alleged
5. are believed
6. is claimed
7. of
8. is regarded

C 1. C 2. B 3. A 4. D

UNIT 16

A
1. not smoking
2. shopping
3. Emiko's
4. Not giving
5. to having
6. seeing
7. being awakened
8. not having been invited

B
1. finishing
2. Having missed
3. coming
4. driving
5. being told
6. seeing
7. having taken
8. mentioning

C 1. B   2. A   3. C   4. D

UNIT 17

A
1. to do
2. to accept
3. to give up
4. smoking
5. to lock
6. locked
7. to confront
8. to be criticized

B
1. strong enough
2. warned you
3. to postpone
4. be typed
5. to have had
6. not to get
7. to have forgotten
8. to finish

C 1. D   2. B   3. A   4. C

UNIT 18

A
1. just don't
2. had we
3. he even thinks
4. only members
5. don't just
6. even he can
7. does Eva
8. comes the train

B
1. are kangaroos
2. ,clearly
3. but he should
4. does our team lose
5. Just members
6. is the money
7. Actually,
8. goes the plane

C 1. C   2. D   3. D   4. A

UNIT 19

A
1. unless
2. Even though
3. in case
4. As
5. Once
6. now that
7. wherever
8. as soon as

B
1. whenever
2. As soon as
3. Even if
4. Because
5. Only if
6. Although
7. Whereas
8. unless

C 1. B   2. A   3. A   4. D

UNIT 20

A
1. Not knowing
2. Caught cheating
3. Having gotten the tickets
4. before leaving
5. On realizing
6. Relaxing
7. Having visited
8. being given

B
1. Having heard
2. while doing
3. Having eaten
4. finishing
5. Having been
6. being taken
7. Fearing
8. Given

C 1. A   2. C   3. D   4. B

UNIT 21

A
1. however
2. though
3. Because
4. consequently
5. besides
6. and
7. or
8. otherwise

B *Possible answers*
1. so
2. besides
3. or
4. consequently
5. Although
6. After
7. Besides
8. consequently

C 1. B   2. C   3. D   4. B

UNIT 22

A
1. rains
2. doesn't
3. rained
4. wouldn't
5. weren't
6. hadn't rained
7. 'd
8. were going to

B
1. wishes
2. wouldn't
3. hadn't
4. have had to
5. wouldn't
6. made
7. wouldn't
8. had listened

C 1. B   2. A   3. C   4. D

UNIT 23

A
1. Without
2. If not
3. If so
4. otherwise
5. With
6. if not
7. without
8. with

B *Possible answers*
1. otherwise
2. If I hadn't
3. call
4. Should that happen
5. But for
6. understand
7. if so
8. likes

C 1. A   2. B   3. C   4. B

9. Game

Answers				
The type of tree that used to grow on Easter Island What is the (Chilean) wine palm?	The ship that sank in the Atlantic in 1912 on its first voyage What is the *Titanic*?	The place in a city or town where one keeps one's money What is a / the bank?	The home country of the first European to see Easter Island What is Holland / the Netherlands?	The name of the people who settled Easter Island Who are the Polynesians?
The animals that have been reintroduced in national parks What are wolves?	The circular object that was not used in moving the Easter Island statues What is the wheel?	The outer covering of a tree What is bark?	The body of water in which Easter Island is located What is the Pacific (Ocean)?	The people in a particular circumstance who have a great deal of money Who are the rich / wealthy?
The material from which the Easter Island statues are made What is stone?	A form of precipitation that is necessary for crops to grow What is rain?	A form of energy that involves the use of radioactive material What is nuclear power?	The device invented by Easter Islanders to move their statues What is the / a canoe rail?	A liquid substance used to produce gasoline What is petroleum / oil?
The place in a city or town where one can mail letters What is a / the post office?	A type of natural phenomenon that devastated the country of Haiti in 2010 What is an earthquake?	The part of the human body that is the seat of intelligence What is the brain?	The nation over which Hurricane Katrina formed What is the Bahamas?	The electronic device invented in 1944 by Farnsworth and Zorinsky What is the computer?
A type of animal killed by wolves in Yellowstone National Park What is the / an elk?	A woodwind instrument that uses a reed and was invented about 1700 What is a / the clarinet?	The people in a particular circumstance who are badly off economically Who are the poor?	A polluting material in the ocean that birds and fish mistake for food What is plastic?	In the Arctic and subarctic region, the part of the soil that doesn't thaw in the summer What is (the) permafrost?

8. Game

Team A

1. **A:** Which country has fewer people, Canada or Mexico?
    B: Canada has fewer people.

2. **A:** Which country has more land area, Canada or the United States?
    B: Canada has more land area.

3. **A:** Which country produces less oil, Venezuela or Mexico?
    B: Venezuela produces less oil.

4. **A:** Which country has no snowfall, Somalia or Tanzania?
    B: Somalia has no snowfall.

5. **A:** Which country has fewer rivers, Libya or Nigeria?
    B: Libya has fewer rivers.

6. **A:** Which country has a smaller number of people, Monaco or Cyprus?
    B: Monaco has a smaller number of people.

7. **A:** Which country produces a large amount of gold, Nigeria or South Africa?
    B: South Africa produces a large amount of gold.

8. **A:** Which city has less rainfall, Aswan, Egypt, or Athens, Greece?
    B: Aswan, Egypt, has less rainfall.

Team B

1. **A:** Which country has fewer people, Great Britain or Spain?
    B: Spain has fewer people.

2. **A:** Which country has more land area, Australia or Brazil?
    B: Brazil has more land area.

3. **A:** Which country produces less oil, the United States or Saudi Arabia?
    B: The United States produces less oil.

4. **A:** Which country has no military, Colombia or Costa Rica?
    B: Costa Rica has no military.

5. **A:** Which country has fewer rivers, Yemen or Turkey?
    B: Yemen has fewer rivers.

6. **A:** Which country has a smaller number of people, San Marino or Kuwait?
    B: San Marino has a smaller number of people.

7. **A:** Which country uses a larger amount of nuclear energy, the Netherlands or France?
    B: France uses a larger amount of nuclear energy.

8. **A:** Which city has less rainfall, Antofagasta, Chile, or Nairobi, Kenya?
    B: Antofagasta, Chile, has less rainfall.

8. Game

Team A

1. **A:** Which island is composed of the nations of Haiti and the Dominican Republic?
   B: Hispaniola is composed of the nations of Haiti and the Dominican Republic.

2. **A:** Which Central American country is bordered by Panama and Nicaragua?
   B: Costa Rica is bordered by Panama and Nicaragua.

3. **A:** Which people are considered by some to be the descendants of Atlanteans?
   B: The Basque people are considered by some to be the descendants of Atlanteans.

4. **A:** Which legendary creature is thought to live in the Himalayas?
   B: The yeti is thought to live in the Himalayas.

5. **A:** Which individual is claimed to have been the assassin of U.S. President John F. Kennedy?
   B: Lee Harvey Oswald is claimed to have been the assassin of U.S. President John F. Kennedy.

6. **A:** Which individuals are regarded as great humanitarians?
   B: Albert Schweitzer and Mother Teresa are regarded as great humanitarians.

Team B

1. **A:** Which Caribbean nation is composed of many islands?
   B: The Bahamas is composed of many islands.

2. **A:** Which Caribbean nation is located about 90 miles south of Florida?
   B: Cuba is located about 90 miles south of Florida.

3. **A:** Which forest creature is said to live in the Pacific Northwest?
   B: Bigfoot is said to live in the Pacific Northwest.

4. **A:** Which lost continent is thought to have been located in the Atlantic Ocean?
   B: Atlantis is thought to have been located in the Atlantic Ocean.

5. **A:** Which planet was thought to be the center of the universe before Copernicus?
   B: Earth was thought to be the center of the universe before Copernicus.

6. **A:** Which presidents are regarded by many as the greatest American presidents?
   B: George Washington and Abraham Lincoln are regarded by many as the greatest American presidents.

9. Conditional Game

Team A

1. **A:** Where would you be if you were in the capital of Honduras?
   B: You would be in Tegucigalpa if you were in the capital of Honduras.

2. **A:** How old would you have to be if you were the president of the United States?
   B: You would have to be at least 35 years old if you were the president of the United States.

3. **A:** Where would you be traveling if the monetary unit were the won?
   B: You would be traveling in North or South Korea if the monetary unit were the won.

4. **A:** Where would you be if you were visiting Angkor Wat?
   B: You would be in Cambodia if you were visiting Angkor Wat.

5. **A:** Who would you have been if you had been the emperor of France in 1804?
   B: You would have been Napoleon if you had been the emperor of France in 1804.

6. **A:** Who would you have been if you had been the first prime minister of India?
   B: You would have been Jawaharlal Nehru if you had been the first prime minister of India.

7. **A:** What country would you have been from if you were Marco Polo?
   B: You would have been from Italy if you had been Marco Polo.

8. **A:** What mountain would you have climbed if you had been with Edmund Hillary and Tenzing Norgay?
   B: You would have climbed Mt. Everest if you had been with Edmund Hillary and Tenzing Norgay.

Team B

1. **A:** How old would you be if you were an octogenarian?
   B: You would be between 80 and 89 if you were an octogenarian.

2. **A:** Where would you be traveling if you were in Machu Picchu?
   B: You would be traveling in Peru if you were in Machu Picchu.

3. **A:** What would you be if you were the largest mammal?
   B: You would be a blue whale if you were the largest mammal.

4. **A:** What country would you be in if you were standing and looking at Angel Falls?
   B: You would be in Venezuela if you were standing and looking at Angel Falls.

5. **A:** Who would you have been if you had been the inventor of the telephone?
   B: You would have been Alexander Graham Bell if you had been the inventor of the telephone.

6. **A:** What kind of creature would you have been if you had been a stegosaurus?
   B: You would have been a dinosaur if you had been a stegosaurus.

7. **A:** What would your occupation have been if you had been Genghis Khan?
   B: You would have been an emperor if you had been Genghis Khan.

8. **A:** Who would you have been if you had been Siddartha Gautama?
   B: You would have been the founder of Buddhism if you had been Siddartha Gautama.

G-AK4

PHOTO CREDITS:
Page 195 (left) Shutterstock.com, (right) Warner Bros./Photofest; **p. 196** Shutterstock.com;
p. 197 Danita Delimont/Alamy; **p. 211** Warner Bros./Photofest; **p. 212** (top) Moviestore collection Ltd/Alamy,
(bottom) AF archive/Alamy; **p. 233** (left) Dale O'Dell/SuperStock, (right) Classic Image/Alamy; **p. 244** AP Images/
The Columbian/Dave Olson; **p. 247** (left) Dale O'Dell/SuperStock, (right) AP Images/Eric Draper; **p. 263** (top left)
Eric Schaal/Getty Images, (top right) Eye Ubiquitous/Alamy, (bottom left) Classic Image/Alamy, (bottom right)
Gianni Dagli Orti/Corbis; **p. 269** (left) Pictorial Press Ltd/Alamy, (right) Julian Hirshowitz/Corbis; **p. 285** Pictorial
Press Ltd/Alamy; **p. 300** Julian Hirshowitz/Corbis; **p. 307** (left) AP Images/Lou Requena, (right) Digital Vision/
Getty Images; **p. 308** Pearson Education; **p. 318** Pearson Education; **p. 323** Shutterstock.com; **p. 324** Tom &
Dee Ann McCarthy/Corbis; **p. 337** AP Images/Lou Requena; **p. 340** AP Images/FILES; **p. 358** Digital Vision/
Getty Images; **p. 371** M.Flynn/Alamy; **p. 372** Bonnie Kamin/PhotoEdit; **p. 377** (left) Corbis RF/Alamy, (right)
Shutterstock.com; **p. 378** Corbis RF/Alamy; **p. 396** Shutterstock.com; **p. 411** (top left) Shutterstock.com, (top
right) Shutterstock.com, (bottom left) Shutterstock.com, (bottom right) Shutterstock.com.

TEXT CREDITS:
Pages 196–197: Bryce, Tim. *Morphing into the Real World: The Handbook for Entering the Work Force.* MBA Press.
Copyright 2007 Tim Bryce. Palm Harbor, FL.
Pages 223, 227: "A Beautiful Mind", from LEONARD MALTIN'S MOVIE AND VIDEO GUIDE 2003 by Leonard Maltin,
copyright ©1991–1999, 2000–2004 by Leonard Maltin. Used by permission of Dutton Signet, a division of
Penguin Group (USA) Inc.
Pages 234–235: Based on information in Mark McGwire, "15 Minutes of Fame," *Biography Magazine,* September
1998; and Richard Severn, " D.B. Cooper: Perfect Crime or Perfect Folly?" *Seattle Times,* November 17, 1996.
Pages 250–251: Based on the article "Body Ritual Among the Nacirema" by Horace Minor (found in *American
Anthropologist,* Vol. 58. Vol. 1 156 pp.18–21).
Pages 270–271: Based on Judith Viorst's essay "Friends, Good Friends, and Such Good Friends" in Alfred Rosa
and Paul Eschholz, eds., *Models for Writers: Short Essays for Composition,* 3rd Ed. New York: St. Martin's Press, 1989.
Pages 323–324: Includes material based on Simon Haydon's "The Only Foul He Saw Was on the U.S." The
Associated Press, June 19, 2010.
Pages 340–341: Based on information in Brad Darrach's "Journey: A Brave Family Changes Horror into Healing
after a Child Dies," *Life,* October 1, 1995, pp. 42+
Page 348: Sutapa Mukerjee, "A Caring Elephant That Died of Grief," *The Seattle Post-Intelligencer*, May 6, 1999,
Copyright: The Associated Press.
Pages 358–359: "How Quickly We Forget" *U.S. News and World Report,* October 13, 1997, p. 52. Reprinted by
permission.
Pages 396–397: Based on information in: "How to Survive a Messy Roommate." http://wikihow.com/Survive-a-
Messy-Roommate.

ILLUSTRATION CREDITS:
Steve Attoe: pp. 251, 406; **Burmar Technical Corporation:** p. 257; **A.J. Garces:** p. 235; **Chris Gash:** p. 260;
ElectraGraphics, Inc./Gene Gonzales: pp.330, 396; **David Klug:** p. 336; **Jock MacRae:** p. 332; **Andy Myer:**
p. 367; **Thomas Newsom:** pp. 387, 388; **Dusan Petricic:** pp. 350, 351; **Susan Scott:** pp. 225, 369

This index is for the full and split editions. All entries are in the full book. Entries for Volume A of the split edition are in black. Entries for Volume B are in red.